Epic

The Storyline of the Bible

James L. Nicodem

M000304461

MOODY PUBLISHERS

CHICAGO

© 2013 by
JAMES L. NICODEM

All Scripture quotations are taken from the *Holy Bible, New International Version*®, NIV®. Copyright ©1973, 1978, 1984 by Biblica, Inc.™ Used by permission of Zondervan. All rights reserved worldwide.

Published in association with the literary agency of Wolgemuth & Associates, Inc.

Edited by Jim Vincent
Interior design: Ragont Design
Cover design: Smartt Guys design
Cover image: Hemera

Library of Congress Cataloging-in-Publication Data

Nicodem, James L., 1956-
   Epic : the storyline of the Bible / Jim Nicodem.
     p. cm. — (The Bible savvy series)
   Includes bibliographical references.
   ISBN 978-0-8024-0633-0
   1. Bible—Criticism, interpretation, etc. 2. Redemption—Biblical
   teaching. 3. Bible stories. I. Title.
   BS511.3.N53 2013
   220.6—dc23

                                                            2012043477

We hope you enjoy this book from Moody Publishers. Our goal is to provide high-quality, thought-provoking books and products that connect truth to your real needs and challenges. For more information on other books and products written and produced from a biblical perspective, go to www.moodypublishers.com or write to:

Moody Publishers
820 N. LaSalle Boulevard
Chicago, IL 60610

3 5 7 9 10 8 6 4 2

Printed in the United States of America

Jim Nicodem has taken on a monumental task—putting the Bible in a thimble-sized summary that gives the reader tremendous insight into the timeline of the greatest story ever told. *Epic* centers on the theme of the Bible—Redemption. Jim shows how from the beginning of time God had a plan to save lost souls from the sin that blackened the perfect world He gave to mankind. In the pages of Scripture God reveals His Son, who would come as our Redeemer. Nicodem inspires us to explore in greater detail the epic story revealed in God's Word.

> Franklin Graham
> President and CEO, Samaritan's Purse and
> The Billy Graham Evangelistic Association

Jim Nicodem's purpose is to lay out, in straightforward, nontechnical language, many of the most important principles of interpretation. He does this so each person may know the foundational principles of biblical interpretation, and so understand many texts. In other words, Jim wants the church he serves, and many other churches, to be filled with men and women who will become better Bible readers.

> D.A. Carson, PhD
> Research Professor of New Testament
> at Trinity Evangelical Divinity School
> Author of *New Testament Commentary Survey*

Jim Nicodem has the gift of taking the complex and—through clear explanations and compelling illustrations—making it highly accessible. If you or someone you know feels intimidated by the Bible, I can't think of a better resource to put in their hands than *Epic* and the Bible Savvy series.

> Nicholas Perrin
> Professor of biblical studies, Wheaton College
> Author of *Lost in Transmission: What We Can Know about the Words of Jesus*

As a university professor on a Christian college campus, I can tell you that biblical illiteracy is on the rise. That's why the Bible Savvy series should be a prerequisite reading for everyone. Jim Nicodem puts the cookies on the bottom shelf by making the epic story of the biblical narrative understandable and accessible. The Bible Savvy series lays out the foundation and context for God's Word and then shows us in plain language how to apply the Bible's teachings to our lives step-by-step. It's phenomenal.

> Les Parrott, PhD
> Seattle Pacific University
> Author of *You're Stronger Than You Think*

The compelling reality about the Bible is that it is full of fascinating details about God and His wise and redemptive oversight of the history of mankind. Unfortunately, the larger, more profound story often gets lost in the details. Like a master storyteller, Jim Nicodem takes us beyond the details and exposes the grand plot of Scripture. Jim's work in the Bible Savvy series will amaze many of us who have lived to master the details and will motivate all of us to stand in greater awe of the One who is navigating history to a good and glorious end.

> Joseph M. Stowell
> President, Cornerstone University

The Bible is one of the most precious possessions to a believer living in a restricted nation. I am constantly amazed by the hunger for biblical teaching expressed by those who face persecution daily. Their sacrificial passion should inspire us to rekindle our quest for biblical understanding. Jim Nicodem's Bible Savvy series is the kind of resource needed to reengage our hearts and minds with God's Word, and renew a hunger for God's truth on par with our persecuted brothers and sisters.

> James E. Dau
> President, The Voice of the Martyrs

Jim has done a masterful job in the Bible Savvy series! In these four concise books, Jim marches with clarity and skill into topics that would be difficult to tackle in a seminary classroom, much less in an American living room. And rather than a monologue, these books create a dialog among the author, the reader, their small group, and the living Word of God. These practical, approachable resources provide foundational training that is greatly needed by nearly every small group and leader I encounter.

> Greg Bowman
> Coauthor of *Coaching Life-Changing Small Group Leaders*
> Past executive director of the Willow Creek Association

Reading the four books in the Bible Savvy series is like getting a Bible college education in a box! The Lord is calling our nation to a Bible reading revolution, and these books are an invitation to be part of it.

> Hal Seed
> Author of *The Bible Questions* and *The God Questions*
> Lead Pastor, New Song Community Church, Oceanside, California

Living in the land of the Bible is considered a privilege by many, but the real privilege is to let the Bible become alive through us, in whatever land we may live. In the Bible Savvy series, Jim Nicodem not only helps us to understand God's plan to save us, but also His desire to change and shape us through His Word and Spirit in order to be a light in this dark world.

> Rev. Azar Ajaj
> Vice President and lecturer, Nazareth Evangelical Theological Seminary

JAMES L. NICODEM

Bible Savvy

Hear from the author by
checking out the videos
on the Bible Savvy Series
with James Nicodem.

biblesavvy.com

MOODY
PUBLISHERS

About the
Bible Savvy Series

I MET THE REAL ESTATE AGENT at my front
door and invited him in. My wife and I were about to put
our home on the market and I had called Jeff as a potential
representative. As he sat down at our dining room table and
opened his briefcase, I noticed a Bible perched on top of other
papers. I asked Jeff if he was a Bible reader and he replied that
he was just getting started. What had prompted his interest?
He'd recently come across a list in *Success, Inc.* magazine of
the most influential books recommended by business leaders.
The Bible had been the most frequently mentioned book on
the list. So, Jeff was going to give it a try.

My real estate agent isn't alone in his new interest in the
Bible. According to a recent survey, 91 percent of those who
have lately begun attending church were motivated to do so
by a desire to understand what the Bible has to say to their
lives.[1] That means nine of every ten visitors to church are intrigued by the Bible! But while they are curious about God's
Word, they're also a bit intimidated by it. The Bible is such
a daunting book, written in ancient times and addressed to
vastly different culture. Is it really possible to draw relevant
insights from it for our lives today? People are returning to
church to find out.

Ironically, while an interest in Bible knowledge can be detected among those who are new to church, it seems to be on the wane among many veteran churchgoers. When my oldest daughter enrolled at a Christian college, the president of the school addressed parents on opening day. He told us that the Bible comprehension exams of each incoming class of freshmen show less and less knowledge of God's Word. And then he added: "These kids are growing up in *your* churches." Evidently, many churches are not doing a good job of teaching committed believers how to read, interpret, and apply the Bible.

The Bible Savvy series has been written to help a wide spectrum of Bible readers—from newbies to seasoned Bible study leaders—get their arms around God's Word. This multi-book series covers four essential Bible-related topics that Moody Publishers has made available in one set as a comprehensive manual for understanding God's Word and putting it into practice. *Epic* is the first of the four-book series.

An added bonus to the Bible Savvy series is the Study Guide that follows every chapter of each book. These questions for personal reflection and group discussion have been crafted by a team of small-groups experts. The Study Guide is also available online at biblesavvy.com and may be downloaded and used for personal study or reproduced for members of a small group.

Four Things You Must Know to
Get the Most out of God's Word

The four books of the Bible Savvy series will give you a grasp of the follwing topics, allowing God's Word to become a rich resource in your life:

1. *The storyline of the Bible.* The Bible is actually a compilation of sixty-six books that were written over a 1,500-year period. But amazingly there is one central storyline that holds everything together. You'll trace this storyline in *Epic* from Genesis to Revelation, learning how each of the sixty-six books contributes to the overall plot.

2. *The reliability of the Bible.* How did God communicate what He wanted to say through human authors? What are the evidences that the Bible is a supernatural book? How do we know that the *right* books made it into the Bible and that the *wrong* books were kept out of it? Isn't a text that was hand-copied for hundreds of years bound to be filled with errors? *Foundation* will give you answers to questions like these—because you won't get much out of the Bible until you're certain that you can trust it.

3. *How to understand the Bible.* People read all sorts of crazy things into the Bible, and have used it to support

a wide variety of strange (and sometimes reprehensible) positions and activities. In *Context* you will learn the basic ground rules for accurately interpreting Scripture. (Yes, there are rules.)

4. *How to apply the Bible.* It's one thing to read the Bible, and it's another thing entirely to walk away from your reading with an application for your life. Even members of Bible study groups occasionally do a poor job of this. Participants leave these gatherings without a clear sense of how they're going to put God's Word into practice. *Walk* will equip you to become a Bible doer.

Do You Have Savvy?

The dictionary defines *savvy* as *practical know-how.* It is my hope and prayer that the Bible Savvy series will lead you into an experiential knowledge of God's Word that will transform your life.

Many people have contributed to my own love and understanding of the Bible over the years—as well as to the writing of this book. I owe a huge debt of gratitude to them. Mom and Dad made God's Word central to our family life, encouraging my siblings and me to memorize big chunks of it.

When I got to high school, I was a bit turned off to church, but I started attending a youth ministry in a neighboring suburb that was led by Bill Hybels. (These were pre–

Willow Creek Community Church days, when dinosaurs roamed the earth.) Bill had (and still has) an incredible ability to open the Bible, read a passage out loud, and then drive home its application to the lives of his listeners. After a year of hearing him teach God's Word in such a life-impacting way, I went away to college and decided to major in biblical studies.

Two professors (among many) fanned the flame of my love for the Bible during my college and seminary years. Dr. Gerry Hawthorne taught me Greek New Testament at Wheaton College, and there are thousands of men and women in ministry around the world today who still remember his simple-but-powerful class devotions. He'd put one verse on the chalkboard (remember chalk?) and then tease out its significance for our lives—often with tears in his eyes. Dr. D. A. Carson taught me the Bible at Trinity Evangelical Divinity School. His books (and occasional phone and email exchanges) continue to shape me today. I aspire to have even a quarter of his passion for God's Word!

After school, as I started out in youth ministry, I began listening to cassette tapes (same era as chalk) by Dr. John MacArthur. John is internationally famous for his verse-by-verse teaching of Scripture. Although he is occasionally more adamant about certain doctrines than I am (we agree on the essentials), his love for the Bible is infectious. John has set the bar high for all pastors who want to faithfully teach their churches God's Word. As my ministry has continued,

11

I have found other communicators who whet my appetite for Scripture—many of them through their books, some of them currently through their podcasts. Thank you Lee Strobel, Joe Stowell, John Ortberg, Mark Driscoll, Francis Chan, Tim Keller, and many others.

Today, my desire to get people into the Bible is fueled by the five thousand-plus eager learners whom I have the privilege of pastoring at Christ Community Church of St. Charles, Illinois, and its regional campuses. I am especially grateful for both the staff and volunteer leaders who oversee almost four hundred Community Groups that are studying God's Word. And one of those leaders, who writes incredible Bible curricula and teaches scores of Bible-hungry women, is my wife, Sue. Her devotion to Scripture is a constant inspiration to me.

Lastly, a special thanks to my faithful assistant, Angee Jenkins, who helped to edit my manuscript, track down footnotes, and protect my writing time; and to my agent, Andrew Wolgemuth, who found a great publisher in Moody to make the Bible Savvy series available to you.

Contents

To watch Jim's personal introduction to Epic,
scan this QR code with your smartphone or go to
www.biblesavvy.com/video#epic1.

Foreword

"WHOEVER TELLS the stories shapes society."

Plato spoke those words in the fourth century BC, and nothing has happened in the subsequent twenty-four centuries to prove him wrong. In fact, given the vast, global influence of our modern storytelling industry, his words seem truer today than ever. *The Lord of the Rings, Gone with the Wind, Harry Potter, The Hunger Games*—nothing captures our collective attention more than a well-told story.

Why is storytelling so powerful? In the words of screenwriting and story expert Robert McKee, "A story is the living proof of an idea." Stories bring ideas to life. They give them flesh. Make them real.

Jesus knew this. When He stood before a crowd with an idea to communicate, He didn't pull out a three-point sermon outline or PowerPoint slides. He told a story. A poor widow, a lost coin, a rebellious son. Jesus communicated His ideas by wrapping them in the flesh of our everyday lives.

And so we hold in our hands the Bible—a vast collection of stories. We all know the big ones like Noah's ark, David and Goliath, Daniel in the lions' den. The images immediately spring to life, for Christian and non-Christian alike. But too many of us, regardless of our familiarity with the stories of the Bible, are blind to the story of the Bible. We miss the forest for the trees. We fail to recognize how the Bible's many individual stories fit together to tell one mega-story. The macro-story. The story of God and us.

The effect of our blindness to *the* story is huge. We can't interpret our lives. We don't understand the world—why it is the way it is. We don't understand suffering, and fail to communicate a compelling vision of redemption to a hurting world. We are living blind. Tragedy strikes, history unfolds, and the world says, "Why? Why is it this way?" And the church, by and large, stands silent, because we have lost our place in the story.

It is time to recapture what we have lost. It is time to pull up chairs, to sit down around the campfire. To retell the story of a world at war—a broken creation—and a fantastic, breathtaking plan to make it whole again.

Join Jim Nicodem as he takes us into God's epic story.

> PHIL VISCHER
> Creator of Veggie Tales and What's in the
> Bible? video series

Introduction:
A Grand Storyline

EVERY STUDENT who has ever taken a high school or college literature class holds one name in high esteem. The name is not Shakespeare, Dickens, or Tolstoy. It is not Hemmingway, Chaucer, or Milton. The name that I'm thinking of is . . . uh . . . Cliff. Cliff is known for his great literary works: *CliffsNotes*.

Now, in case you're not familiar with these masterpieces, let me briefly (pun intended) explain that *CliffsNotes* are condensed versions of famous novels. For example, the nine-hundred-page *Nicholas Nickleby* by Charles Dickens is reduced by *CliffsNotes* to a thirty-five-page quick summary. (We'll call it *Nick*.) The *CliffsNotes* of *War and Peace*, a mammoth novel by Leo Tolstoy, can be read in half an hour.

English teachers hate *CliffsNotes*. But if you're a student, cramming the night before a big test, on a book you have only partly read, *CliffsNotes* can be a lifesaver. (Of course, you lose the awe-inspiring benefits of reading a classic work.) On the other hand, the worst thing you could discover about your unread book is that it's not available in *CliffsNotes*! (You're in trouble.)

Wouldn't it be great if the Bible, the greatest book of all time, was available in *CliffsNotes*? It actually is. But the *Cliffs-Notes* version is 224 pages long! The fact is: it's tough to find a brief summary of the Bible's contents. Even the condensed *Reader's Digest Bible* (and believe it or not, there is such a thing) is 767 pages long.

Wrapping your mind around a book this long is a daunting task. But that is just what you're going to do in this opening book of the Bible Savvy series. *Epic* is a comprehensive-but-concise presentation of the Bible's grand storyline.

{ 1 }

Redemption Prompted

I NEED TO SEE the big picture—especially when I'm trying to figure out travel directions. If I am about to drive through New York City, for example, the two- by three-inch GPS picture on my iPhone of the immediate vicinity will not suffice. I want an AAA road map of the entire city at a glance—the kind that opens up to three feet wide and can never be refolded the right way.

God has given us a road map for our lives. It's called the Bible. God's Holy Word. The Bible is the best place to turn for direction for our lives. But we need to have a sense of the Bible's big picture in order to understand its individual parts. So, how are we going to get a sense of that big picture? We won't find it summarized in a couple of paragraphs on the back cover of our Bible, right above a picture of the book's author. (God won't hold still while His photo is taken.)

No, the Bible is not like other books. In fact, the Bible is not "a" book. It's actually a compilation of sixty-six books in one. Sixty-six books that were written over a period of 1,500 years, penned by forty different authors. And those forty different authors lived in ten different countries, worked in more than twenty different occupations (including king, shepherd, general, tax collector, fisherman, and doctor), and wrote in three different languages (Greek, Hebrew, and Aramaic).

What are our chances of ever being able to get a sense of the Bible's big picture, the Bible's *storyline*? And speaking of the Bible's storyline, does it even *have* a clear storyline? After all, the Bible mentions, by name, 2,930 different characters. Is it really possible that all these people belong to the same drama, that they're part of the same plot?

Yes, the Bible has a storyline: a single, overarching, comprehensive storyline. A storyline that amazingly ties the whole book together, from Genesis to Revelation. And once we grasp that storyline, we'll be able to make sense of the Bible's individual parts. We'll be able to use God's road map to gain direction for our lives.

But before we dive into the Bible's opening book of Genesis, let me say a word about the general theme of the Bible's storyline. We can capture this general theme in one word, *redemption*. Look up *redemption* in the dictionary, and one of the first definitions you'll see is *deliverance* or *rescue*.

The Rescue

The Bible is a rescue story. It begins with a crisis. There are people in grave danger. Who will save them? A lot of good stories begin this way. This is what immediately grabs our attention. This is what hooks us.

If you were ever a fan of the blockbuster TV series *24*, you know what I'm talking about. Each season the show began with an emergency. Lives were at stake. There was a plot in motion to assassinate the president, or suicide bombers were on the loose, or a nuclear bomb was about to be detonated, or a deadly virus was about to be released. These situations called for the rescue efforts of super-agent Jack Bauer.

Now, not every story that we read or watch begins with that much of an adrenalin rush. But a lot of good stories *do* begin with people in dire straits. And those dire straits prompt a rescue effort.

The Bible is no exception to this pattern. In fact the Bible opens with the mother of all crises. A crisis so big that it prompts the greatest rescue effort in the history of humanity. That rescue effort—*redemption*—is the theme of the Bible's storyline. After the description in Genesis 1 of an awesome God creating earth and its inhabitants, Genesis 2–3 tells us about the crisis that prompted the rescue operation. I encourage you to grab your Bible and follow along as I identify five stages to: *Redemption Prompted.*

The Command

In the first chapter of Genesis, the opening pages of the Bible, God creates the world and everything in it. This includes the original human couple, Adam and Eve. Mister and missus are then placed in a virtual paradise, called the garden of Eden. We pick up the story in Genesis 2:15–17: "The Lord God took the man and put him in the Garden of Eden to work it and take care of it. And the Lord God commanded the man, 'You are free to eat from any tree in the garden; but you must not eat from the tree of the knowledge of good and evil, for when you eat of it you will surely die.'"

This command in Genesis 2:17 immediately raises a couple of objections in the minds of some readers. First off, it seems so silly, so arbitrary: *Don't eat from this tree!* C'mon. That's the best that God could come up with? I mean, this is the very first prohibition that we come across in the Bible. We expect something significant, right?

Hebrew scholars tell us that it's worded exactly like some of the famous Ten Commandments. You remember the Big Ten? They include, "You shall have no other gods before me. . . . You shall not murder. You shall not commit adultery" (Exodus 20:3, 13–14).

But . . . *You shall not eat from this tree?* In the words of an old *Sesame Street* jingle: "One of these things is not like the others." Is this really God's best shot for the Bible's opening prohi-

22

bition? How random! If God didn't want Adam and Eve to eat from that tree, why did He put the tree in the garden of Eden to begin with? Was He deliberately trying to trip them up?

May I suggest that objecting to God's command along these lines reveals a rebellious streak in our hearts? It reveals a resistance to the notion that God is *God*. As God, He has the right to command us to do whatever He pleases. If some of God's commands seem silly or arbitrary to us, the problem is not with *God*; it's with *us*.

Let me illustrate what I'm saying here. Last summer, I was looking for a place to take my family on vacation, and so I emailed a friend of mine who lives on Cape Cod. I asked him if he knew of any inexpensive rental cottages on the Cape. Preferably something near the ocean. My friend is a retired banker, a wealthy man. He emailed me back, saying: "My wife and I have a vacation house up in Maine. Why don't we go there for a week, and you and your family can have our house on the Cape?" That sounded reasonable to me.

When we got there, we realized it was a really sweet deal. Their house is massive. It has a beautiful swimming pool, a private theatre, and a gorgeous view of the ocean. Soon after we arrived we spotted a piece of paper on the kitchen counter, explaining where we could find everything. And in the middle of all this information, my friend had given us a directive: "Please water the house plants while you are here."

My immediate thought was: *What a stupid directive! Doesn't he know we're on vacation? With all his money, he could've hired somebody to do the watering.* So we just let the house plants wither and die.

Of course we didn't! It would have been foolish and ungrateful to defy my friend's instructions.

And yet, when it comes to *God's* commands, we're constantly pushing back. It's as if we reserve the right to determine which commands deserve our obedience and which commands are worthy of disdain.

A second objection that people have, when they read the "Don't eat from this tree" prohibition in Genesis 2:17, is that the penalty seems overly severe. What does our Bible say would happen to Adam and Eve if they ate from the Tree of the Knowledge of Good and Evil? They would *surely die.*

The death sentence? Are you kidding me? For eating an apple? (Actually, the Bible never says that this was an apple tree. That's just how artists have depicted it.)

What's the deal with the death sentence? It's really quite simple to explain. For the first two chapters of Genesis, the Bible has been referring to God as the source of all life. He brought the world into existence, creating stars and oceans and forests and wild animals. And when He created Adam, God "breathed into his nostrils the breath of life, and the man became a living being" (Genesis 2:7).

If God is the source of Adam's *life* (and of ours), what would be the natural consequence of unplugging from God by rejecting His commands? Death. Isn't that what happens when you're vacuuming your house and the plug pulls out? The vacuum dies, right? Well, people who unplug from God—the source of life—die.

The Con Job

The main characters in this drama now begin to distort God's original command. As you read Genesis 3:1–6, see if you can detect the truth-twisting that's going on:

Now the serpent was more crafty than any of the wild animals the Lord God had made. He said to the woman, "Did God really say, 'You must not eat from any tree in the garden'?"

The woman said to the serpent, "We may eat fruit from the trees in the garden, but God did say, 'You must not eat fruit from the tree that is in the middle of the garden, and you must not touch it, or you will die.'"

"You will not surely die," the serpent said to the woman. "For God knows that when you eat of it your eyes will be opened and you will be like God, knowing good and evil."

When the woman saw that the fruit of the tree was

good for food and pleasing to the eye, and also desirable for gaining wisdom, she took some and ate it. She also gave some to her husband, who was with her, and he ate it.

Who is the serpent in this story? Satan. Now, the fact is Genesis 3 doesn't tell us who the serpent is. But the last book of the Bible identifies the serpent for us (Revelation 12:9): "The great dragon was hurled down—that ancient serpent called the devil, or Satan, who leads the whole world astray."

So the serpent who approaches Eve in Genesis 3 is indeed Satan—God's archenemy! But please note in verse 1 that God *made* Satan. It's important for us to understand that even though God and Satan have been engaged in a cosmic battle of good

SATAN IS *NOT* God's equal. God is the Creator of all things, so Satan is a created being.

vs. evil since the beginning of time, Satan is *not* God's equal. Satan is *not* God's exact polar opposite. God is the Creator of all things. Satan is a created being. God is omnipotent, omniscient, and omnipresent. Satan is none of those things.

And because Satan lacks God's power, he must fight his battles using trickery and deceit. The Genesis account refers to him as *more crafty* than any of God's other creatures. Just look at the first words out of Satan's mouth to Eve: "Did God really say . . . ?" (v. 1) There's something subtly sinister about this question. Satan's use of the word *really* drips with sarcasm. Can you detect his *you've-got-to-be-kidding-me* attitude? Although God has just given Adam and Eve a fairly straightforward command, Satan is about to twist and distort that command so as to get them to disobey it.

Why? Because, if Adam and Eve disobey the command, they unplug from the source of life. They die. Satan is out to destroy the pinnacle of God's creation. And he uses trickery—a con job—to accomplish his goal.

Satan's Three Deceits

Let me note three strategies with which Satan deceitfully counters God's original prohibition (strategies that he's still using on us today).

The first is *exaggeration*. His first deceit is a misleading question: "Did God really say, 'You must not eat from any tree in the garden'?" Is Satan accurately quoting God? No. There was only *one* tree that God said not to eat from. So why is Satan exaggerating God's Word? To make God's command look severe, overly demanding, unreasonable, ridiculous.

Once Satan has us believing that God's commands are severe, overly demanding, unreasonable, or ridiculous, we feel like we have the right to disobey them. Don't we? Like when we drive 45 mph in a 30 mph zone because it's *so stupid* to drive the speed limit on that wide-open stretch of road. Like when we come in at midnight (if we're high school age), even though our parents have told us that curfew is 11 p.m., because it's *so lame* to go home by 11 p.m. When we exaggerate God's commands, we make them easier to dismiss, because they're so over-the-top.

Look at how Eve quickly picks up on Satan's bad habit of exaggerating God's Word. She starts to do it herself. In the middle of verse 2, Eve says (my summary): "It's only the tree in the middle of the garden that we're not to eat from—and we're not supposed to touch it either, or we'll die." Not supposed to *touch* it? When did God say not to *touch* that tree? He didn't. Now Eve is exaggerating.

A second clever strategy that Satan uses to counter God's command is flat out *denial of consequences.* In verse 4, Satan promises Eve: "You will not surely die." Satan's denial of the death sentence that God had attached to His command (Genesis 2:17) is even stronger in the original Hebrew. Satan actually begins his sentence with the word *not.* His denial is literally: "NOT—you will surely die!"

Isn't it interesting that the very first doctrine Satan ever contradicts is the doctrine of divine judgment? "God doesn't punish sin. Disobedience to God doesn't unplug you from the source of life. There's no such thing as spiritual or eternal death." People are still buying this lie today. We all buy it to some extent. We convince ourselves that God will shrug His shoulders at our sin. We don't really expect to pay for sin in any significant way.

A third strategy Satan uses to counter God's command is the promise that *disobedience will bring tremendous satisfaction.* That deceit remains today a great weapon in Satan's arsenal. He guarantees Eve that the forbidden fruit will make her

SATAN IS IN the business of dressing up evil and trying to pass it off to us as something wonderful.

"like God, knowing good and evil" (v. 5). That sales pitch was actually half-true. Eve would know good and evil if she ate the fruit. But not like God.

God knows evil like a cancer doctor knows cancer. But Eve would know evil like a cancer victim knows cancer. Do you see the difference? If Eve ate the fruit, she would know evil from personal experience. That wouldn't be a good thing, even though Satan tried to dress it up as if it would be tremendously satisfying.

Satan is still in the business of dressing up evil and trying to pass it off to us as something wonderful. "You'd feel much better if you got some revenge." "You'd really enjoy a shopping spree." "You'd laugh yourself silly over this raunchy movie." "You'd be a lot happier if you got out of your difficult marriage." "You'd loosen up with a few more beers."

Eve fell for Satan's con job. She ate from the tree that God had said not to eat from. So did her husband Adam. And we've been falling for Satan's con job ever since.

The Cover-Up

What happened after Eve and then Adam bit into the fruit? According to Genesis 3:7–13:

> Then the eyes of both of them were opened, and they realized they were naked; so they sewed fig leaves together and made coverings for themselves.
>
> Then the man and his wife heard the sound of the Lord God as he was walking in the garden in the cool of the day, and they hid from the Lord God among the trees of the garden. But the Lord God called to the man, "Where are you?"
>
> He answered, "I heard you in the garden, and I was afraid because I was naked; so I hid."
>
> And he said, "Who told you that you were naked? Have you eaten from the tree that I commanded you not to eat from?"
>
> The man said, "The woman you put here with me— she gave me some fruit from the tree, and I ate it."

Then the Lord God said to the woman, "What is this you have done?"

The woman said, "The serpent deceived me, and I ate it."

This is the cover-up—also called the Shame and Blame Game. This is what sin always leads to in our lives.

First, there's shame. Adam and Eve were embarrassed by their nakedness, and so they tried to cover it up with fig leaves. (I'll bet *that* was pretty uncomfortable.) We're still trying this same approach today. We don't use fig leaves. But we do our best to hide our sinfulness from other people, to keep them from finding out the worst about us. We'd be mortified if others knew some of the things we've thought, said, or done.

Adam and Eve not only tried to hide their shame from each other, they tried to hide it from God. When they heard the sound of God walking in the garden (v. 8), they hid from Him. How crazy is that? Hiding from God? I was in a clothing store with my wife, Sue, recently. A little boy was standing next to a rack of dresses. He pulled one of the dresses across his face and, with 90 percent of his body still showing, he called out to his mom, "Come and find me!" How childishly amusing. How very like our own attempts to hide from God.

The psalmist dumps a bucket of cold water on those of us who are inclined to try this approach. He addresses God with the rhetorical question (Psalm 139:7–8): "Where can I go from your Spirit? Where can I flee from your presence? If I go up to the heavens, you are there; if I make my bed in the depths, you are there." We have no chance of hiding from God—even though our *shame* drives us away from Him.

So, hounded by our shame we resort to blame. We try to cover up our sins by blaming them on other people, blaming them on our circumstances, blaming them on our personality, blaming them on our upbringing.

Adam blamed Eve. Look at verse 12: "The woman," Adam says. "She gave me some fruit from the tree, and I ate it." *The woman*. I'm sure that Adam spit that out with disgust. But ironically, when God first created Eve and brought her to Adam, Adam looked at this beautiful naked lady and joyfully exclaimed (Genesis 2:23): "She shall be called 'woman.'" My grad school Hebrew teacher said that the proper translation of this exclamation should probably be: "She shall be called 'Whoa! Man!'" But in Genesis 3, it's no longer "Whoa! Man!" It's now a derisive "the woman," as Adam blames Eve for his sin.

> WE TRY TO COVER up our sins by blaming them on other people, on our circumstances, on our personality, or on our upbringing.

And Adam doesn't just blame Eve. He blames God! Look

again at verse 12: "The woman *you put here* with me—she gave me some fruit from the tree" (italics added). So, it's *God's* fault for putting Eve in the garden with Adam in the first place.

Of course, Eve also participates in the blame game, so don't get the idea that it's just men who like to shift responsibility for their wrongdoing to others. Whom does Eve blame (v. 13)? "The serpent deceived me, and I ate."

You may be old enough to remember the comedian Flip Wilson. He made famous the gag line, "The devil made me do it!" Evidently, Flip got the line from Eve.

This is the Shame and Blame Game in action. Rather than cover up, we all need to participate in a frank self-assessment. I love the familiar story about British writer G. K. Chesterton, in this regard. Early in the twentieth century, a prominent London newspaper asked a variety of famous writers to submit articles that would address the question: "What's wrong with the world?" Chesterton's response was quite brief: "I am."[1]

The Consequences

I find it fascinating that the consequences of Adam's sin and Eve's sin seem to be gender related. The penalties seem to track with how God has uniquely wired men and women. See what you think about that as you read the rest of the story (Genesis 3:16–19, 23):

To the woman he [God] said, "I will greatly increase your pains in childbearing; with pain you will give birth to children. Your desire will be for your husband, and he will rule over you."

To Adam he said, "Because you listened to your wife and ate from the tree about which I commanded you, 'You must not eat of it,' "cursed is the ground because of you; through painful toil you will eat of it all the days of your life. It will produce thorns and thistles for you, and you will eat the plants of the field. By the sweat of your brow you will eat your food until you return to the ground, since from it you were taken; for dust you are and to dust you will return." . . .

So the Lord God banished him from the Garden of Eden to work the ground from which he had been taken.

Adam and Eve faced some pretty stiff consequences for their disobedience. Let's start with Eve. Her sin had negative repercussions on the important relationships in her life. As a mother, she would experience great pain in childbirth (v. 16). And as a wife, she and Adam were going to struggle in their marriage.

What does God mean when He says to Eve, "Your desire will be for your husband"? Wouldn't that be a good thing? Unfortunately, God isn't using the word *desire* here in a positive sense. He's not talking about Eve's sexual desire or emotional desire for Adam. God is warning Eve about a sin-corrupted desire, a desire to control Adam.

This same word—*desire*—pops up again in the very next chapter of Genesis. God warns Cain, who's extremely angry with his brother, "Cain, watch out!" Why? Because sin "*desires* to have you." In other words, sin wants to control Cain, manipulate Cain, make Cain do its bidding. This is the same Hebrew word for *desire* that's used of Eve in Genesis 3. Her sin-corrupted bent will now be to control her husband. And what will be Adam's response to that? The last line of Genesis 3:16 says that Adam will push back. Adam will *rule* Eve. In other words, Adam will be domineering. Needless to say, their marriage is now going to be characterized by power struggles—something that still troubles married couples today.

Well, if Eve's sin is going to have negative relational consequences, what about Adam's sin? God tells Adam that he is now going to experience futility in his work. Adam will try to make a living off the land, but the land will not cooperate (vv. 17–19). Isn't it interesting that because Adam disobeyed God by eating forbidden fruit, getting something to eat is now going to be a difficult task? (God uses the word *eat* five times in His reprimand of Adam.)

So, Eve will struggle with relationships, and Adam will

struggle with work. I won't suggest that these struggles are entirely gender exclusive. But they do seem to touch on important priorities of women and men. And much worse than these consequences, Adam and Eve will now be banished from the garden of Eden, the place where they had experienced such a close relationship with God. One Bible commentator writes about their life-after-banishment: "They had breathed the air of God's presence. Now it was

THE WORST PART about sin is that it cuts us off from a relationship with God.

impossible. For them, their new state must have been like life without oxygen. They were perpetually short of spiritual breath. They could never get enough of God."[2]

That's the worst part about sin. It cuts us off from a relationship with God. This is spiritual death. Do you remember how God had warned Adam and Eve that if they ate from the Tree of the Knowledge of Good and Evil, they would *surely die*? Maybe you're wondering why they didn't die—not immediately—after eating the fruit in Genesis 3. The answer is: They *did* die. They died spiritually. Their relationship with God died. And eventually spiritual death would result in physical death and eternal death.

These are the consequences of sin! Brokenness in relationships. Futility at work. Alienation from God. This is what prompted God's intervention, specifically God's *redemption*. (Remember the theme of the Bible's storyline?) Adam and Eve needed to be rescued, as do we.

The Coming of Christ

If you saw the 2004 movie *The Passion of the Christ*, you might have been confused by the opening scene. Jesus is praying in the garden of Gethsemane, shortly before His arrest and crucifixion. And as He prays, a snake approaches Him, slithering along the ground. Jesus spots the snake, leaps to His feet, and stomps on the snake's head until it is dead. Do you recall the Bible saying anything about Jesus duking it out with a snake in Gethsemane?

Well, you won't find that scene depicted in Matthew, Mark, Luke, or John, the four biographies of Jesus. But you will find it described indirectly in Genesis. Note the words with which God curses the serpent for leading Adam and Eve into sin: "I will put enmity between you and the woman, and between your offspring and hers; he will crush your head, and you will strike his heel" (3:15).

What is God saying here? He's telling Satan that one day Eve's offspring (i.e., a human being) will totally destroy him ("crush your head"), even though this person will be mortally wounded in the process (Satan will "strike his heel"). This is a description, amazingly, of what happened between Satan and

37

Jesus at the crucifixion. Let me explain.

Satan had hoped to destroy Adam and Eve by leading them into sin. Their sin unplugged them from the source of life, bringing about their spiritual death, which potentially would result in their physical and eternal death. Satan's plan is the same for every member of the human race. He wants to bring about our death. But Jesus was willing to die in our place. He suffered the consequences of our sin. And because Jesus is the eternal Son of God, His sacrificial death is of infinite worth. It becomes a gift of life to all who put their trust in Him. So Jesus defeated Satan at the cross. Satan may have struck Jesus' heel, but Jesus crushed Satan's head. Just as Genesis 3:15 promised.

There's another hint of redemption in Genesis 3, which can be observed only through the lens of the Christian faith. When Christians celebrate Jesus' death at Communion services (also known as the Eucharist or Lord's Supper), the bread that they eat represents the body of Christ. His body was hung on a cross to pay for our sins. When Jesus first taught His disciples how to celebrate Communion, He handed them the bread with these words: "Take and eat; this is my body" (Matthew 26:26). *Take* and *eat*. Where else are these two verbs coupled together in Scripture?

In Genesis 3:6, we read that Adam and Eve "took . . . and ate" the forbidden fruit, introducing sin and death into the world. What a disaster! But help was on the way. One day Jesus Christ would arrive on the scene. And just before He gave His life for us, He would break bread with His followers and say: "Take and eat."

Do you see the connection? You and I—just as Adam and Eve—have personally feasted on sin. This puts us under the sentence of death, unless we personally feast on Christ. Have you ever done that? Have you ever taken Jesus Christ into your life by faith? You *take and eat* of Jesus when you ask Him to save you from your sins, rescuing you from both their consequences and control.

Study Guide

The *Study Guide* questions at the end of each chapter have been designed for your personal benefit. *All* questions can be used for personal study and, if you're part of a discussion group, for preparation for your group meeting. If you are part of a small group, you will find that the questions preceded by the group icon (🗨) are especially useful for discussion. Your group leader can choose from among those questions when the group meets.

Icebreakers (for groups)

- How good is your sense of direction? Describe a time when you got lost.
- How significant a role—as a road map for life—did the Bible play in your family as you were growing up.

1. 🗨 What is the theme of the Bible's storyline and what does it mean? Why is it important to understand this theme as you read the Bible?

2. What does God promise to *redeem* people from in the following verses?
   Exodus 6:6 (compare with John 8:34, 36)

   Psalm 49:7–9, 15   Psalm 107:2

   Luke 21:25–28   Galatians 3:10, 13

   Titus 2:11–14   1 Peter 1:18, 19

3. When God prohibits Adam from eating the forbidden fruit, the death penalty for violating this command seems overly severe (Genesis 2:17). But why is death (spiritual, physical, and eternal) a natural consequence for disobeying God's commands?

4. It is difficult to take God's commands seriously if we are unfamiliar with them. On a separate sheet of paper, see how many of the Ten Commandments you can list—without looking them up in your Bible. Then read Exodus 20:1–17 and add to your list any that you missed. Once you're done, circle the top three commandments that pose the biggest challenge to you.

5. Read Genesis 3:1–6. What are the three strategies Satan used to undermine God's command and entice Adam and Eve to sin? (⚌) Describe how Satan has used (or is using) one of the Genesis 3 strategies on you.

What other "schemes" (Paul's word in Ephesians 6:11) does Satan use to tempt you to disobey God?

6. Adam blames Eve and God for his disobedience. Eve blames the serpent. With one or two of your most frequent sins in mind, *who* or *what* do you tend to blame for your disobedience? (⚌) Why is it our natural inclination to cover up our sins instead of owning up to them?

7. What were the consequences of Adam and Eve's sin?
    (•••) What other consequences for sin have you (or others) experienced?

8. Summarize the references to Christ's coming redemption that appear in Genesis 3.

(•••) When it comes to sin, we have all responded to the invitation to "take and eat." Have you also responded to the invitation to "take and eat" Christ by confessing your sins and asking Him to forgive them, and then receiving Him into your life by faith? If yes, briefly describe how this happened for you. If no, what has kept (is keeping) you from doing this?

{ 2 }

Redemption Prepared

BUTCH COLBY LOVES to get ready for Christmas. Back in 1980, Butch put up a few strings of lights on his house. And he enjoyed the experience so much that each year since he's expanded his display. In 2005, he was stringing over 55,000 lights! It added $500 to his monthly electric bill. But Butch didn't mind. The local community calls him Mr. Santa Claus.

Now, it takes a lot of work to put up that many lights. So each year Butch recruits a team of neighbors who spend all of their November weekends preparing the display—a display that airline passengers can see when they fly over his house.[1]

But Butch's preparation for the holiday season doesn't begin to compare with the way that God prepared for the very first Christmas—the Christmas God sent His Son to rescue the world. God's preparation for the big event began two thousand years before that starry night in Bethlehem. And it's described for us in the pages of the Bible's Old Testament. It's quite a story. I'm calling it *Epic*, because it's ginormous in scope and revolves around an amazing Hero.

So far, we've learned that the theme of the Bible is *redemption*. That is, the storyline traces a rescue effort—the greatest rescue effort in the history of humanity. This was prompted, we learned in chapter 1, by our sins. Our sins have corrupted our character, damaged our relationships, and brought a sense of futility to our lives. But worst of all, they have alienated us from God and rendered us spiritually dead.

Jesus Christ came to earth to rescue us from our sins. The Scriptures tell us He took upon Himself the punishment of death that our sins deserved (e.g., Isaiah 53:5–6; Romans 4:25; 1 Peter 2:24). To all who surrender their lives to Him, Jesus promises freedom from sin's control and the power to live in a way that is God-pleasing and

ABRAHAM is referred to as the "friend of God." That says a lot about this guy.

fulfilling. How did God pave the way for Jesus' arrival in this world? How did God prepare for that first Christmas? That's the topic of our study in this chapter.

God's preparation began two millennia before Jesus came to planet Earth, when God chose a man named Abraham. Abraham gave birth to a people. And those people gave birth to Jesus. Abraham's people were Jesus' ancestors.

Abraham is arguably the most important person in the Bible after Jesus. Almost one-fourth of the book of Genesis—

fourteen chapters—is devoted to telling his story. On three separate occasions in the Bible, Abraham is referred to as the *friend of God*. (If we're known by the friends we keep, that says a lot about this guy.)

Even the New Testament continues to talk him up. Romans, Galatians, Hebrews, James—these books all point to Abraham as a role model for us in terms of his faith and obedience. In fact, if you've put your faith in Jesus Christ, the apostle Paul says that Abraham is your spiritual father (Romans 4:16). How did he come by *that* title?

Abraham and the Big Ask

To begin to answer that question, let's look at the first three verses of Genesis 12, where Abraham's story begins:

> The Lord had said to Abram, "Leave your country, your people and your father's household and go to the land I will show you. I will make you into a great nation and I will bless you; I will make your name great, and you will be a blessing. I will bless those who bless you, and whoever curses you I will curse; and all peoples on earth will be blessed through you." (Genesis 12:1–3)

This exchange between God and Abraham takes place when Abraham is known as Abram. I'll explain the name

47

change to you a little later; for now I'll call him Abraham. Up to this point, Abraham has *not* been a follower of the one true God. He has worshiped idols, just like everybody else in his hometown of Ur.

But God appears to Abraham and asks him to do something that would take an incredible amount of faith to do. God wants Abraham to leave his country, his people, and his father's household. That's a big ask! God wants Abraham to relocate eight hundred miles away to a place where he would have no hope of staying in contact with his relatives and friends by phone or Facebook or a quick flight home.

What does God promise Abraham in exchange for taking such a huge step of faith? Three things: *a people*, *a place*, and *a purpose*. Each of these elements would play a critical role in the redemption that God was preparing for the world—a redemption that would reach fulfillment with the arrival of Jesus Christ.

In this chapter, we'll trace the promises made to Abraham about a people, a place, and a purpose. They recur in the pages of the Old Testament, and we'll cover twenty-two of the Old Testament's thirty-nine books. So let me recommend that you keep your finger in Genesis 12 of your Bible, as well as turn to the table of contents at the beginning of your Bible. I want you to see how the first twenty-two Old

Testament books fit together and how they contribute to the Bible's storyline.

Abraham and a People

Look again at the first half of Genesis 12:2, where God says to Abraham, "I will make you into a great nation and I will bless you." Abraham is seventy-five years old when God makes this promise to him. And he doesn't have any kids yet! But God says He will make Abraham into a great nation and Abraham believes God. A few chapters later in Genesis (15:5), God underscores this promise by taking Abraham outside on a clear night and asking him to count the stars. Of course, there are too many stars to count. God says: "That's how many descendants you're going to have" (author paraphrase). And once again, Abraham believes God.

Twenty-five years later (we're talking about a quarter-of-a-century interlude!), after Abraham has turned one hundred, God finally delivers on this promise. Isaac is born. That's when God changes Abram's name to Abraham, because Abraham means "father of many."

Father of *many*? At the time, it sounded like a wee bit of an overstatement, but Abraham kept on putting his faith in God. Well, Isaac has a son named Jacob. And Jacob has a son named Joseph, as well as eleven other sons. And these boys eventually become the heads of the twelve tribes of Israel.

The book of Genesis tells the stories of Abraham, Isaac, Jacob, and Joseph, guys who are often referred to as the "patriarchs," the early fathers.

After Joseph, one generation follows another . . . and another . . . and another. Almost two millennia later a baby is born through this ancestry, in Bethlehem, by the name of Jesus.

The gospel of Matthew, the first book in the New Testament, opens with a recitation of the genealogy of Jesus. And guess who's at the top of the list? Abraham!

So God fulfilled His promise to make Abraham into a great nation. And through Abraham's descendants, God provided the world with a Redeemer: Jesus Christ. This means that the Old Testament people of Israel formed the coming Redeemer's family tree. That was a very special

GOD EXPECTED the people of Israel to behave like a uniquely chosen people. They were to be set apart.

privilege for them. So God expected them to behave like a uniquely chosen people. They were to be set apart from all other peoples. They were to be qualitatively different.

The Bible has a word for qualitatively different. It's the word *holy*. God wanted His people, Jesus' ancestors, to be holy. God wanted them to be special, set apart. In order to provide them with a standard of holiness, God gave His people laws to follow. There are over six hundred laws spelled out in the first five books of the Old Testament.

Such laws remind me of a new high school basketball coach who seeks to shape his players into champions. He begins by putting some high standards in place. Rules to train by and later play by. (If you've seen Gene Hackman in the movie *Hoosiers*, you know how this is done.)

Now imagine *you're* the coach. Your rules cover everything from showing up on time for practice, to working out in the weight room, eating a healthy diet, maintaining a B average in schoolwork, dressing up on game day, demonstrating sportsmanship on the court, and so on. Why all the rules? Because you want your players to look and behave and carry themselves like champions—like a breed apart.

God wanted His people to be a breed apart (i.e., holy). So He gave them His laws. You will find them in the first five books of the Old Testament. The first book of the Bible, which we've been reading from, is Genesis. Genesis was written by Moses, who also wrote the next four books: Exodus, Leviticus, Numbers, and Deuteronomy.

Turn to your Bible's table of contents and you'll spot them. Now put a bracket beside these opening five Old Testament books (it's OK to write in your Bible) and label them: *Books of the Law.*

Three Kinds of Laws for Abraham's People

There are some great stories in these first five books. But a significant portion of Genesis through Deuteronomy is devoted to laying out the rules that God wanted His people to live by. As you read these books, you will encounter basically three kinds of laws. First, there are *moral* laws. Moral laws help people to determine right from wrong. They're timeless. They apply to everybody. The moral laws that we're most familiar with are contained in the Ten Commandments: prohibitions against murder, stealing, adultery, dishonesty. But there are additional moral laws sprinkled throughout the pages of Genesis through Deuteronomy.

In his book *This Is My God* (Doubleday), author Herman Wouk claims that the Jews' best contribution to the civilized world has been their moral laws. Wouk, an acclaimed novelist and a Pulitzer Prize winner for *The Caine Mutiny*, is also an orthodox Jew. He believes that God's promise to make Abraham into a blessing to all peoples on earth was fulfilled when Abraham's descendants gave the world a set of moral laws to live by.

I can't agree with Wouk on this score. The Jews' best contribution to all peoples has been Jesus! However, it's worth noting that the Old Testament's moral laws are also truly a gift to everyone. They're universally applicable and beneficial, even today. That's why we shouldn't ignore the first five books of our Bible. (When was the last time you read Leviticus?)

The second kind of laws that we find in Genesis through Deuteronomy are *ceremonial* (or *religious*) laws. Many of the ceremonial laws have to do with the offering of sacrifices, the regulation of the priesthood, and the furnishing of the tabernacle (which was the forerunner of the temple). These sorts of ceremonial laws are now obsolete. They're no longer in force.

Here's why: In Old Testament times, sacrifices were required by God as a payment for sins. This is how people gained forgiveness after disobeying God's moral laws. But once Jesus died on the cross to pay for sins, animal sacrifices were no longer necessary. Jesus became the supreme sacrifice for those who put their faith in Him. Similarly, priests are no longer needed because Jesus became our high priest, the only Mediator needed between God and us. And, finally, the tabernacle is no longer an indispensable building. It's now personified as a group of people—the people who follow Jesus and gather regularly to worship Him.

You may be thinking: If the laws that governed sacrifices, priests, and the tabernacle are now obsolete, why waste time reading about them in the Old Testament? I'm glad you asked.

Here's the benefit of familiarizing ourselves with the ceremonial laws today. When we read about the gory animal sacrifices, we're reminded of how disgusting our sins are. We're reminded that God hates sin so much that He requires the laying down of a life to pay for it. Eventually, that would be Jesus' life.

And when we read about the priests, and all the purification rituals they had to go through before they could serve as mediators for the people, we're reminded that our priest—Jesus—is perfect. And He's on constant duty as our advocate before God the Father. And when we read about the tabernacle and its elaborate furnishings, and

OUR PRIEST—Jesus—is perfect. And He's on constant duty as our advocate before God.

the huge religious festivals that took place there, we're reminded that God deserves enthusiastic, reverent, celebrative worship from us.

So, these ceremonial laws give us a deeper understanding and appreciation of Jesus Christ and our relationship with Him.

One final word about ceremonial laws. Besides the laws about sacrifices, priests, and the tabernacle, there are ceremonial laws in the Old Testament that do nothing but drive home the point that God's people are to be different from other people—holy. They are to be totally devoted to God and eager to stay far away from sin. How did God remind His people of their different-ness?

God used a wide variety of ceremonial laws to keep this truth constantly in front of Abraham's descendants. Some of these laws had to do with diet (what they could and couldn't eat), some of these laws had to do with clothing (what they could and couldn't wear), and some of these laws had to do with hygiene. The keeping of these kinds of ceremonial laws constantly reminded God's people that they were to be holy.

Here's the third major category of Old Testament laws: *civil* laws. These laws are somewhat dated because they were used to govern society in ancient Israel. They are laws that have to do with the protection of private property, the redressing of injuries, the guidelines for marriage and divorce, the care of widows and orphans, the fair treatment of people who work for you, and so forth. Because we don't live in ancient Israel, these laws don't apply to us today. At least, not directly. But if we will look for the principles behind each of these civil laws, we will be able to make an indirect application of them to our contemporary lives. More about this when we get to *Context* (the third book in the Bible Savvy series) and learn how to interpret the various literary types— including laws—that we find in Scripture.

Let's review. God prepared for the big rescue operation that would culminate in the sending of Jesus Christ by making three promises to a guy named Abraham two thousand years before Christ came to earth. The first promise had to do with people: God would make Abraham into a great nation, a people who would be the ancestors of the coming Redeemer. This special privilege required that these people be qualitatively different from other people. Holy, or set apart. So God gave them moral, ceremonial, and civil laws to live by. These laws are found in the first five books of the Old Testament.

Abraham and a Place

God's big rescue effort would need a launching pad. A place from which the rescue could be staged. Let's go back to Genesis 12. At the end of verse 1, God instructs Abraham: "Go to the land I will show you."

Briefly (this is my *Reader's Digest* version), Abraham completed an eight-hundred-mile journey to the land of Canaan. When he arrived, he found no real estate For Sale signs there. So he lived the rest of his life as a squatter on property that didn't belong to him.

Several generations later a famine in the land forced Abraham's descendants to relocate in Egypt, where his great-grandson Joseph had managed to get a job as Pharaoh's right-hand man. (Actually, God got him the job. Read the incredible story for yourself in Genesis 37–50.) Joseph was able to supply the family with food, keeping Jesus' family tree alive.

Everything was looking good for God's people. But some years later a new pharaoh came to power, and he didn't know anything about a former top employee named Joseph. So, God's people were made to be slaves, and their slavery extended for four hundred and thirty years, until a liberator by the name of Moses arrived on the scene. Moses' job was to get God's people out of Egypt and back to Canaan—back to the place that God had promised to Abraham and his descendants.

Flip back to your Bible's table of contents. The Old Testament Books of the Law, especially Exodus and Numbers, tell the story of Israel's deliverance from bondage in Egypt and their travels back to the land of Canaan (which has been nicknamed the *Promised Land*). At the very end of the Books of the Law, God's people are not quite there. They're on the east side of the Jordan River, looking westward into Canaan. Longingly. They haven't arrived. They still don't have a place of their own, as God had promised Abraham.

Which takes us to the next book in your table of contents: the book of Joshua. This book was named after Moses' successor, a military general who would lead God's people across the Jordan River and into the Promised Land.

The book of Joshua is filled with battles between God's people and the inhabitants of the land (the Canaanites). If you liked the *Lord of the Rings* trilogy, you'll love Joshua. But it's only fair to acknowledge that a lot of people who read Joshua are deeply disturbed by all the violence. Especially because it's *God* who commands His people to inflict this violence on others.

ARE GOD'S PEOPLE no better than religious extremists who advance their cause with the sword?

What's going on here? Is this just another example of religious jihad? Are God's Old Testament people no better than the religious extremists who advance their cause with the sword? Let me answer that question as briefly as I can. There are three major differences between the Israelites' conquering of Canaan and religious jihad. (A fuller explanation of these differences is available in Christopher Wright's book *The God I Don't Understand* [Zondervan].)

Difference #1: The conquering of Canaan involved a very limited period of warfare. God didn't intend warfare to be an ongoing activity for His people. Compare that, if you would, to militant Islam, whose wars of aggression have been going on for hundreds of years.

Difference #2: The conquering of Canaan was God's method of punishing the local inhabitants for their wickedness. The Bible says that the inhabitants of Canaan were an unbelievably evil people, known for horrific practices such as infant sacrifice. So, just as God used a flood during the days of Noah to wipe out wicked people, He used warfare during the days of Joshua to do the same thing.

Difference #3: The conquering of Canaan was not motivated by religious bigotry, since God threatened to bring a similar disaster on His own people if they ever became as wicked as the Canaanites. Joshua warned the people about this very danger in his farewell address at the close of the book (Joshua 24:11, 20).

Now, go back to your Bible's table of contents. After Joshua you see Judges. Yes, Canaan has been conquered; and God's people finally have a place of their own. But the possession of the land doesn't last for long. In a few short years, God's people start behaving wickedly, and so God allows an enemy nation to come in and defeat Israel in battle. God's people lose control of their land and are subjugated in virtual slavery.

This lasts for several decades, until the people repent of their sins and cry out to God for help. So God sends them a deliverer—a judge (hence, the name of the Old Testament book). Now, when you see the word *judge*, don't think of a guy who wears a black robe and sits behind a tall bench. An Old Testament judge was a combination of military hero, political statesman, and judicial leader. Israel's first judge, Othniel, led God's people to victory on the battlefield. The land was back in their own hands. They had their *place* once again.

But, as had happened previously, that didn't last for long. The people quickly returned to their sins. In fact, the book of Judges records one cycle after another in which: the people behave wickedly; God sends an enemy to take away their land and oppress them; they cry out to God for help; God sends them a deliverer; and the people return to wicked behavior. Round and round the cycle goes.

One of the few bright spots during the period of Judges was a woman named Ruth. Ruth led an exemplary, godly life, even though the people around her didn't. Ruth's story is told in the book after Judges. What d'ya think it's called? Yup: the book of Ruth.

After being led by judges for a few hundred years, God's people decided that they wanted a king. Israel's first king was Saul, followed by David and Solomon.

UNDER THE leadership of three kings, God's people reclaimed their land.

You may have heard of these three kings, who reigned around 1050 to 930 BC. This has been called Israel's Golden Age. Under the leadership of these three kings, God's people reclaimed their land. They even expanded their territory. Under King Solomon, there would be few skirmishes, as peace prevailed.

One day the prophet Nathan delivered this message from God to King David:

"Now I will make your name great, like the names of the greatest men of the earth. And I will provide a place for my people Israel and will plant them so that they can have a home of their own and no longer be disturbed. Wicked people will not oppress them anymore." (2 Samuel 7:9–10)

Did you catch that reference to God providing His people with a *place*? This portion of God's promise to Abraham was finally fulfilled during the reigns of Israel's first kings. And it was in this land that the world's Redeemer, Jesus Christ, would eventually be born. Redemption was being prepared.

Take another look at your Bible's contents page. If you want to read about Saul, David, and Solomon, Israel's first kings, you'll find their stories in the books of 1 and 2 Samuel, and the first half of the book of 1 Kings.

God promised Abraham a people, a place—and one more thing in preparation for redemption. What was that?

Abraham and a Purpose

Let's take one last look at Genesis 12. In the second half of verse 3, God promises Abraham: "All peoples on earth will be blessed through you." Let me note something really important here. God did not choose a people and give them a place of their own just so they could enjoy an exclusive relationship with God.

God wanted to bless *all peoples on earth* through Abraham and his descendants. How would this happen? Two ways. First, Abraham's line, as I've already pointed out, would one day produce a Redeemer who would rescue people from their sins. Jesus is the ultimate fulfillment of God's promise to Abraham that *all peoples on earth* would be blessed through him. Jesus is the Savior of all who put their trust in Him.

Second (and don't miss this one), God always intended that the people of Israel would make a relationship with *Yahweh*, the one true God, look so appealing that other peoples would want to make Israel's God *their* God. In other words, Abraham and his descendants would be a blessing to all peoples on earth by lighting the way to God. This was to be their mission, their calling, their purpose.

So, how did they do? Well, they got some good momentum going during Israel's Golden Age. They built God a beautiful temple—and even foreign people came from miles around to see it. Besides that, King David and King Solomon were known and admired, far and wide, for their godly wisdom. When Solomon first came to power (you may remember this story), God appeared to him in a dream and offered to give him anything he wished for. Do you remember Solomon's request? (1 Kings 3) Solomon asked for wisdom. And God gave it to him. A wisdom so great that it attracted leaders from other nations to Solomon's God. (See 1 Kings 4:34.)

On a recent trip to Israel, my tour group stopped at a promontory point, overlooking ancient Gibeon. We could see the likely spot where Solomon had prayed for wisdom. When our guide finished his presentation and invited the group to move on, I lingered behind for a few minutes of meditation. I wanted to repeat Solomon's wisdom-seeking prayer for myself. Not just so I can be a better leader, dad, friend, counselor. But so others will be drawn to the God who provides such wisdom. That's how it worked for Solomon.

The Quest for Wisdom, Then and Now

Return once more to your Bible's table of contents. Go down the list of Old Testament books and skip ahead until you come to Job. Do you see Job? Job begins a section of five books that are referred to as the *Books of Wisdom*.[2] Make a bracket around Job through Song of Songs and label it: *Books of Wisdom*.

David and Solomon wrote a lot of this stuff. Not all of it, but a lot of it. These books are intended to make God's people wise in the everyday affairs of life. Job is a book about wisdom in the midst of personal suffering. Psalms teaches the wisdom that comes from knowing and worshiping God. Proverbs is filled with wisdom sayings about all sorts of practical topics. Ecclesiastes has a lot to say about wisdom and vocational calling. And Song of Songs is about wisdom in romance and marriage.

When God's people behave wisely—I'll say it one more time—they point others to the God who's behind their wisdom. This fulfills the purpose that God gave to Abraham, the mission of blessing all peoples by directing them to God. Israel's Golden Age was characterized by this sort of attractive wisdom.

But the Golden Age didn't last. After Solomon, the spiritual life of Israel headed south. Solomon's son, Rehoboam, was not a wise king. And so there was a mutiny. Ten of the twelve tribes of Israel in the north broke away and formed their own country. They called it . . . *Israel* (pretty original, eh?). And Israel's capital became Samaria. The two tribes that were left in the south called their severely reduced country *Judah*. And Judah's capital city remained Jerusalem.

A Purpose Forfeited

Israel, the northern kingdom, endured one wicked king after another. When God finally had enough of this, He allowed the superpower of Assyria to destroy Israel and carry many of her people into its land as captives. The year was 722 BC.

Now, instead of being a light and blessing that would attract people from surrounding nations, a large part of Abraham's people were taken captive. Later others from Israel would follow. The people had ignored God's purpose, and now, for a time, forfeited it.

Judah, the southern kingdom, fared a little better. Occasionally a good king would take the throne and inspire the nation to turn to God. But these revivals never lasted. About 135 years after Israel fell, Judah fell. God allowed the superpower of Babylon to destroy Judah and carry many of her people into captivity. The year was 586 BC. Seventy years later, these captives were granted permission to return from exile to Judah. And they did their best to rebuild their homeland.

Time to mark up your Bible's table of contents again. If you want to read about the ups and downs of Israel and Judah (mostly the downs of all the kings who followed Solomon), you'll find this part of the story in the second half of 1 Kings and all of 2 Kings. The next two books, 1 and 2 Chronicles, are a repeat of all the material that's covered in 1 and 2 Samuel and 1 and 2 Kings. It would take me too long to fully explain the reason for the repeat, but in short, the Samuels and the Kings were written as God's people were *heading into exile* to remind them of the wicked behavior that had occasioned such punishment. The Chronicles were written years later, as God's people were *returning from exile*, to remind them of God's continuing grace in spite of their former sins. It's the same material, but with two different slants.

After the Chronicles, you'll see Ezra, Nehemiah, and Esther. These books cover the history of God's people as they return from captivity and rebuild their homeland. Now, put a bracket around twelve books—beginning all the way back at the book of Joshua and continuing down to the book of Esther—and label them the *Books of History*.

We just covered the first twenty-two of the Old Testament's thirty-nine books: Books of the Law, Books of Wisdom, and Books of History. Unfortunately, we are not leaving the Bible's storyline in a good place as we close this chapter. God has been preparing to redeem the world by setting apart a *people*, with a *place* of their own, whose *purpose* is to point others to God.

But God's people have not been cooperating. They've been making a mess of things. Does this ruin the *Epic* storyline?

God's Unconquerable Plan of Redemption

Well, the good news is, God's plan of redemption cannot be thwarted. God still had an "ace up His sleeve" (if it's OK to use that expression about God). God still planned to send a Savior through this line of wayward people. A Savior to fulfill His promises to Abraham. A Savior who would be a blessing to all peoples on earth who put their trust in Him.

When we put our trust in Jesus today, we inherit the promises that were given to Abraham. We become part of

God's *people*. We are guaranteed a *place* in God's eternal new heaven and new earth. And we are given the fantastic *purpose* in this life of pointing others to our Savior and God.

Study Guide

Icebreaker (for groups)

What family traditions do you observe in preparing for Christmas?

1. What is Abraham commended for in the following passages?

   Romans 4:18–21 and Galatians 3:6–9

   Hebrews 11:8–10

   James 2:20–22

2. Abraham's life illustrates how genuine faith and obedience go hand in hand. Describe a situation in which *your* faith was tested by requiring a demonstration of personal obedience.

3. What threefold promise did God make to Abraham?

4. List the three kinds of laws that are sprinkled throughout the first five books of the Old Testament. 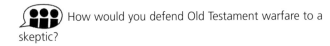 Explain the extent to which each kind of law is applicable to our lives today.

5. Why is reading through the ceremonial laws of Leviticus still worthwhile for us?

6. Who led Israel in initially conquering and occupying the Promised Land? What is disturbing about the contents of the Old Testament book that bears his name?

 How would you defend Old Testament warfare to a skeptic?

7. What cycle repeats itself, again and again, in the book of Judges? Do you see any parallels here to the Christian life? Explain.

8. What is God's purpose for His people? How was this purpose somewhat fulfilled during Israel's Golden Age? Give some examples of how today we might attract unbelievers or repel them from Christ.

Attract:

Repel:

9. List the five *Books of Wisdom* and note the topic that each one covers.

   Circle the one that you could use most in your life right now, and explain why.

10. What lesson(s) might we learn from what happened to Israel in the Old Testament?

{ 3 }

Redemption Prophesied

WHEN SHE WAS eight years old, Jeane Dixon accepted a crystal ball from a traveling gypsy, who announced that Jeane would one day become an advisor to powerful people. In the late 1950s, Jeane predicted that a Democrat would win the next presidential election, but that he would be assassinated while in office. John F. Kennedy, a Democrat, was elected president of the United States in 1960 and shot to death in 1963.

Jeane became an instant celebrity. She was called a modern-day prophet. Soon she became a syndicated columnist, writing an astrological advice column for hundreds of newspapers. President Nixon consulted her, as later did first lady Nancy Reagan. Some of Dixon's biggest predictions made the headlines when they came true, such as the communist takeover of China and the suicide of Marilyn Monroe. But it turned out that Dixon was wrong far more often than she was right. And some of her mis-predictions were whoppers. My favorite was her prediction that scientists would soon develop a "sun" pill that would contain a concentrated dose of solar energy and yield great health benefits. (Did you take your sun pill today?)

Overall, Jeane Dixon was not really a great prophet. But in this chapter, we're going to take a look at sixteen guys who *were*. Their names comprise the titles of the closing books in the Bible's Old Testament. The *Books of Prophecy* begin with Isaiah and conclude with Malachi. On your Bible's contents page, locate and label these *Books of Prophecy*.

If you happened to count these books while you were labeling them, you may have noticed that there are actually seventeen. Is my math off? No, sixteen prophets wrote a total of seventeen books in this section. Do you see the book of Lamentations? There's nobody named Lamentations in the Old Testament. It would be a bummer of a name. A lamentation is a poem or song of distress. The book of Lamentations was written by the previous guy on the list, Jeremiah, who was grieving over the destruction of Jerusalem. The other sixteen Books of Prophecy are all named after the prophets who composed them.

It's interesting to note that there are more Books of Prophecy than of any other kind of Old Testament literature. If you have been labeling, you'll be able to count five *Books of the Law* (Genesis–Deuteronomy), twelve *Books of History* (Joshua–Esther), and five *Books of Wisdom* (Job–Song of Songs). Compare that to a whopping seventeen *Books of Prophecy* (Isaiah–Malachi).

Introducing the Major and Minor Prophets

Let me give you some general background on the Books of Prophecy and on the men who wrote them. Bible scholars break these books down into two categories: the Major Prophets and the Minor Prophets. There are four major prophets: Isaiah, Jeremiah, Ezekiel, and Daniel. Why are these guys called the major prophets? Were they the Big Leaguers? Are their books the most important books of prophecy? Nope. Their books are just the longest books of prophecy.

So, four major prophets, which leaves us with twelve minor prophets (Hosea through Malachi). Please understand that these sixteen guys were not the only prophets in Israel during their day. There were scores of others, even big shots like Elijah and Elisha. But these sixteen men were the only ones who wrote Old Testament books, getting their names in your Bible's table of contents.

We don't learn very much about these prophets themselves from the books they wrote. We do know that they worked at a variety of occupations, since prophesying was not a full-time gig. Ezekiel, for example, was a priest. Daniel was a government employee (working for a pagan superpower). Amos was a fig-tree farmer. Zephaniah was a member of the royal family, the descendant of a king. But we don't have too many details about their lives.

Poetry and Oracles

These prophets frequently wrote in poetry. Do you read poetry on a regular basis? (I didn't think so.) Most of us are not big into poetry, so we may find the Bible's Books of Prophecy a bit more challenging to read than other parts of God's Word. And making it even more difficult, Hebrew poetry doesn't rhyme like a lot of English poetry. The only way you'll be able to tell you're reading poetry in the Bible is that the format for poetic line changes from an even left margin to indented lines, like with the verses of a poem.

Something else that you'll encounter in the Books of Prophecy is oracles. Oracles are just another way of referring to speeches. Now, imagine sitting down and reading all of the president's speeches from this past week—with no introductions, no context (you don't know who he's addressing, or what the occasion is), and no sense of where one speech ends and the next one begins. That's the challenge you'll face when reading large portions of the Books of Prophecy.

None of this should discourage you before you start. After you've read *Context*, the third book in the Bible Savvy series, you will feel more confident when encountering both poetry and oracles in the Books of Prophecy.

One final introductory comment about the sixteen major and minor prophets, before we jump into a discussion about their contribution to the Bible's storyline. This is kind of funky. Besides writing and prophetic pronouncements, a third creative communication tool the prophets used was drama. I like to think that the church I pastor is pretty hip, because we use visual arts like drama, video, and sermon props. Well, some of the Bible's prophets got there far ahead of us. They understood that a picture is worth a thousand words. So they sometimes acted out their messages.

Isaiah walked around naked for three years (you read that right), to drive home the point that Israel should trust God instead of their ally, Egypt, when facing conflicts with other nations. Why naked? Because Assyria would soon conquer Egypt and carry the Egyptians away as naked captives. How foolish to count on Egypt's future help. Ezekiel shaved his entire head (look at a photo of me and you'll see why I like this guy) and divided the hair into three piles. The first pile he burned, the second pile he jabbed with a sword, and the third pile he tossed into the wind. The point? If God's people didn't turn from their wickedness, destruction of their homeland would follow. Jeremiah went to a pottery shop and drew attention to the fact that the potter sometimes crumpled up his lump of clay and started over. This was a picture of what God was about to do to disobedient Israel. Pretty creative stuff, eh?

Preachers of Repentance

All the prophets played three major roles during their ministry. These three roles made a huge contribution to the Bible's storyline, God's plan of redemption. As we will see, they acted as preachers of repentance, predictors of world events, and proclaimers of the coming Christ.

If you look up the word "prophecy" in the dictionary, this is what you'll find: *a prediction of something to come.* So if you've never read the Bible's Books of Prophecy, you might expect that this is exactly what you'd find in them: lots of predictions about coming events. But surprisingly, only about one third of the prophets' writings are predictive in nature.

THE PROPHETS proclaimed what God said about people's sins and the consequences of those sins.

The other two thirds are appeals to people to turn from their sins and follow God. The prophets mainly acted as preachers of repentance.

So, the prophets were not primarily *foretellers* (predictors of future events). They were mostly *forth-tellers.* They told forth (or proclaimed) what God said about people's sins and the consequences of those sins. They began many of their messages with the words: "This is what the Lord says . . ." And there were three major themes to their forth-telling.

First, *they reminded people of God's laws.* In chapter 2 we explored the three kinds of laws in the Old Testament: moral, ceremonial, civil. The prophets focused most of their efforts on reminding God's people about the moral laws. If people didn't know these laws, or were ignoring these laws, there was a good chance that they were flagrantly disobeying God.

Let's read one of Jeremiah's oracles to get a feeling for the way in which an Old Testament prophet hammered home God's laws.

This is the word that came to Jeremiah from the Lord: "Stand at the gate of the Lord's house and there proclaim this message: . . .

"'This is what the Lord Almighty, the God of Israel, says: Reform your ways and your actions, and I will let you live in this place. . . . If you really change your ways and your actions and deal with each other justly, if you do not oppress the alien, the fatherless or the widow and do not shed innocent blood in this place, and if you do not follow other gods to your own harm, then I will let you live in this place, in the land I gave your forefathers for ever and ever. But look, you are trusting in deceptive words that are worthless.

"'Will you steal and murder, commit adultery and perjury, burn incense to Baal and follow other gods you have not known, and then come and stand before me in this house, which bears my Name, and say, "We are safe"—safe to do all these detestable things?'" (Jeremiah 7:1–10)

This oracle has much in common with those of many of the prophets. First, Jeremiah is addressing people who consider themselves to be believers. They're God's people. They've got Star of David stickers on their vehicles. Second, it's obvious they think that going to the temple guarantees them God's favor. Sure, they're disobeying God's laws. But God doesn't care about that as long as they show up each week for church, right? Finally, these people are guilty of a variety of sins—everything from following other gods, to adultery, to not caring about orphans, widows, and immigrants ("the alien").

This reminder of God's laws can have powerful application to believers and churchgoers today. We can ask ourselves whether we are ever guilty of the same kinds of sins. Do we ever follow after other gods by making our jobs, our personal possessions, or even our kids and their activities our number one priority? Are we guilty of adultery or other sexual sins that God's Word condemns, such as lusting (over pornography or attractive people) or fantasizing about sleeping with someone we're not married to? And what about not caring for hurting people: orphans, widows, immigrants? What are we doing to provide for their needs? Are we familiar with the commands of God that address matters like these?

As preachers of repentance, the prophets' first duty was *to remind people of God's laws.* Second, as preachers of repentance, they were *to warn their listeners of God's blessings and curses.*

AS PREACHERS of repentance, the prophets were to warn the people of God's blessings and curses.

Blessings are the consequences of obedience to God's laws, while curses are the consequences of disobedience.

Moses emphasized this correlation at the end of his book of Deuteronomy. *Deuteronomy* literally means "second" (Greek: *deuteros*) "law" (*nomos*), and this book restates the laws that God had given His people years earlier at Mt. Sinai. After Moses recapped these laws, he drove home the blessings and curses that accompany them.

Deuteronomy 28 begins with these words: "If you fully obey the Lord your God and carefully follow all his commands I give you today, the Lord your God will set you high above all the nations on earth. All these blessings will come upon you and accompany you if you obey the Lord your God" (vv. 1–2).

I won't spell out all the blessings that follow in this

passage. But Moses makes clear that obeying God's laws typically brings rewards such as health, prosperity, food, and protection from enemies.

Conversely Moses warns of the dangers of disobedience: "However, if you do not obey the Lord your God and do not carefully follow all his commands and decrees I am giving you today, all these curses will come upon you and overtake you" (v. 15).

Significantly, the ensuing section, which lists curses for disobedience, is three times as long as the one that itemizes blessings for obedience. Evidently, God does not take it lightly when His people disregard His laws. The curses that Moses mentions consist of what one Bible scholar refers to as the "D" list: disease, death, drought, danger, defeat, deportation, and disgrace. This is not a road we want to take.

Just a footnote to the blessings and curses of Deuteronomy 28. In order to help God's people remember these two lists, Moses gave them instructions for rehearsing the blessings and curses once they got to the Promised Land. They were to assemble six of the twelve tribes of Israel on Mt. Gerazim and the remaining six tribes across a valley on Mt. Ebal. The crowd on Mt. Gerazim was then to shout out the blessings of Deuteronomy 28 and the crowd on Mt. Ebal was to shout back the curses. Like a giant pep rally! ("We've got spirit, yes we do! We've got spirit, how 'bout you!") Sue and I stood on Mt. Gerazim last summer. While we didn't shout out any blessings, we enjoyed imagining this big event.

Centuries after Moses, the Old Testament prophets were still drilling God's people with the blessings and curses that result from obedience and disobedience to God's laws. A familiarity with Deuteronomy 28 would greatly increase our understanding of this aspect of the prophets' role as preachers of repentance.

A third part of that role (after reminding people of God's laws and warning them about blessings and curses) was that *they urged people to turn away from their sins and return to God.* The Hebrew word for turn or return is *shuv*. There are a lot of *shuvs* in the

TO HELP GOD'S people remember, they would rehearse the blessings and curses once they got to the Promised Land.

writings of the prophets. Consider the following examples (i.e., look for the references to turn or return):

> **Jeremiah:** "This is what the Lord says: Look! I am preparing a disaster for you and devising a plan against you. So turn from your evil ways, each one of you, and reform your ways and your actions." (18:11)

Ezekiel: "Repent! Turn away from all your offenses; then sin will not be your downfall. . . . As surely as I live," declares the Sovereign Lord, "I take no pleasure in the death of the wicked, but rather that they turn from their ways and live. Turn! Turn from your evil ways! Why will you die, O house of Israel?" (18:30; 33:11)

Hosea: "Return, O Israel, to the Lord your God. Your sins have been your downfall! Take words with you and return to the Lord. Say to him: 'Forgive all our sins and receive us graciously.'" (14:1–2)

Joel: "Rend your heart and not your garments. Return to the Lord your God, for he is gracious and compassionate, slow to anger and abounding in love, and he relents from sending calamity." (2:13)

You get the idea. As preachers of repentance, the prophets were constantly exhorting their listeners to turn, to do a 180-degree about-face. After reminding people of God's laws and warning them about blessings for obedience and curses for disobedience, the prophets urged them to turn away from their sins and return to God.

Faithful pastors are today's preachers of repentance. Although it may not win me any popularity contests, I plan to keep on reminding those at our church about God's laws, the biblical standards of right and wrong. And I plan to keep on warning our people (me included) that obedience leads to blessings and disobedience leads to curses. We must never think that we can disobey God, in big or small ways, and get away with it.

Finally, I plan to keep on urging all of us to turn from our sins and return to God, again and again and again. I hope you've found a church whose pastor is committed to this kind of forth-telling.

Predictors of World Events

Even though the prophets were primarily forth-tellers, they were also foretellers. They did predict the future. The remaining one third of their material was foretelling. What sorts of things do you think they foretold? What topic do you think *most* of their predictions were about? C'mon, take a guess.

Did you guess the first coming of Jesus Christ? Well, the prophets did have some very significant things to say about Christ's advent (which we'll explore shortly), but less than 2 percent of their predictions had to do with that future event.

Maybe you guessed that the prophets' hottest topic was the end times (what theologians refer to as *eschatology*). Nope. Less than 1 percent of the prophets' predictions had to do with the end times. I find that interesting, because I frequently hear from some who attend our church that they'd like a sermon series or a small group Bible study on the Books of Prophecy so that they might learn about how the world will end. Little do they know that this topic is barely on the radar in Isaiah through Malachi.

So what was all their foretelling about? More than 90 percent of the prophets' predictions had to do with world events that were about to happen in the immediate future of the prophets themselves. In other words, while these events were in *their* future, they are in *our* past. And that means if we want to understand the majority of the prophets' predictions, we need to know something about Bible history, since most of what they predicted has already taken place a long time ago!

With that in mind, here's a quick review of the Old Testament history mentioned in the previous chapter. In our review, I'll place all the major and minor prophets (with the exception of Obadiah and Nahum) onto this historical timeline.

After Israel's Golden Age (that era when Israel's first three kings, Saul, David, and Solomon, reigned), the kingdom began to unravel. This was about 900 BC. Solomon's son, Rehoboam, was a foolish ruler. His hardheaded leadership style incited a mutiny. Ten of Israel's twelve tribes seceded from the kingdom. They formed their own country in the north, which they called *Israel*, and made Samaria their capital city. Meanwhile, the two remaining tribes in the south formed the severely diminished country of *Judah* and kept the city of Jerusalem as their capital.

Things didn't go well for the northern country of Israel. They endured one wicked king after another. So, finally, in 722 BC, God allowed the superpower of Assyria to invade and conquer them. Now, this is where the writing prophets begin to pop up. As things were getting worse and worse in Israel, and as D-Day (722 BC) approached, God sent a couple of prophets to warn the people of their impending danger. These two prophets, Amos and Hosea, predicted what would happen if the northern country didn't turn around.

In fact, God even sent a prophet to Nineveh, the capital of Assyria, to put the brakes on Israel's major nemesis. And the Assyrians experienced a spiritual revival, which temporarily kept them from marching against God's people. Do you know that prophet's name? Jonah. Jonah chose not to go to Nineveh the first time God sent him. But after spending three days and nights as whale-food, he had a change of heart.

A quick side note here. If you'll look at your Bible's table of contents for a minute, please note something about the names of the three prophets I just mentioned. Amos, Hosea, and Jonah are the seventh, fifth, and ninth names among the guys who penned the Books of Prophecy, even though they were the first ones to arrive on the historical scene. What does that tell you? The Old Testament Books of Prophecy are not arranged chronologically. Too bad! That would make following the timeline so much easier. But this is why you need a good study Bible that provides a one- or two-page historical introduction for each of these books. (Throughout the Bible Savvy series you'll find me recommending the *NIV Study Bible*. This is my favorite, although the *ESV Study Bible* is a close runner-up.)

Back to our quick review of Old Testament history. After the northern country, Israel, was wiped out in 722 BC, the southern country, Judah, lasted another 135 years. And that's because Judah, you'll recall, occasionally had a good king. And those good kings brought about spiritual revivals. But those revivals never lasted for long. Finally, by 587 BC, Judah had become so wicked that God allowed the new superpower on the block, Babylon, to invade and conquer Judah.

As the time of collapse approached, more writing prophets warned what would happen if the people of Judah didn't straighten up. Isaiah and Micah had actually started warning Judah's residents about impending judgment almost two centuries earlier. Now, as the year 587 drew

ISAIAH AND MICAH started warning Judah's residents about impending judgment almost two centuries earlier.

ever closer, their voices were joined by those of Joel, Zephaniah, Habakkuk, and Jeremiah.

Jeremiah includes one blood-chilling story about the approaching Babylonian invasion in his prophetic book.

Jeremiah writes his predictions about what Babylon is going to do to Judah on a scroll, and he gives the scroll to his personal aide, Baruch, who later reads it to the king's officials. Once they hear the words of doom, the officials warn Baruch and Jeremiah to hide.

Evidently they know something about the king. Later King Jehoiakim listens as his secretary reads from the scroll. The king has a blaze going in the fireplace of his winter apartment. And each time the secretary finishes reading a few columns of Jeremiah's scroll, the king takes his pocketknife, slices off those columns, and feeds that part of the scroll to the fire (Jeremiah 36:1–26). In other words: "You can take your prophecy and stick it in your ear, Jeremiah."

But Jeremiah's predictions came true. Babylon invaded and conquered Judah. And thousands of Judah's citizens were taken away as captives to Babylon. The prophets Daniel and Ezekiel were among those captives. Their books are filled with all sorts of predictions about world events from this era.

God's people endured seventy years of exile in Babylon. When Babylon was superseded by Persia, Persia's King Cyrus allowed God's people to return to their homeland. Many of them did. And they began to rebuild the temple, as well as the walls of Jerusalem.

But it wasn't long before the people lost interest in these building projects. It wasn't long before they became more interested in their personal concerns than in God's work. It wasn't long before they began to drift spiritually.

So God sent three prophets, by the names of Haggai, Zechariah, and Malachi, to get the people back on track. Interestingly, one of the things that had caused the people who were rebuilding the temple to lose interest in the project was that their new temple was just a shadow of the one that **SOLOMON'S TEMPLE had been glorious. The rebuilt temple looked like a Lego construction by comparison.** had formerly stood there. Solomon's temple had been glorious. Their rebuilt temple looked like a Lego construction by comparison.

But the prophet Haggai motivated them to keep on rebuilding with an amazing prediction. This is Haggai's word from God: "'I will shake all nations, and the desired of all nations will come, and I will fill this house with glory,' says the Lord Almighty. . . . 'The glory of this present house will be greater than the glory of the former house,' says the Lord Almighty. 'And in this place I will grant peace'" (Haggai 2:7, 9).

Haggai prophesied that one day God would send someone—"the desired of all nations"—to that rebuilt temple, whose presence would fill the temple with greater glory than the glory it had had in the days of Solomon. Who do you think that someone would be? Jesus Christ. What a prediction!

Proclaimers of Christ

That takes us to the third and final role of the prophets. They were preachers of repentance, predictors of world events, and *proclaimers of Christ*. Although only one third of what the Old Testament prophets wrote was predictive in nature, and of this one third, less than 2 percent of those predictions had to do with the coming of Jesus Christ, those predictions about the Christ [Heb. *Messiah*] in the Books of Prophecy are truly amazing. They comprise the third key role of the prophets.

How amazing are these prophecies of the coming Christ? Keep in mind that the final prophet, Malachi, lived about 430 BC. That means that every one of the predictions about Jesus in the prophets was made before that time—hundreds and hundreds of years before He came to earth.

Here's just a brief sampling of those prophecies, beginning with Isaiah in the eighth century BC. The prophet used the word *salvation* twenty-six times in his book. He wrote so much about the anticipated Savior that his book is sometimes referred to as the *fifth Gospel* (after the New Testament Gospels of Matthew, Mark, Luke, and John).

Shortly after Jesus began His public ministry, He visited the synagogue in His hometown of Nazareth where He was asked, as a visiting rabbi, to read some Scripture. And when He finished, He said, in essence: "I'm the fulfillment of what I just read to you" (see Luke 4:21). Significantly, Jesus had read from the book of Isaiah (specifically 61:1–2).

Here are just two examples of Isaiah proclaiming Christ:

For to us a child is born, to us a son is given, and the government will be on his shoulders. And he will be called Wonderful Counselor, Mighty God, Everlasting Father, Prince of Peace (9:6). (Note that a human child will be born who will be divine; He will be called "Mighty God.")

But he was pierced for our transgressions, he was crushed for our iniquities; the punishment that brought us peace was upon him, and by his wounds we are healed. We all, like sheep, have gone astray, each of us has turned to his own way; and the Lord has laid on him the iniquity of us all. (53:5–6)

One of the things that confused the readers of Isaiah for hundreds of years before Jesus came to earth was that the prophet spoke of the coming Redeemer as both a victorious king (as we read in Isaiah 9:6) *and* a suffering servant (Isaiah 53:5–6). How could the same person fill both of those roles? Well, when Jesus came to earth the first time, He arrived as a suffering servant, who gave His life on the cross in payment for our sins. But when He returns a second time, at some point in the future, He will come as a victorious king. Wow!

Of course, Isaiah wasn't the only prophet who proclaimed Christ. Daniel predicted the exact time of Christ's coming (9:24). Micah said that the coming Redeemer would be born in the small village of Bethlehem (5:2). Zechariah was second only to Isaiah in the number of predictions about the coming Redeemer. He prophesied, among other things, that Christ would ride triumphantly into Jerusalem on the back of a colt (9:9), but would later be betrayed for thirty pieces of silver (11:12–13) and have His body pierced in death (12:10).

These are stunning predictions. And this is how the Old Testament portion of the Bible's storyline wraps up. So far, we have observed redemption prompted, prepared, and prophesied. It's now time to move to the New Testament and this *Epic* storyline's high point.

*To watch Jim's midpoint comments about Epic,
scan this QR code with your samrtphone, or go to
www.Biblesavvy.com/video/#epic2.*

Study Guide

Icebreaker (for groups)

Are you into poetry? Why or why not? If you are a fan of poetry, who is your favorite poet and/or what is your favorite poem?

1. How are the Major Prophets different from the Minor Prophets? What are some of the general characteristics of Old Testament prophetic literature?

2. As forth-telling "preachers of repentance," what were the three main emphases of the prophets' sermons? Why do you think they began their messages by reminding the people of God's laws?

3. Make a list of all the laws that Jeremiah refers to in 7:1–10. Circle the ones that are still applicable to our lives today. What does this exercise tell you?

4. Jeremiah's audience tended to ignore God's laws due to their mistaken assumption that their disobedience was compensated for by their attendance at the temple. In what ways do we dismiss the importance of obeying God's laws today?

5. Read Deuteronomy 28:1–68 and make a list of the blessings that accompany obedience and the curses that accompany disobedience.

   Blessings of Obedience   *Curses of Disobedience*

6. Why do you think the portion of Deuteronomy 28 that spells out curses is three times the length of the portion that spells out blessings?

So many Christian sermons and books today are slanted in the opposite direction—emphasizing the *positive* (blessings), almost to the exclusion of the *negative* (curses). Why do you think that's the case? What is the potential downside of this imbalance?

7. God repeatedly pleads with His people to *turn* from their sins and *return* to Him. What do the following references tell you about this *God* who constantly urges us to repent? (These verses are printed out in chapter 3, so you don't have to look them up.) Why should such a profile encourage us to regularly confess and forsake our sins?

Jeremiah 18:11; Ezekiel 18:30; Ezekiel 33:11;

Hosea 14:1–2; Joel 2:13

Where is a good place to find a quick summary of each writing prophet's historical context? How will this help you better understand the books they wrote?

8. Why is it important to understand Old Testament history (not end-times events) when reading the *predictive* prophecies in Isaiah–Malachi?

9. What do the following prophecies proclaim regarding Christ's first coming?

   Daniel 9:24

   Micah 5:2

   Zechariah 9:9; 11:11–12; 12:10

   Isaiah 53:5–6

   Why do you think God prophesied Christ's coming— as opposed to just having Him show up?

{ 4 }
Redemption Purchased

DO YOU LIKE treasure hunts? Years ago, when I was a college student, I went to my campus mailbox one day to find a little note that read: "Welcome to the April Fool's Treasure Hunt." Yes it was April 1, and the note informed me to look under the sink in the men's room for the opening clue. The note was signed by my girlfriend.

My immediate reaction was to write it off as a gag. I suspected that there was probably a group of young women watching from around the corner, hoping to see me take the bait and head into the men's room. No way was I going to fall for the prank.

But my curiosity eventually got the better of me. Looking both ways to make sure I wasn't being spied on, I slipped into the men's room. I stood in front of the mirror, pretending to comb my hair. Then I deliberately dropped my comb, bent to pick it up, and checked out the underside of the sink. There *was* a note!

And for the next two hours, note after note directed

me around campus until I ended up back at the student post office, where the final note instructed me to ask the lady at the counter for my prize. It turned out to be a Mickey Mouse kite. Not wanting my girlfriend to get the last laugh, I assembled the kite and hung it out a third floor window of that building, along with a sign professing my love for this young lady. It must have worked, because she's now my wife.

For the past three chapters we have been on an *Epic* treasure hunt through the thirty-nine books of the Old Testament. Clue after clue has pointed us to the greatest prize of all time: a coming Redeemer. Someone who would deliver humanity from the consequences and tyranny of sin.

The hints that would lead us to this Redeemer first appeared in the garden of Eden, when God announced to Satan that he would one day be crushed by a descendant of Eve. Years later, God told Abraham that through his offspring all peoples on earth would be blessed—another allusion to the coming Redeemer. And although Abraham's progeny did a terrible job of behaving like the family tree of a great Savior, prophets continued to reiterate God's promise to send a worldwide redeemer through this lineage.

The last prophet, Malachi, wrote his Old Testament book around 430 BC. And then everything became very quiet. In fact, the next four centuries have been referred to by Bible scholars as "the silent years," because God stopped sending messengers with news about a redeemer. Not that life itself was silent in the locale that had been identified as the Redeemer's future birthplace. Israel was in constant turmoil, as conquerors came and went.

The Persians, who had allowed God's people to return from Babylonian captivity to their homeland, were eventually defeated by Alexander the Great. Alexander unified his kingdom through the promotion of the Greek language and culture (a process known as *hellenization*), which indirectly resulted in the publication of a Greek version of the Old Testament (called the *Septuagint*). The Bible became a popular book. But God's people, for the most part, lived under the oppression of one cruel foreign regime after another, culminating in Roman subjugation after General Pompey conquered Jerusalem in 63 BC.

Four Gospels Herald the Christ

Finally, God broke His silence by sending His Son into the world. No Bible books had been produced since Malachi's Old Testament contribution. But now the period between the Old and New Testaments comes to an end with the publication of four biographies about Jesus of Nazareth, the Christ. These Gospels (*gospel* means "good news") open the New Testament, which is made up of twenty-seven books in all. (More about how these books came to be written and collected into one volume can be found in *Foundation*, the second book in the Bible Savvy series.)

Why four Gospels? Wouldn't one suffice? Good question. The answer is that these biographies were written for different audiences. Each audience had its own needs, culture, and level of biblical understanding. The basic facts about Jesus' life and ministry don't change from one Gospel to another, but their packaging does.

Matthew, for instance, is written predominantly for Jewish readers. It opens by tracing Jesus' genealogy back to Abraham. It's full of quotations from the Old Testament. Instead of referring to the kingdom of *God* (which would have offended orthodox Jews who avoided direct usage of God's name), Matthew talks about the kingdom of *heaven*. And this Gospel is organized around five prominent speeches of Jesus, just as the Old Testament is headlined by five books of Moses, a Jewish hero.

Mark, the second Gospel in our New Testament (although probably the first one that was written), is aimed at Gentiles. John Mark, the author, takes time to explain Jewish customs to the uninitiated. And Mark talks a lot about suffering, a topic of interest to Gentile Christ followers, since the apostle Peter (Mark's mentor) had recently been crucified in Rome in a growing wave of persecution against believers.

Luke, like Matthew, provides us with an opening genealogy for Jesus. But Luke's genealogy stretches all the way back to Adam, the first man! It's obvious that Luke wants to present us with a redeemer who is relevant to everyone. This emphasis reflects Luke's global perspective. He was a traveling companion of the apostle Paul, taking the good news of Jesus to every corner of the then-known world.

The fourth Gospel, John, clearly states its objective in 20:30–31: "Jesus did many other miraculous signs in the presence of his disciples, which are not recorded in this book. But

JOHN AIMS TO make believers out of spiritual seekers, so his Gospel focuses on seven of Jesus' miraculous signs.

these are written that you may believe that Jesus is the Christ, the Son of God, and that by believing you may have life in his name." John, one of Jesus' original twelve disciples, aims to make believers out of spiritual seekers. That's why his Gospel focuses on seven of Jesus' miraculous signs, which point to the Redeemer's identity as the Son of God.

Four Gospels with four distinct portraits of Jesus Christ. But they present us with one Savior and one common theme: *Redemption Purchased.* This is the climax of the Bible's *Epic* storyline. This is where redemption becomes a reality, not just something that's been prompted, prepared, and prophesied.

Open your Bible to the table of contents and write *Redemption Purchased* next to the New Testament books of Matthew, Mark, Luke, and John. Now, let's talk about what this means.

Jesus' Mission

I recently read a biography of one of my favorite U.S. presidents: Rutherford B. Hayes. (I'll bet you were expecting me to say George Washington or Abraham Lincoln.) While Hayes is unknown to most Americans, I've become familiar with his life because my wife grew up in his hometown of Fremont, Ohio, where his mansion and presidential library sit on twenty-five acres of parkland. Hayes was actually a pretty amazing guy. The author of his biography took 533 pages to tell his life story (including the tale of having five horses shot out from underneath him during the Civil War).

But interestingly, it's not until page 520 that the events leading up to Hayes' death are mentioned. And the death itself is only described in the final two pages of the book. That means about 2 percent of this biography is dedicated to Hayes' final days, and less than .4 percent portrays his actual death.

Let's compare that to the Gospel biographies of Jesus Christ. The four Gospels devote a significant portion of their narratives to detailing Jesus' final week: His triumphal entry into Jerusalem; His famous Last Supper; His agonizing prayer in the garden of Gethsemane; His arrest and bogus trials; His torture and brutal death on the cross; and His resurrection. John, in fact, devotes so much of his Gospel to these events, that his biography of Jesus is sometimes referred to as "a passion [i.e., death] narrative with an introduction." The description of crucifixion week begins in chapter twelve of John's twenty-one chapters. In other words, just beyond the midpoint of the book!

Why do Matthew, Mark, Luke, and John focus so much attention on Jesus' death? Because Jesus Himself, during His earthly ministry, focused so much attention on His upcoming death. Mark's Gospel is instructive on this point. In Mark 8, shortly after performing some spectacular miracles, Jesus asks His disciples, "Who do people say I am?" (Mark 8:27). The disciples throw out several responses they've heard noised about. But when Jesus asks them who *they* think He is, Peter answers enthusiastically: "You are the Christ" (v. 29).

This is a momentous occasion. This is the first time that Jesus has been identified accurately by His disciples. A cause for celebration? No, it actually serves as an intro to a sobering lecture from Jesus about His upcoming death. "He then began to teach them that the Son of Man must suffer many things and be rejected by the elders, chief priests and teachers of the law, and that he must be killed and after three days rise again. He spoke plainly about this" (vv. 31–32). This is only the first of three times that Jesus will bring up the topic of His death in Mark's Gospel. (See also Mark 9:31 and 10:33–34.)

Was Jesus just a gloomy, glass-half-empty kind of guy? Why was He so fixated on dying? Because that was the heart of His mission. Jesus spelled out His God-given assignment to His disciples: "The Son of Man did not come to be served, but to serve, and to give his life as a ransom for many" (Matthew 20:28). Later in Matthew's Gospel, as Jesus passed the cup of wine among His disciples at the Last Supper, He said: "This is my blood of the covenant, which is poured out for many for the forgiveness of sins" (26:28).

So Jesus' death was central to His mission of delivering people from their sins. How did dying accomplish this purpose? How did the Cross result in people being forgiven sin's penalty and ransomed from sin's power? How should we explain Jesus' atonement? Theologians have wrestled with this issue for centuries and several popular theories have been proposed along the way.

Some picture Jesus' death as primarily a defeat of Satan and the liberation of people from his diabolical control. This is called the *Christus Victor* view of the atonement. It is certainly supported by the Genesis 3:15 statement that one day a descendant of Eve would crush Satan's head. The apostle Paul describes Jesus' fulfillment of this prophecy in Colossians 2:15: "Having disarmed the powers and authorities, he made a public spectacle of them, triumphing over them by the cross."

Although the *Christus Victor* view is supported by verses like this one, I question whether it is the most prominent depiction of the atonement in the Bible. Besides that, it seems to focus too much attention on the conquered foe and not enough on those who've been liberated from his tyranny.

A second popular view of Jesus' death is that it serves as *an example* to us. This view comes in a variety of flavors. Some see the greatest value in Jesus' example as being the love He showed us at the cross. This love, they say, has the power to melt our hard hearts and motivate us to love God in response (see 1 John 3:16; 4:10). Others who hold the example view of the atonement emphasize the revulsion it produces in us toward sin. When we observe what sin did to Jesus, nailing Him to a cross, our only fitting response is to put an end to sin in our own lives (see Hebrews 12:3–4). Still another variety of the example view of Jesus' death points out how it calls us to a selfless and sacrificial lifestyle (see 2 Corinthians 5:15 and 1 Peter 2:21).

While it cannot be denied that Jesus, in His death, is a role model for us, along the lines of what I've just described, I believe that it would be wrong to choose *example* as the explanation of the atonement's primary purpose. Keep in mind that the theme of the Bible's storyline is redemption. God is on a rescue mission. He is out to save us. But if the goal of

Jesus' death on the cross was principally to provide us with an example to follow, the inference would be that we are somehow responsible for saving ourselves. Yes, Jesus gets the credit for setting an example to which we may aspire. But it's now up to us to take the ball and run with it. I hardly think this is the picture that the Bible paints of redemption.

There's a third view of the atonement that I believe most adequately sums up how Jesus accomplished His mission by dying on the cross. This view sees Jesus' death in terms of *sacrifice*. He paid the penalty that our sins

SACRIFICE is the central focus of the cross.

deserved—the forfeiture of life. While some evangelical Bible scholars are willing to accept this as "a" view of the atonement, they insist that we balance it with other views, such as those I've just described.

One writer even likened this balancing act to the way we use a bag of golf clubs. We don't (I'm summarizing his argument) use the same club off the tee, in the fairway, and on the putting green, do we? Just as we choose from an assortment of golf clubs based upon the shot that's required, so we should select our view of the atonement based upon its relevance to the situation at hand.

This analogy rightly recognizes that Jesus' death achieved a variety of goals, yet it does not do justice to *sacrifice* as the primary aim of the atonement. Sacrifice is not just a one-among-equals golf club. It is the central focus of the cross.

Why do I say that? Because the Old Testament, in preparing us for Jesus' cross, constantly emphasizes the importance of atoning sacrifices. The very first sacrifice occurred when God provided animal skins to cover a guiltily cowering Adam and Eve. Abraham, too, learned the importance of sacrifice when God commanded him to place his son, Isaac, on an altar, but then provided a ram to take Isaac's place. (You can read the gripping account in Genesis 22.) And Moses codified an extensive sacrificial system in his *Books of the Law*.

Most poignantly, the prophet Isaiah used the language of sacrifice to spell out the coming Redeemer's mission, when he wrote: "But he was pierced for our transgressions, he was crushed for our iniquities; the punishment that brought us peace was upon him, and by his wounds we are healed. We all, like sheep, have gone astray, each of us has turned to his own way; and the Lord has laid on him the iniquity of us all" (Isaiah 53:5–6).

What would be the Redeemer's mission on earth? To die. To sacrifice His life in payment for the sins of others. No wonder Jesus' biographers—Matthew, Mark, Luke, and John—devoted so much of their Gospels to the events leading up to and including the Cross. Jesus purchased our redemption by laying down His life. As the apostle Peter puts it: "For you know that it was not with perishable things such as silver or gold that you were redeemed . . . but with the precious blood of Christ, a lamb without blemish or defect" (1 Peter 1:18, 19).

Jesus' Qualifications

Victor Lustig was one of the most clever, notorious con men who ever lived. Without a doubt his greatest feat was the selling of the Eiffel Tower in 1925. (I'm not making this up!)

One day while reading his newspaper in Paris, Lustig spotted an article indicating that the French government was facing difficulty in maintaining the Eiffel Tower in the postwar economy. This gave the cunning Lustig an idea. Posing as a government official, he invited several CEOs of scrap metal businesses to a meeting. He explained to them that the Eiffel Tower would be sold to the highest bidder, who could then haul it away. One of the businessmen fell for the ruse, and Lustig was soon on a train for Vienna with a suitcase full of cash.[1]

Would we believe somebody who offered us the Eiffel Tower? I hope not! Then why would we believe somebody who offers us redemption from sin and eternal life? What is it about Jesus Christ that assures us that He could actually deliver the goods? The Bible answers this question by spelling out the unique attributes that qualify Jesus to serve as the world's Redeemer: He is the only one in history who is both fully God and fully human.

Why is such a profile necessary for the role of Redeemer? To understand the requirements of one to redeem the human race, we begin with the "fully man" nature of Jesus. In order to pay for our sins, Jesus had to be one of us. Jesus had to be a human to represent humans. People had sinned and so a real person must die. The writer of Hebrews explains the necessity of Jesus' humanness as follows: "Since the children [i.e., we] have flesh and blood, he too shared in their humanity so that by his death he might destroy him who holds the power of death—that is, the devil—and free those who all their lives were held in slavery by their fear of death. . . . For this reason he had to be made like his brothers in every way . . . that he might make atonement for the sins of the people" (Hebrews 2:14–15, 17).

On the other hand, if Jesus had been only human, His sacrifice would have been of limited worth. This is easy to illustrate. If a soldier throws himself on a grenade, his sacrifice saves the lives of all the men who are in his bunker. But it doesn't save the lives of every soldier in the army. Get it? The sacrifice of a finite being can only be finite in its effectiveness. But what if someone's life was, by nature, infinite? What if someone was, let's say, *God*? Because of Jesus' divine nature, His sacrifice on the cross was of limitless worth. It purchased redemption for everyone, in every time and place, who puts their trust in Jesus as Savior and Lord.

Matthew on Jesus' Dual Nature

Now this is great theory—that Jesus, being fully God and fully man, is uniquely qualified to be our redeemer. But do we have any evidence to support this dual-nature notion? It's time to return to the Bible's epic storyline and see what Jesus' biographers had to say about Him in this regard. We'll do a quick survey of one of the Gospels, Matthew's, considering four passages that attest to Jesus' God-man qualifications for being the Redeemer.

Let's begin with a familiar passage about Jesus' birth:

This is how the birth of Jesus Christ came about: His mother Mary was pledged to be married to Joseph, but before they came together, she was found to be with child through the Holy Spirit. Because Joseph her husband was a righteous man and did not want to expose her to public disgrace, he had in mind to divorce her quietly.

But after he had considered this, an angel of the Lord appeared to him in a dream and said, "Joseph son of David, do not be afraid to take Mary home as your wife, because what is conceived in her is from the Holy Spirit. She will give birth to a son, and you are to give him the name Jesus, because he will save his people from their sins."

All this took place to fulfill what the Lord had said through the prophet: "The virgin will be with child and

will give birth to a son, and they will call him Immanuel"—which means, "God with us." (Matthew 1:18–23)

Do you see evidence of both Jesus' human and divine
natures in this passage? Humanly speaking, Jesus was born
to a man and a wom-
an, Joseph and Mary. **THE SIGNIFICANCE of this**
Mary was Jesus' actual **name [Immanuel] is that it**
biological mother. And **means** *God with us*. **Jesus**
Joseph, even though he **is** *God* **with us!**
didn't contribute any
DNA to the baby, is recognized in these verses as Jesus' legal
father. That's why the genealogy that opens Matthew's Gospel (1:1–17) traces Jesus' ancestry from Abraham to *Joseph*.
For all intent and purposes, Joseph was Jesus' dad.

In addition to having human parents (one biological and
the other legal), Jesus' humanity is underscored in this text by
the angel's proclamation to Joseph that Jesus would "save *his*
people from their sins" (italics added). Jesus, clearly, belonged
to a people. He was one of them.

On the other hand, there was a divine aspect to Jesus'
birth. Mary was a virgin. She had not been impregnated by
Joseph. Nor by any man, for that matter. Where, then, did the
baby come from? Not once, but twice, we are told by Matthew that Jesus was conceived in Mary by the Holy Spirit.

This accounts for Jesus' nature as God. And to make sure that we have not missed this point, Matthew quotes a seven-hundred-year-old prophecy from Isaiah about a virgin giving birth to a child who would be called *Immanuel.* The significance of this name is that it means *God with us.* Jesus is *God* with us!

Now, let's fast-forward from Jesus' birth to the inauguration of His ministry. The big press conference that announced this new phase of His life was a baptism celebration. Here's how Matthew tells the story:

> Then Jesus came from Galilee to the Jordan to be baptized by John. But John tried to deter him, saying, "I need to be baptized by you, and do you come to me?"
>
> Jesus replied, "Let it be so now; it is proper for us to do this to fulfill all righteousness." Then John consented.
>
> As soon as Jesus was baptized, he went up out of the water. At that moment heaven was opened, and he saw the Spirit of God descending like a dove and lighting on him. And a voice from heaven said, "This is my Son, whom I love; with him I am well pleased." (Matthew 3:13–17)

Why did Jesus get baptized? Before you answer that question, let me point out that the others who were getting dunked by John the Baptist were doing so as a sign of their repentance from sin. "Confessing their sins, they were baptized"

(v. 6). John made sure that everyone understood, "I baptize you with water for repentance" (v. 11). So, was Jesus' baptism a public renunciation of personal sin? That hardly seems possible, since the Gospels paint a picture of Him as faultless. Throughout His ministry, even His antagonists were unable to pin any moral wrongdoing on Him.

If Jesus, then, did not get baptized as an act of repentance, we must conclude that He had some other reason for doing so. Jesus' own explanation was a rather cryptic, "It is proper for us to do this to fulfill all righteousness" (v. 15). Most evangelical Bible scholars hold that Jesus' baptism was a God-ordained means of identifying **JESUS' BAPTISM underscored His humanity.** with the people He had come to save. He was qualified, as a divinely approved human being, to serve as their representative. Jesus' baptism underscored His humanity.

But it also showed signs of His deity. The Christian God, as you know, is believed to be triune: Father, Son, and Spirit. One God, three persons. Together they form the Godhead, or the Trinity. Although the Bible never uses the word *Trinity*, depictions of such a God pop up throughout Scripture. We see one here at Jesus' baptism. The *Father's* voice expresses, from heaven, His love for His *Son*. And the *Spirit* settles on Jesus in the form of a dove. This is a snapshot of the three-in-one God, and Jesus is in the middle of the picture. Certainly this affirms His God-ness.

Have you ever witnessed a baptism like this one? We baptize hundreds of people at my church every year, but I have never heard God the Father audibly blessing anyone, nor seen the Spirit descending on anyone's shoulder. Jesus definitely belongs in a category of His own: a man who is God.

Now, let's jump ahead into the thick of Jesus' ministry for a third look at His dual nature. Here's an incident from a typical day in the life of the Redeemer:

> Jesus stepped into a boat, crossed over and came to his own town. Some men brought to him a paralytic, lying on a mat. When Jesus saw their faith, he said to the paralytic, "Take heart, son; your sins are forgiven."
>
> At this, some of the teachers of the law said to themselves, "This fellow is blaspheming!"
>
> Knowing their thoughts, Jesus said, "Why do you entertain evil thoughts in your hearts? Which is easier: to say, 'Your sins are forgiven,' or to say, 'Get up and walk'? But so that you may know that the Son of Man has authority on earth to forgive sins . . ." Then he said to the paralytic, "Get up, take your mat and go home." And the man got up and went home. When the crowd saw this,

they were filled with awe; and they praised God, who had given such authority to men. (Matthew 9:1–8)

We will assume Jesus' humanity, as we consider this passage, and concentrate instead on two evidences of His deity that are apparent here. The first is His implicit claim to be able to forgive sins. Jesus' offer of absolution to the paralytic really riled the religious leaders. They called it *blasphemy*, because forgiving (in the ultimate sense) is something only God can do. Jesus was making Himself out to be God. Of course, this would only be blasphemy if Jesus were *not* God. If Jesus was indeed God, forgiving the paralytic would be His legitimate prerogative. Jesus' claim to be able to do so would make absolute sense.

(By the way, Jesus makes claims that put Him on par with God in many other places in the Gospels. One of the most dramatic is His announcement to the Jews: "Before Abraham was born, I am!" [John 8:58]. No doubt Jesus was referring to His eternal preexistence as God. And the stinger to this claim was the *I am* at the end of it, since *I AM* was the name by which God revealed Himself in the Old Testament. Jesus' listeners got the message. Once again, they were certain it was blasphemy. And this time they decided to do something about it, picking up rocks to stone Jesus. But He slipped away from them.)[2]

Not only did Jesus claim the ability to forgive sins, something that only God could do, but Jesus also revealed His divine nature in a second way. He healed the man! And this is not an isolated healing on the part of Jesus. There are thirty miracle-cure stories in the four Gospels. These healings demonstrate Jesus' power over sickness. And He did other kinds of miracles as well, that showcased His power over nature (walking on water, multiplying a few loaves and fish to feed thousands, stilling a storm at sea), over evil forces (casting out demons), and even over death (resurrecting, among others, His friend Lazarus). Only God has power like this!

JESUS' MIRACLES showed His power over sickness . . . over nature . . . over evil forces . . . even over death.

One final episode from Matthew's Gospel that reveals the fully-God, fully-man nature of Jesus. This is taken from Jesus' final moments on the cross:

> And when Jesus had cried out again in a loud voice, he gave up his spirit.
>
> At that moment the curtain of the temple was torn in two from top to bottom. The earth shook and the rocks split. The tombs broke open and the bodies of many holy people who had died were raised to life. They came out

of the tombs, and after Jesus' resurrection they went into the holy city and appeared to many people.

When the centurion and those with him who were guarding Jesus saw the earthquake and all that had happened, they were terrified, and exclaimed, "Surely he was the Son of God!" (Matthew 27:50–54)

Jesus' humanity is on full display here. He dies, just as every man and woman dies. But Jesus' deity is also on display. We see it in the earthquake. We see it in the tearing of the temple curtain, which indicated that God's presence—previously off-limits in the Holy of Holies—would now be accessible. We see it in the people who were raised back to life, stepped out of their tombs, and returned to business-as-usual in Jerusalem. We see it in the anticipation of "Jesus' resurrection" (the full story of which is told in the next chapter). And we see it in the conclusion of the Roman centurion and other bystanders, who exclaimed, "Surely he was the Son of God!"

If Jesus needed to be fully God and fully man in order to qualify as the Redeemer, He certainly filled the bill, as our quick survey of Matthew's Gospel attests.

Jesus' Followers

My local newspaper recently carried the story of a man who returned a bank bag with thousands of dollars in it. He said that he'd found it on the street and wanted to do the honest thing by bringing it back. The guy became an instant celebrity. His integrity was praised by everyone from Oprah Winfrey to a spokesman at the Vatican. Invitations poured in for guest appearances on talk shows and news broadcasts.

But then it got ugly. It was discovered that the do-gooder's story was phony. He hadn't found the bag of money on the street. He'd lifted it from the counter at the bank. Later on, when remorse set in, he felt compelled to return the money. His tall tale was necessary to cover his tracks. What a disappointment to discover that a modern-day hero was really an imposter.[3] (At least he didn't try to sell anyone the Eiffel Tower.)

We began this chapter with the story of Victor Lustig to illustrate how important it was that Jesus prove His qualifications as Redeemer. The phony money returner also reminds us how important it is that *we* prove *our* qualifications as those who are redeemed. Woe to those who profess themselves to be true followers of Jesus but lack the life-transformation to back it up!

It would be a huge oversight to sum up the contents of the four Gospels and what they contribute to the Bible's *Epic* storyline without making mention of the teachings of Jesus. If you are a true follower of Jesus, your faith in His works should be reflected in your obedience to His words. "If anyone loves me," Jesus observed, "he will obey my teaching. My Father will love him, and we will come to him and make our home with him" (John 14:23). We are wasting our breath if we claim that Christ lives in us and yet we have little desire to discover His commands in Scripture and make feeble efforts to put them into practice.

Yes, the Gospels focus on the Cross. But they also give us an extensive sampling of what Jesus taught His followers about everyday life. *Take care of the poor. Pray hard. Forgive your enemies. Be faithful to your spouse. Use your income to advance God's cause in the world.* And so on.

The famous Sermon on the Mount (Matthew 5–7) lays out high standards for those who are citizens in Christ's kingdom. More than thirty parables end with poignant punch lines we are to apply to our lives. Neither should we ignore the life lessons that accompany Jesus' miracles, nor the long discourses about how to prepare for the end times.

All of this teaching is meant to shape those who are genuinely redeemed. If we have truly been rescued by Jesus from the consequences and power of sin, our lives will show it! You've probably heard this point expressed in the form of a question: "If you were arrested for being a Christ follower, would there be enough evidence to convict you?" Good question to ponder.

Study Guide

Icebreaker (for groups)

Describe a time in your life when you really, really wanted something—but couldn't afford it. How would you have felt if somebody had purchased that item for you?

1. List some of the characteristics that make each of the four Gospels distinct from the others.

    Matthew   *Mark*   *Luke*   *John*

2. Why do Matthew, Mark, Luke, and John devote a disproportionate amount of their Gospels to describing the events surrounding Jesus' death?

3. Describe the following three views of the atonement. Explain why each of the first two views is not the *best* interpretation of Jesus' death (although both make valid points). What evidence is there in Scripture that the third view is the central focus of the cross?

Victor

Example

Sacrifice

What impacted you most as you read these (all three) descriptions of Jesus' mission?

4. Do you ever wrestle with the thought that you have been too gullible in accepting the Bible's affirmation that Jesus is fully God and fully man? Explain.

In terms of the atonement, why is it important that Jesus be both fully God and fully man?

5. What evidences do you see in the following four passages for Jesus' deity and humanity?

                              Deity   *Humanity*

Matthew 1:18–23

Matthew 3:13–17

Matthew 9:1–8

Matthew 27:50–54

6. Occasionally you will hear someone make the assertion that Jesus Himself never claimed to be God. List three quotes from the lips of Jesus that make a case for His deity.

7. (icon) Besides the importance of Jesus' deity and humanity for the atonement, why else might you be glad to have a Savior who is both God and man?

God

Man

8. (icon) Ask the average person about what Jesus taught and they're likely to reduce it to: *"We're supposed to love each other."* Yes, Jesus taught that. But He also taught a whole lot more. Unfortunately, many of us are familiar with Jesus' miracles and the events that surrounded His birth and death, but are sketchy when it comes to His teaching. Read Matthew 5–7 (yes, all three chapters). This is Jesus' famous Sermon on the Mount. List at least five demands that Jesus makes of His followers in this sermon.

9. What evidences might you expect to see in a person who is truly a Christ follower?

 What transformations has Christ brought to *your* life?

{ **5** }

Redemption Proclaimed

DURING THE 2011 Christmas season many church-es across America attached GPS tracking devices to Baby Jesus. (I read this in my news magazine, so it must be true.) It seems that every year a number of outdoor nativity scenes are vandalized. And often the statue of Baby Jesus is stolen.

So churches began using a high-tech method to protect their property. Jesus was wearing a GPS device, and churches could track wherever vandals took Him.

We're about to track where people took Jesus during the first century, as we follow the spread of Christianity. Not by GPS, of course, but by the New Testament.

We are in the midst of tracing the Bible's storyline from Genesis to Revelation. What's the theme of this epic adven-ture? (I'm all about interactive learning. So you may not con-tinue reading until you have said out loud, and with enthusi-asm: "Redemption!") This is an account of the greatest rescue effort in history.

As a quick review, recall that this rescue was *prompted* by the human race being in deep trouble. Adam and Eve had introduced sin into the world, and death quickly followed—spiritual, physical, and eternal death. Only God could rescue humanity from this fate. The Bible's Old Testament tells us how His plan of redemption was *prepared* and *prophesied*. Then the New Testament's opening four Gospels explain how Jesus Christ *purchased* this redemption.

Let's continue our study of the New Testament by tracking those early Christ followers, who discovered redemption for themselves when they surrendered their lives to Jesus and then *proclaimed* the good news of that redemption to everyone who would listen. Turn in your Bible to the book of Acts, plant your finger there, and then flip to the table of contents. Do you see Acts? Acts is the solo New Testament book of history. You can write *Book of History* next to it.

Acts: The Story of the First Christ Followers . . .

Do you remember how many Old Testament *Books of History* there are? (More opportunity for reader interaction. I hope you said aloud: "Twelve! Joshua through Esther.") Those Old Testament books cover almost one thousand years of history. But the New Testament needs only *one* book of history, because it covers only *one* generation: the very first generation of Christ followers.

Acts picks up the story right after Jesus' return to heaven. In fact, Acts was written by the same guy, Dr. Luke, who wrote one of the four biographies of Jesus' life and ministry. Luke's Gospel tells the story of Jesus' life, death, and resurrection. Luke's book of Acts tells the story of the first generation of Christ followers, who proclaimed the good news of Jesus far and wide. These two works were originally the first and second halves of the same volume.

. . . And 21 Letters to the Christ Followers

Just a brief introductory word about the twenty-one books that follow the book of Acts: Romans through Jude. Every one is an epistle. What's an epistle? When a class of Sunday school children was asked that question, a little boy replied: "An epistle is the wife of an apostle." Not quite. An epistle is a letter. These letters were written by first-century Christian leaders to various groups of Christ followers. They explain both the basic doctrines of the Christian faith as well as how Christ followers are expected to live in light of what they believe. To keep their role in mind, write *Epistles* next to these books, Romans through Jude.

The first thirteen of these letters (Romans through Philemon) were written by the apostle Paul, an early convert to Christianity. The next letter, Hebrews, was written by an undisclosed author. Then comes the epistle of James, who was a son of Mary and Joseph, and a stepbrother of Jesus. Interestingly, he didn't believe in Jesus until after Jesus' resurrection. But

James eventually became the leader of the church in Jerusalem, which was the headquarters for early Christianity.

The book of James is followed by two epistles from the pen of Peter and three epistles from the pen of John. These two guys, as you probably know, were among the original group of Jesus' twelve disciples. Finally, there's Jude's letter. The author of Jude is a toss-up, since Jude is both the name of one of Jesus' twelve disciples (not to be confused with Judas, who betrayed Jesus), as well as the name of another stepbrother of Jesus. It was probably Jude the stepbrother who wrote the epistle.

Now, let me make a somewhat obvious point here about how the book of Acts fits together with these twenty-one epistles. As noted, Acts is a history of first-century Christianity, and the epistles were all written during this era. That means that these letters were written *by* people and *to* people who are described in the book of Acts. For example, we can read about Paul proclaiming the good news of Christ in the city of Philippi in Acts 16. And then we can flip over to Philippians and read the letter that Paul wrote to these Christians some time later. So, the epistles all fit somewhere into the history of the book of Acts.

The Key Verse of Acts and the Epistles

Enough introduction to Acts and the epistles. We're now ready to unpack the key verse for this portion of the Bible. It's Acts 1:8. And I contend that it's the key verse because it serves as an outline for Acts' storyline, which, in turn, is the backdrop for the twenty-one letters to the churches. These words were spoken by Jesus several weeks after His resurrection and just seconds before He ascended back to heaven. This is the gist of what theologians refer to as Jesus' Great Commission: the big assignment that Jesus gives to everyone who wants to follow Him. (The Great Commission is also recorded, in some form, in all four Gospels.[1]) Here it is:

"But you will receive power when the Holy Spirit comes on you; and you will be my witnesses in Jerusalem, and in all Judea and Samaria, and to the ends of the earth."

One extremely important word appears in this verse that's worth exploring: *witnesses*. Jesus wants His followers to be witnesses. Some form of this word appears thirty-nine times in the book of Acts. Being *witnesses*, without a doubt, is the theme of this book. And now you can understand why I'm calling this portion of the Bible's overall storyline "Redemption Proclaimed." Because that's what witnesses do. They proclaim that Jesus can redeem people from their sins. He can rescue them from certain death. Let's take a look at four aspects of this job—this *Great Commission*—that witnesses engage in.

The Message of Witnesses

If you want to know what message the first-century Christ followers were proclaiming, read the ten sermons or sermon excerpts that are recorded in the book of Acts: five by Peter, one by Stephen, and four by Paul. In addition to these ten sermons, there are at least thirty summaries of what early Christians communicated to the people they talked with. The same topic comes up again and again in these sermons and conversation summaries. Their basic message? *Jesus.*

A typical example of this can be found in Acts 14:3, where we're told that Paul and Barnabas went into a synagogue in the city of Iconium and spoke "boldly for the Lord [and] the message of his grace." That's it in a nutshell. It didn't matter where these Christ followers were, or who they were talking with; they always found a way to bring things around to Jesus.

Oh, they might approach the topic in different ways with different audiences. But the main topic never changed. When Paul was talking with Greek philosophers in Athens, he spoke of Jesus from the standpoint of reason and experience. When Paul was talking with Jewish worshipers in some synagogue, he presented Jesus from the standpoint of Old Testament history and Scripture. But the heart of the message was always the same: Jesus.

These early witnesses were like the parents of a newborn, who only want to talk about their baby. Or the guy who's just fallen in love and only wants to talk about his girlfriend. Or the football-crazed fans who only want to talk about their quarterback. (Think Green Bay Packers.) These early witnesses couldn't stop talking about Jesus. But it wasn't Jesus' life in general that they talked about. There's not a lot of biographical material on Jesus in the sermons and conversation summaries that we find in the book of Acts.

No, they talked mostly about Jesus' death and resurrection. Why? Because it was Jesus' death and resurrection that had purchased redemption for those who would put their trust in Him. Jesus' death paid sin's penalty and Jesus' resurrection proved that He had the power to give others new life. Listen to this excerpt, from one of Peter's first sermons:

Men of Israel, listen to this: Jesus of Nazareth was a man accredited by God to you by miracles, wonders and signs, which God did among you through him, as you yourselves know. This man was handed over to you by God's set purpose and foreknowledge; and you, with the help of wicked men, put him to death by nailing him to the cross. But God raised him from the dead, freeing him from the agony of death, because it was impossible for death to keep its hold on him. (Acts 2:22–24)

What did Peter preach about? Jesus! Specifically, Jesus' death and resurrection. Yet one other element was common to what the early Christians had to say about Jesus. Often they would let their audience know that these listeners were the guilty party behind Jesus' death. Do you see that in the middle of the verses you just read? "You, with the help of wicked men, put him to death by nailing him to the cross."

That's a strange way to win the hearts of your listeners, right? Blame them for Jesus' death! In fact, the message was the same to every audience, for everyone on the planet has had something to do with Jesus' death. If everyone is a sinner, and Jesus died to pay sin's penalty, then everyone is guilty of contributing to Jesus' death. That was the message of these early witnesses: "Jesus died for *your* sins and rose again to give you new life. So own up to your sins, turn your back on your sins, and trust Jesus to forgive your sins. Then follow Him."

This was the passionate message of early followers of Jesus. It should be the passion of all of us who are Christ followers. We need to be working Jesus into our everyday conversations with people. People hear ad nauseam from us about our love for skiing, pizza, dogs, working out, the Cubs (the sign of a true Chicagoan), and even our nails (just recently, I overheard two women going on and on about this topic).

Do people hear from us about our love for Jesus? Jesus is the message of witnesses.

The Outspokenness of Witnesses

By definition, witnesses must speak. They can't get their message across without using words. The reason that I make this obvious point is that I hear Christ followers rationalizing all the time that even though they don't *talk* about Jesus at work, or at school, or at the health club, or in the neighborhood, they try to *live* the Christian life in front of others.

Living the Christian life is good. That's what gives our message credibility. It's so important, it is the subject of the next point in this chapter. But living the Christian life must never become an excuse for not talking about Jesus. Being a witness requires words. The early Christian witnesses spoke up. In fact, it was impossible to keep them quiet.

One dramatic example of this occurs after a beggar, crippled from birth, sees Peter and John walking into the temple and asks them for some money. Instead of giving him a handful of loose change, Peter heals him. The crowd of onlookers goes wild. They start praising God for what they have seen (Acts 3:1–10). But the local religious authorities are not so happy. You see, Peter had healed the crippled beggar "in the name of Jesus" (v. 6)—the same Jesus whom the religious authorities had recently conspired to put to death. They don't know what to do with Peter and John. Here's the confrontation that ensued:

> "What are we going to do with these men?" they asked. "Everybody living in Jerusalem knows they have done an outstanding miracle, and we cannot deny it. But to stop this thing from spreading any further among the people, we must warn these men to speak no longer to anyone in this name."
>
> Then they called them in again and commanded them not to speak or teach at all in the name of Jesus. But Peter and John replied, "Judge for yourselves whether it is right in God's sight to obey you rather than God. For we cannot help speaking about what we have seen and heard." (Acts 4:16–20)

These early witnesses wouldn't shut up and couldn't be shut down. And it wasn't just the leaders, like Peter and John, who were so outspoken. Every Christ follower was sharing the good news about Jesus. And whenever their enthusiasm for this task waned, God rekindled it. An instance of rekindling is recorded in Acts 8. By this point witnesses had permeated the entire city of Jerusalem with the message of Jesus. Unfortunately, however, that's as far as they'd gone. But the

Great Commission, you'll remember, had instructed them to begin witnessing in Jerusalem and then continue on to Judea and Samaria until they reached the ends of the earth.

There was more work to be done. So God lit a fire under these Christ followers—the fire of persecution. Look at what happened next: "On that day a great persecution broke out against the

GOD LIT a fire under these Christ followers— the fire of persecution.

church at Jerusalem, and all except the apostles were scattered throughout Judea and Samaria. . . . Those who had been scattered preached the word wherever they went" (Acts 8:1, 4).

Who was it that God scattered by persecution? Please note: it wasn't the apostles (v. 1). It was all the Joe Six-Pack Christians (six-pack referring to Coke). Your average, run-of-the-mill Christ followers were scattered. And what did they do after they fled the area? *They preached the word in towns that had not heard the good news about Jesus.* This is what you're going to find, again and again and again, in the book of Acts: outspoken witnesses.

Of course, the apostles were active too. The entire second half of the book describes three adventuresome journeys that were undertaken by the apostle Paul for the sole purpose of spreading the word about Jesus. Paul, bound and determined to spread the word, couldn't be stopped from traveling far and wide to proclaim Christ. Indeed, he accepted hardship for the sake of telling others about Jesus. Listen to what Paul wrote to the believers in Corinth, one of the cities he visited:

Five times I received from the Jews the forty lashes minus one. Three times I was beaten with rods, once I was stoned, three times I was shipwrecked, I spent a night and a day in the open sea, I have been constantly on the move. I have been in danger from rivers, in danger from bandits, in danger from my own countrymen, in danger from Gentiles; in danger in the city, in danger in the country, in danger at sea; and in danger from false brothers. I have labored and toiled and have often gone without sleep; I have known hunger and thirst and have often gone without food; I have been cold and naked. (2 Corinthians 11:24–27)

Now, does any Christ follower who's reading this want to complain about how hard it is to talk about Jesus with family members, or coworkers, or fellow students, or friends? At Christ Community Church, where I serve as the lead pastor, we have a specific strategy for getting the word out about Christ. I'm sure it's not original with us. But if you're a witness who needs to become more outspoken, please consider the *invest-inform-invite* strategy.

First, those of us who are Christ followers must *invest* in relationships with people who need Jesus. We can't always hang out in our holy huddles of fellow believers. When was the last time you had some neighbors over for dinner? Who are you spending time with who doesn't know Christ? Invest! Working, as I do, at a local church, I am continually challenged during the week to connect with those who don't know Christ. That's why I work out at a local health club and why I collect canned goods for the town food pantry from my neighbors every few months. These are venues for developing relationships with spiritual seekers.

Second, we need to *inform.* There are two stories we should be ready and willing to tell others. There's the general story of Jesus and how He came to rescue people from their sins. And then there's the personal story of how we our-

DO YOU KNOW how to tell these two stories: Jesus' story and your own story?

selves decided to surrender our lives to Christ. Do you know how to tell these two stories: Jesus' story and your own story? Jesus' story is often best told with the help of an evangelistic tool, such as Campus Crusade for Christ's *Four Spiritual Laws* booklet. Find a variation of this booklet that works for you, something that uses helpful diagrams and Bible verses to communicate the gospel to others.

My wife, Sue, visited the hairdresser a few weeks ago, where she ran into her friend Kim, who owns the shop. Kim is a relatively new believer and she loves to talk to her customers about Jesus. She broke into a smile when she saw Sue, because she'd just gotten stuck in a gospel presentation to a customer and needed some help.

Sue and the customer slipped into a back room, both of them draped in smocks and hair plastered with coloring chemicals. (What a picture!) My wife reached into her purse, pulled out a little gospel booklet, and walked through it page by page with this woman who couldn't stop crying over the truth she was hearing. That's the inform step of witnessing in action!

Third, after witnesses invest (in relationships with spiritual seekers) and inform (telling both Jesus' story and their own), they *invite*. They invite people to weekend services or outreach events at their church, where the message of Jesus will be presented in a clear and creative fashion. Or, they invite their friends to their small group, where the Bible will be discussed and applied. Or, they invite those who would never darken the door of a church to participate in a church-sponsored community service project, where they will rub shoulders with Christ followers as they care for the needy.

Invest. Inform. Invite. Because Jesus expects His witnesses to be outspoken.

The Credibility of Witnesses

A few years ago the British government funded an exhibition by a Polish artist. The government gave him a grant, but when the exhibition opened, there wasn't anything there. The display area was empty.

The Polish artist, asked to explain his "work," said that his show consisted of (you're gonna love this): "a painting that hasn't been painted yet; an invisible sculpture; and a movie shot with no film in the camera."[2]

If I were the British government, I'd ask for my money back! How can that guy claim to be an artist and have nothing to show for his work? The Bible raises a similar question about people who claim to be Christ followers but who have nothing to show for Christ's supposed work in their lives.

In contrast, the first-century Christ followers had credibility with their listeners as they talked about Jesus. Their priorities, values, morals, and behavior gave evidence of having been transformed by Christ. They were visual, as well as verbal, witnesses, as is seen in the following passage:

All the believers were together and had everything in common. Selling their possessions and goods, they gave to anyone as he had need. Every day they continued to meet together in the temple courts. They broke bread in their homes and ate together with glad and sincere hearts, praising God and enjoying the favor of all the people. And the Lord added to their number daily those who were being saved. (Acts 2:44–47)

You'll find lots of other passages like this one in the book of Acts, describing Christ followers who back up their good *news* with good *deeds*. Witnesses whose mouths are filled with *truth* and whose lives are filled with *proof*. I love the story of Dorcas (Acts 9) in this regard. Dorcas was a skilled seamstress. But rather than use her sewing ability just to make clothes for profit, Dorcas also provided garments free of charge for poor people.

One day Dorcas died. And when the apostle Peter got the news, he went to her house to express his condolences and found it jammed with mourners. They had come out of love for this woman and they were showing each other clothes that Dorcas had made for them. Well, God did a miracle that day. Peter prayed over Dorcas and she revived. But equally amazing, when Peter used that opportunity to tell all those mourners about Jesus, many of them became Christ followers. What influenced their decision? Dorcas's life. That's what I call the credibility of a witness.

This is why God gave us the New Testament epistles. These letters are full of instructions about how Christ followers should live, so that our message is attractive to others instead of repulsive. When you read through the epistles, you'll come across admonitions to *tell the truth; care for widows; serve your spouse; settle business disputes without resorting to lawsuits; treat your employees with dignity; discipline your children* . . . And on and on it goes.

If we're going to have credibility as witnesses, then our lives must be "Exhibit A"—proof that backs up our truth. This is why it's so important to major in Bible application, not just Bible knowledge. Whenever we're done reading God's Word, or studying it in a small group, or hearing it taught in a sermon, we need to immediately determine how we're going to put into practice what we've just learned.

> **OUR LIVES must be "Exhibit A"—proof that backs up our truth.**

The Reach of Witnesses

Let's return to our key verse one last time: Acts 1:8. Jesus challenged His followers to be His witnesses, starting in Jerusalem, and then moving to the surrounding areas of Judea and Samaria, and eventually reaching the ends of the earth. One Bible scholar says that Acts 1:8 serves as the table of contents for the book of Acts. It's the outline that Dr. Luke follows in describing the spread of the good news about Jesus.

It all begins in Jerusalem, where the key player is Peter and the primary audience for the good news is Jews. But in

Acts 8, persecution drives Christ followers out of Jerusalem. They are scattered throughout Judea and Samaria. They start sharing the good news with non-Jews, or, I should say, with half-Jews. Samaria was filled with people who had descended from Jews who intermarried with Gentiles. This is now the target audience. And Peter is no longer the central character in the drama. That role passes to a guy named Philip.

In Acts chapter 9 the reach of the witnesses goes one step further, when a Jew named Paul becomes a Christ follower (Acts 9:1–19; see also 13:9) and ends up taking the good news to Gentiles across the then-known world. Paul went on three missionary journeys (as Bible scholars refer to them). If your Bible has maps at the back, there's probably a map that lays out those three missionary journeys in three different colors.

Paul visited places in what is modern-day Turkey, cities like Ephesus (to which he later wrote the epistle of Ephesians), and regions like Galatia (to which he later wrote the epistle of Galatians). Paul also visited places in what is modern-day Greece: cities like Corinth and Philippi and Thessalonica (to which he later wrote the epistles of 1, 2 Corinthians, Philippians, and 1, 2 Thessalonians).

Eventually Paul made it to Rome, the capital city of the empire. This last trip wasn't on one of his missionary journeys. Paul went to Rome, all expenses paid, as a prisoner. He'd been arrested in Jerusalem for his faith in Christ and was transported to Rome to stand trial. But that was OK with Paul because he'd always wanted to proclaim the good news of Jesus in the empire's capital. In fact, years before he arrived in Rome, he'd actually written a letter to believers there whom he'd never met (the epistle of Romans).

Jesus wants His witnesses to reach the whole world with the good news of His redemption, because Jesus wants to rescue people everywhere. And most churches provide opportunities to play a role in that worldwide rescue effort. At our church, we have international partners in places like Sierra Leone (West Africa), Bangladesh, Brazil, the Czech Republic, Haiti, and Nicaragua. Every year some four hundred of our people use vacation time to serve one of these partners on a "Go Team" trip. We all have the opportunity, as well, to financially support our international ministries.

How big a reach do *you* have for Jesus? Does it stretch around the world via praying and giving and perhaps going on short-term mission trips? This global reach is cultivated at home. How are you doing as a witness with neighbors, extended family, coworkers, and friends? Do you bring Jesus up in conversations? Do you invest, inform, and invite? Does your life provide proof for your truth?

Study Guide

Icebreaker (for groups)

Recall the last time you received some really good news. What was it? What motivated you to share that good news with others?

1. What is the relationship between the book of Acts and the twenty-one New Testament epistles? Why is *witnesses* considered to be the key word in Acts?

2. Read Acts 2:22–24. What was the favorite message of first-century Christ followers? What aspect of this message did they especially emphasize? Why?

Is this a message that you find easy to bring up in conversation? Why or why not? Why must our message be *verbal* (with our *lips*), not just *visual* (with our *lives*)?

3. (image) Read Acts 4:16–20. What compelled Peter and John to speak boldly about Christ? What other motivations come to mind that should stimulate us to be more outspoken in sharing Christ with others?

4. According to Acts 8:1, 4, how did God prompt the spread of the gospel after it had become stalled in Jerusalem? Who did the spreading and why is that significant? How might God use a similar tactic to make *us* gospel-spreaders?

5. What is meant by each of the steps in the *invest-inform-invite* strategy?
   Invest

   Inform

   Invite

Which of these three steps is easiest for you? Why? Which is most difficult? Why? What could you do to improve at the step you find most difficult?

6. What was it about the early Christ followers in Acts 2:44–47 that gave credibility to their witness? (Give specifics.)

We sometimes glibly express a hope that people will see the difference Jesus makes in our lives. What sorts of differences might cause them to sit up and listen to our message?

7. (icon) As a sampling of a New Testament epistle, read through the letter of Philippians (a brief four chapters). Note anything Paul says to these Christ followers that you would imagine might make their lives and witness more attractive to unbelievers. Write down five to six of these insights.

8. Following the outline of Acts 1:8, what would be *your*: *Jerusalem?*

   Judea and Samaria?

   Ends of the earth?

9. How can you personally participate in the spread of the gospel around the world? Which of these means are you currently engaging in and to what extent?

{ 6 }

Redemption Perfected

A FEW YEARS AGO I came across an interesting article in the arts section of the *New York Times*. It was about the restoration of a painting by the seventeenth-century baroque artist Diego Velázquez.[1] As the court painter for the king of Spain, Philip IV, Velázquez painted a full-length portrait of the king back in the early 1600s.

In the early twentieth century, the New York City Metropolitan Museum of Art purchased the portrait. But decades later, art critics began calling into question whether the piece was truly an original by Velázquez. It didn't *look* like a masterpiece. The varnish was discolored. Layer upon layer of repainting covered up whatever had been there in the first place.

Eventually, the portrait's status was officially downgraded. It was no longer referred to as a Velázquez. The critics concluded that it must have been the work of a studio assistant, and not the master himself.

However, a few years ago, someone at the museum suggested that the Metropolitan's chief paintings conservator try to restore the King Philip portrait, to see what lay beneath the discolored varnish and layers of repainting. He did. And to everyone's amazement, it was immediately apparent that this was, indeed, the work of Diego Velázquez. The painting was recognized once again as a masterpiece.

This account bears resemblance to the *Epic* storyline of the Bible. When God first created the world, according to the opening chapters of Genesis, His work was a masterpiece. But then Adam and Eve introduced sin into that world and the masterpiece was seriously marred. Sin has not only marred people. It has also marred everything else that God made. The apostle Paul says that all of creation is currently in bondage to decay (Romans 8:21).

God's Rescue Plan

But the good news is that God has a plan to rescue creation—people especially—from the ravages of sin. God's rescue plan is called *redemption*, and redemption is the theme of the Bible's storyline. (I hope that all this is sounding familiar by now.) So far, we've traced the redemption theme through sixty-five of the Bible's sixty-six books. We've looked at redemption prompted, prepared, prophesied, purchased, and proclaimed.

In this chapter, we're going to look at the very last book of the Bible, the book of Revelation. And our topic is *redemption perfected*. We're going to get a glimpse of what God's masterpiece will look like when it's fully restored.

The Scope and Subject of Revelation

Let me make a few introductory comments about the book of Revelation. First, I have the space to cover just a few of Revelation's highlights. Last year I asked a friend of mine, who is a very bright New Testament scholar and the author of a new eight-hundred-page commentary on Revelation, to teach an hour-and-a-half seminar on this book of the Bible to my church's staff. Well, there are twenty-two chapters in Revelation and about an hour into his presentation he was only on chapter three! (He never made it to the end.)

Second, Revelation is a type of biblical literature called "apocalyptic." This would be a good time to turn to your Bible's table of contents and write "Apocalypse" next to Revelation. So, our New Testament is made up of four *Gospels*, one *Book of History*, twenty-one *Epistles*, and one *Apocalypse*. Apocalyptic literature describes future events in highly symbolic language. This is what makes the book of Revelation so hard to understand. In fact, the great reformer and Bible scholar John Calvin, who wrote commentaries on most of the books of the Bible, refused to write a commentary on Revelation because of the difficulty in interpreting it.

And the highly symbolic language isn't the only thing that makes Revelation tough to interpret. Here's a third introductory comment about the book: Bible scholars don't agree about the time frame that Revelation is describing. Some think

EMPEROR DOMITIAN wanted everyone to call him "Lord." Christ followers obviously had a problem with that.

that it's a book about the future, but others believe it's actually a book about the past. Let me explain.

Revelation has a lot to say about Christ followers who are persecuted for their faith, and how God will eventually overthrow their persecutors. Such persecution was already under way back in the first century. The apostle John wrote Revelation about AD 95. At that time, the Roman emperor Domitian was beginning to enforce the cult of emperor worship. He wanted everyone to call him "Lord." Christ followers obviously had a problem with that. So, many of them were killed.

John wasn't put to death, but he was exiled to a Mediterranean island called Patmos, where he wrote the book of Revelation. As a result, some Bible scholars argue that Revelation is a highly symbolic description of Domitian's persecution of believers and the eventual overthrow of the Roman Empire several hundred years later. In other words, Revelation is about past historical events.

But other Bible scholars contend: "No, Revelation is about events that are much more cataclysmic than anything that's already happened in history. Revelation is about the rise of evil powers at the end of the world, and about how Jesus Christ will destroy those evil powers and set up His eternal kingdom." I personally agree with these Bible scholars who interpret Reve-

REVELATION APPLIES to Christ followers in every era who are being persecuted for their faith.

lation in a futuristic sense, although I readily acknowledge that this book applies to Christ followers in every era who are being persecuted for their faith. Revelation is an encouraging reminder that Jesus Christ wins in the end and all His faithful followers are rewarded!

Let me take you through five events described in the book of Revelation that lead up to Jesus' eventual victory. This victory will be the culmination of the Bible's storyline. The rescue effort that began back in Genesis will finally be completed. God's masterpiece will be fully restored. *Redemption perfected!*

But before we can get from here to there: five big events.

The Great Tribulation

We will begin our study of Revelation in chapter 6, but here's a brief summary of chapters 1 through 5. In chapter 1 John describes an amazing vision of Jesus Christ, who currently lives and reigns in heaven. In chapters 2 and 3 John then records seven letters from this exalted Christ to seven first-century churches. The gist of the letters is that these Christ followers shouldn't give up or compromise their faith under persecution. One day Christ will reward His faithful followers.

In chapters 4 and 5 John paints a picture of an impressive celebration in heaven as believers and angels together worship Jesus Christ. At the height of this worship, God the Father hands Jesus a scroll with seven seals on it. That scroll represents God's plan for the end of the world. Only Jesus is qualified to break the seven seals and put these world ending events into motion.

Here's what happens next, as observed by John:

I watched as the Lamb opened the first of the seven seals. Then I heard one of the four living creatures say in a voice like thunder, "Come!" I looked, and there before me was a white horse! Its rider held a bow, and he was given a crown, and he rode out as a conqueror bent on conquest.

When the Lamb opened the second seal, I heard the second living creature say, "Come!" Then another horse came out, a fiery red one. Its rider was given power to take peace from the earth and to make men slay each other. To him was given a large sword. (Revelation 6:1–4)

When Jesus breaks the first two seals on this scroll, bad things begin to happen on earth. This is the onset of what Bible scholars call the *Great Tribulation*. Near the end of time, life will become really awful on this planet. For starters, there will be widespread wars. The breaking of seal number one releases a rider on a white horse, who is holding a bow and is "bent on conquest" (v. 2). Seal number two lets loose a fiery red horse, whose rider takes peace from the earth and makes men slay each other (vv. 3, 4). This is one bad dude with a ginormous sword. Watch out for widespread wars.

Natural disasters will also mark the Great Tribulation. If we were to keep reading in Revelation 6, we'd discover that the breaking of seal number three sends a black horse to earth, whose rider brings famine. Opening seal four releases a pale horse with more famine and some plague to go with it. Seal six (I'll come back to seal five in a moment) says nothing about a colored horse. Phew! Just a tremendous earthquake—yikes! There will be natural disasters of every kind.

What else? A third characteristic of the Great Tribulation

CHRIST FOLLOWERS will be persecuted, some to the point of death, for their allegiance to King Jesus.

will be the persecution of Christ followers. Back to seal five. When Jesus breaks open this seal, John sees a huge crowd of men and women in heaven who have recently been martyred for their faith. Christ honors them by giving them white robes. This is a common occurrence during the Great Tribulation: Christ followers being persecuted, some to the point of death, for their allegiance to King Jesus.

The entire seventh chapter of Revelation describes these dedicated Christ followers. John says that they number 144,000. That number is probably not to be taken literally. Keep in mind that apocalyptic language is highly symbolic. This is especially true of numbers. You math wizards can verify the following: $144,000 = 12 \times 12 \times 10^3$. The number 12 represents God's people (twelve tribes of Israel in the Old Testament, twelve apostles in the New Testament). And the number 10 signifies completion.[2] In other words, 144,000 is a way of saying that all of God's people will suffer some degree of persecution during the Great Tribulation.

And John's still not finished with that theme. If we skip ahead to Revelation 11, John describes two high-profile Christ followers who are put to death for their faith. Jesus calls them "my two witnesses" (v. 3). Many Bible scholars hold that these two witnesses will be a couple of believers who gain international recognition during the Great Tribulation. (Others argue that these two witnesses are a symbolic reference to Christ followers in general during this period.) When the two witnesses are killed, the rest of the world parties! People actually celebrate the murder by exchanging gifts with each other (vv. 9–10). This gives us some idea of how hated Christ followers will become during the Great Tribulation.

One chapter later, Revelation 12, the story is told (very symbolically) of how Satan tried to destroy Jesus, when Jesus came to earth the first time. But because Satan didn't succeed in his efforts and Jesus was able to return to heaven, Satan turned his fury like a fierce dragon on Jesus' followers! You get the idea. There's a lot in Revelation about the persecution of Christ followers. This will reach a climax during the Great Tribulation.

Widespread wars, natural disasters, the persecution of Christ followers—and now a fourth characteristic of this end-times period: the rise of the Antichrist. The actual title *Antichrist* doesn't appear in the book of Revelation. That's the name that John gives to this guy in his epistle of 1 John. (See 1 John 2:18.) In Revelation, the Antichrist is referred to as *the beast from the sea* (13:1). John describes a charismatic leader, who initially gains recognition by accomplishing some miraculous feats.

THE ANTICHRIST temporarily puts an end to global conflicts. But eventually he turns out to be a cruel dictator.

Most notably, he brokers a few peace treaties that temporarily put an end to global conflicts. But that peacemaking is just a ruse to gain control. Eventually the guy turns out to be a cruel dictator. See if you can wade through the following highly symbolic description of Public Enemy Number One:

> And I saw a beast coming out of the sea. He had ten horns and seven heads, with ten crowns on his horns, and on each head a blasphemous name. The beast I saw resembled a leopard, but had feet like those of a bear and a mouth like that of a lion. The dragon gave the beast his power and his throne and great authority. One of the heads of the beast seemed to have had a fatal wound, but the fatal wound had been healed. The whole world was astonished and followed the beast. Men worshiped the dragon because he had given authority to the beast, and they also worshiped the beast and asked, "Who is like the beast? Who can make war against him?" (Revelation 13:1–4)

Now, if you're around during the Great Tribulation, don't expect to see a ten-horned, seven-headed beast being interviewed on CNN. What you *will* see, if you're still here, is a charismatic leader who gradually gains worldwide prominence. The horns represent his military power and the multiple crowns represent the spread of his rule. Where does this guy originate from? The sea (v. 1)! But once again, this is not a literal description. Don't expect some slimy monster to step out of the surf and onto the beach. The sea is symbolic. In Old Testament times, God's people were mostly landlubbers. They were terrified of the Mediterranean Sea. The sea represented all that was evil. That's why the Antichrist is said to come from the sea.

What about the fact that this guy resembles a leopard, a bear, and a lion (v. 2)? These three animals represent empires that once ruled the world. Alexander the Great and his Greek army were as swift as a leopard. Before them were the bear-like Persians. Before them were the lion-esque Babylonians. In other words, the Antichrist will be a world dominator.

Who is the dragon that gives the beast his power and authority? Satan! And later on, in Revelation 13, we're told that Satan will also give power and authority to another beast, who will become a spokesman for the beast from the sea. That leaves us with an *unholy* trinity: the dragon (Satan), the beast from the sea (the Antichrist), and a second beast (the Antichrist's spokesman). What an affront to the true Trinity! What's worse, verse 4 tells us that people will worship this evil trio during the Great Tribulation.

There's one last characteristic of the end times to be noted in Revelation: rampant wickedness. In chapter 17, we read about another key player in this highly symbolic drama. It's a woman named *Babylon*. She shows up riding on the back of the beast from the sea. What are we to make of her? Well,

Babylon was also the name of an ancient empire. An ancient empire that was known for its idolatry, its excessive materialism, and its moral decadence.

Such rampant wickedness is going to be in full swing during the Great Tribulation, along with widespread wars, increasing natural disasters, the persecution of Christ followers, and the rise of the Antichrist.

This doesn't sound like "redemption perfected," does it? So let's keep going! What's the next big event that will lead to the restoration of God's masterpiece?

The Second Coming

There are 1,845 references to the second coming of Christ sprinkled throughout the Old Testament, according to one Bible commentator.[3] (I didn't stop to count them. I'll take his word for it.) If that number is anywhere near correct, then there are three times as many references to Christ's *second* coming as there are to His *first* coming. And yet we make a much bigger deal out of His *first* coming, celebrating it at Christmastime every year.

Jesus' second coming should be huge to us. In the book of Revelation, the second coming is described in chapter 19. Now, some people believe that this second coming takes place in two stages. The first stage occurs before the Great Tribulation, when Jesus returns secretly to whisk His followers off the planet (i.e., before the really bad stuff begins). These Bible scholars call this the *rapture*. But the book of Revelation makes no clear reference to a secret rapture. Revelation seems to depict Christ's second coming as a one-stage event that takes place *after* the Great Tribulation.

Even though I don't believe in a pretribulation rapture, there are a number of scholars, commentators, radio Bible teachers, and popular authors who do. And if you want to follow their take on things, that's fine with me. This is not a doctrine of the faith that all Christians must agree on. I hope the fans of a rapture turn out to be correct. Personally, I would love to leave town before the Great Tribulation hits.

Before we look at the Revelation 19 passage that describes Christ's return to earth, let's learn where His return will take place. Several chapters earlier in Revelation, John mentions that at the end of the Great Tribulation the rulers of this earth will gather at a place called *Armageddon*. They will gather in defiance of God and for the purpose of stamping out all Christ

THE RULERS of this earth will gather at a place called *Armageddon* for the purpose of stamping out all Christ followers.

followers. Revelation 16:16 is the only place in the Bible where this battlefield is mentioned by name. *Armageddon* means

Mount of Megiddo. And *Megiddo* means *slaughter.* We should anticipate that a horrific battle is going to take place here.

I've visited this location on several trips to Israel. It's a vast plain in the northern part of the country, fifty-five miles north of Jerusalem. Napoleon described it as the perfect theatre for war. Over two hundred major battles have been fought at Armageddon throughout history.[4] This is where Jesus will face off against the armies of this world upon His return to earth. And this is what the showdown will look like:

> I saw heaven standing open and there before me was a white horse, whose rider is called Faithful and True. With justice he judges and makes war. His eyes are like blazing fire, and on his head are many crowns. He has a name written on him that no one knows but he himself. He is dressed in a robe dipped in blood, and his name is the Word of God. The armies of heaven were following him, riding on white horses and dressed in fine linen, white and clean. Out of his mouth comes a sharp sword with which to strike down the nations. "He will rule them with an iron scepter." He treads the winepress of the fury of the wrath of God Almighty. On his robe and on his thigh he has this name written: KING OF KINGS AND LORD OF LORDS. (Revelation 19:11–16)

Read the rest of this chapter on your own sometime. But did you notice *how* Jesus triumphs over this vast array of enemy armies? It doesn't take a protracted battle for Jesus to gain the victory. All it takes is for Jesus to speak a word. The first mention of this is in verse 15: "Out of his mouth comes a sharp sword with which to strike down the nations." If you look at verse 21, you find the same thing. Only it's put a bit more gruesomely: "The rest of them were killed with the sword that came out of the mouth of the rider on the horse, and all the birds gorged themselves on their flesh."

When Jesus returns to earth, He merely speaks a word and it's all over for His enemies.

The Millennial Kingdom

What's next after this cataclysmic battle? John describes in the first half of Revelation 20 a millennial kingdom. This is such a cool part of the story. You've just got to read John's words for yourself:

And I saw an angel coming down out of heaven, having the key to the Abyss and holding in his hand a great chain. He seized the dragon, that ancient serpent, who is the devil, or Satan, and bound him for a thousand years. He threw him into the Abyss, and locked and sealed it over him, to keep him from deceiving the nations anymore until the thousand years were ended. After that, he must be set free for a short time.

I saw thrones on which were seated those who had been given authority to judge. And I saw the souls of those who had been beheaded because of their testimony for Jesus and because of the word of God. They had not worshiped the beast or his image and had not received his mark on their foreheads or their hands. They came to life and reigned with Christ a thousand years. (Revelation 20:1–4)

Did you notice the repetition of the phrase *a thousand years* in this passage? It pops up three times in the first four verses of Revelation 20 (and twice more in verses 5–6). That's why this period is called the millennial kingdom: *mille* is Latin for a thousand; and *annum* means year. Jesus Christ is going to reign upon this present earth for a thousand years before He establishes a new heaven and new earth. Will this millennial kingdom last for a *literal* thousand years? Many Bible commentators think so. Others believe a thousand in this case is another one of those symbolic numbers. This may be a way of saying that the millennial kingdom will last a long, long time.

Some Bible scholars believe that the symbolic language of this passage goes beyond merely its reference to a thousand-year period of time. *Amillennialists* hold that Revelation

20 is not at all a literal description of some future reign of Christ. It's a figurative description of Christ's *current* reign in heaven, along with those followers of His who have left this earth through death. And the depiction of Satan being thrown into the Abyss in the opening verses of this chapter, they say, is a vivid portrayal of Jesus' defeat of Satan at the cross. This explains why Satan is currently powerless to stop the spread of the gospel on earth.

But it seems to me that this amillennial picture of Satan's current status does not do justice to what we read about our enemy in the rest of the New Testament. First Peter 5:8 describes Satan as a roaring lion, looking for people to devour. First John 5:19 says that the world is presently "under the control of the evil one." The apostle Paul warns us in Ephesians 6:11–13 to put on the armor of God in order to protect ourselves against the devil. Does this sound to you as if Satan is currently locked up in some deep pit? No! Well, that means that Revelation 20 must be pointing to a future era when Christ will return and definitively put an end to Satan's troublemaking by tossing him into the Abyss. Then Christ will reign unchallenged upon earth for a thousand years: the millennial kingdom!

Now, before we move on, there is a compelling objection that amillennialists raise against the notion of a millennial kingdom that must be addressed. Amillennialists just don't see the purpose of a millennial kingdom. If Jesus is ultimately going to reign over a new heaven and a new earth, why doesn't He just start doing that the minute He comes back? Why stick a thousand-year reign upon this present earth in front of that?

Do you follow the objection? Maybe an analogy would help. Have you ever been to a concert of your favorite rock band? Before they play, you're forced to listen to some lame warm-up band, right? But you didn't come for the warm-up band. Why doesn't somebody get them off the stage and get the *real* band up there pronto? Can you guess where I'm going with this? To the amillennialists, the millennial kingdom sounds like a mediocre warm-up band. "Let's cut to the chase," they say. "Let's get the new heaven and the new earth on stage."

This seems like a valid objection to the millennial kingdom position. So, let me give you three quick reasons for Jesus' future thousand-year reign on earth. First, the millennial kingdom will demonstrate what the present world could have been like if Adam and Eve (and the rest of us) had *not* rejected God's rule. Our sin, you recall, is the reason that the present world is such a mess. But when Jesus asserts His reign during the millennial kingdom, the world will be an amazing place to live.

Second, the millennial kingdom will demonstrate that

Satan is beyond reformation. At the end of this period, Jesus will let Satan out of the Abyss. You know what Satan **A THOUSAND years in jail won't reform Satan, the deceitful yet powerful "ancient serpent."** will do next? (You can read it for yourself, if you'll go back to Revelation 20 and continue.) Satan will immediately lead a revolt against Christ! Obviously, a thousand years in jail won't reform Satan, the deceitful yet powerful "ancient serpent" (Revelation 12:9).

Third, the millennial kingdom will demonstrate the natural tendency of the human heart toward rebellion against God. Are people basically *good* or basically *bad*? A lot of modern psychology says basically good. It's a bad environment that makes people bad. The Bible disagrees. The Bible says that we've all got a sinful nature. The millennial kingdom proves that point because, when Satan is let out of the Abyss and leads a revolt against Christ, his army is made up of people who've just been enjoying themselves in Christ's wonderful kingdom. How quickly our hearts turn against God.

This is why Jesus came to earth the first time: to rescue us from ourselves. To die on the cross in payment for our sins, so we could be forgiven and receive new hearts from Him. What happens after the millennial kingdom?

The Final Judgment

The final judgment is described in the second half of Revelation 20. John is still our narrator:

> Then I saw a great white throne and him who was seated on it. Earth and sky fled from his presence, and there was no place for them. And I saw the dead, great and small, standing before the throne, and books were opened. Another book was opened, which is the book of life. The dead were judged according to what they had done as recorded in the books. The sea gave up the dead that were in it, and death and Hades gave up the dead that were in them, and each person was judged according to what he had done. Then death and Hades were thrown into the lake of fire. The lake of fire is the second death. If anyone's name was not found written in the book of life, he was thrown into the lake of fire. (Revelation 20:11–15)

Let me sum up this depiction of the final judgment with five quick observations. First, the judge will be Jesus Christ. John doesn't explicitly state that in Revelation 20, but we know it to be the case from other Scriptures. In 2 Corinthians 5:10, for example, the apostle Paul says that "we must all appear before the judgment seat of Christ."

So, the judge is Jesus. Revelation 20 pictures Him sitting

upon a great white throne. He's so intimidating that the earth and sky flee from His presence (v. 11). This is not sweet Baby Jesus in a manger. This is not compassionate Jesus healing the sick. This is not sacrificial Jesus nailed to a cross. This is fearsome Jesus sitting on His judgment throne.

A second observation: Everyone will be judged. In the first half of verse 12, John reports: "And I saw the dead, great and small, standing before the throne." We'll all be there. You may be standing next to Billy Graham or the janitor at your office building. You may be rubbing elbows with Oprah or your next door neighbor. Nobody will be missing at this command performance.[5]

A third observation: The evidence against us will be a comprehensive record of everything we have ever done . . . or *not* done. We read in the second half of v. 12: "And books were opened. Another book was opened, which is the book of life. The dead were judged according to what they had done as recorded in the books."

Here's a scary thought: God is keeping a meticulous record of every sin we've ever committed. Every time we ream somebody out, ignore a needy person, take something that doesn't belong to us, lie, lust, turn a deaf ear to God's voice, spend our money entirely on ourselves . . . it all gets recorded in God's book. And this scary thought is made scarier by the realization that "the wages of sin is death" (Romans 6:23)!

A fourth observation: Our only hope is to have our names found written in the book of life. Did you catch that in the second half of verse 12? God has a book of life. After Christ the Judge reviews the evidence against us in the book that records our sins, He checks to see if our name is writ-

NOBODY IN Scripture talks more about hell than Jesus Himself.

ten in the book of life. Here's the most important question that you'll ever need a right answer to: *How do you get your name in the book of life?*

Although we quoted the first half of Romans 6:23 earlier and found that "the wages of sin is death," the second half of the verse holds great promise: "but the gift of God is eternal life through Christ Jesus our Lord." Eternal life is a gift that's received through Christ. You get your name in the book of life by putting your trust in Jesus, the one who paid for your sins on the cross. If you've never surrendered your life to Him, do so today. Because there are horrible consequences for not having your name in the book of life.

A fifth observation (verbatim from verse 15): "If anyone's name was not found written in the book of life, he was thrown into the lake of fire." This is *not* where you want to spend eternity. The lake of fire is hell. Please don't dismiss hell as a minor Bible doctrine that runs counter to the kinder, gentler teaching of Jesus. Nothing could be further from the truth. Nobody in Scripture talks more about hell than Jesus Himself. He frequently warns people to avoid hell by turning from their sins and putting their faith in Him.

What's the alternative to hell? We are finally at the conclusion of the Bible's *Epic* storyline.

The New Heaven and the New Earth

I love Gary Larson's twisted sense of humor. He's the creator of the *Far Side* cartoons. One of his cartoons pictures a guy sitting on a cloud, angel wings on his back, a blank expression on his face. He's got nothing to do. And the caption reads: "Wish I'd brought a magazine." This is how a lot of people imagine heaven. Boring!

But that's nothing like the picture we get of heaven in the closing chapters of Revelation (21, 22). For starters, heaven is not going to be just heaven. God is going to create a new heaven *and* a new earth. And this new earth, where Christ followers will spend eternity, will reflect the best of what this current earth has to offer—minus all the bad stuff. John sounds blown away as he tries to describe this for us in the opening verses of Revelation 21:

Then I saw a new heaven and a new earth, for the first heaven and the first earth had passed away, and there was

173

no longer any sea. I saw the Holy City, the new Jerusalem, coming down out of heaven from God, prepared as a bride beautifully dressed for her husband. And I heard a loud voice from the throne saying, "Now the dwelling of God is with men, and he will live with them. They will be his people, and God himself will be with them and be their God. He will wipe every tear from their eyes. There will be no more death or mourning or crying or pain, for the old order of things has passed away."

He who was seated on the throne said, "I am making everything new!" Then he said, "Write this down, for these words are trustworthy and true." (Revelation 21:1–5)

You absolutely must sit down and read all of Revelation 21 and 22 for yourself sometime soon (like before today is out). Because this is the culmination of the Bible's *Epic* storyline and there's way too much good stuff in these chapters for me to even mention here, let alone unpack. And I would encourage you to do your reading from an *NIV* (or *ESV*) *Study Bible*. John uses a lot of highly symbolic language for which you'll want to have the benefit of a Bible with explanatory footnotes.

Let me close with one brief example of this highly symbolic language, since it depicts the greatest characteristic of the new earth. In Revelation 21:16 the capital city of the new earth is measured by an angel, who finds it to be 12,000 stadia long by 12,000 stadia wide by 12,000 stadia high (stadia were ancient units of measurement). It's a gigantic cube. What's behind the cube-shaped symbolism here? Some Bible teachers would object: "This isn't symbolism. These are the literal dimensions of the new earth's capital city."

But to me it makes no more sense to see the kingdom as a giant cube than to see the Antichrist as an actual ten-horned, seven-headed beast. This is symbolism. If so, what does it symbolize? Well, we find one other object described as cube-shaped in the Bible: the Holy of Holies in the Old Testament temple.[6] That was the place where God manifested His presence. Of course, only the high priest could enter the Holy of Holies. And he could only go in once a year, on the Day of Atonement.

So, what will be the greatest characteristic of the new earth, with its cube-shaped capital city? God's presence will be fully manifested there. And it won't just be a high priest who will be able to savor God's presence. We'll all enjoy it. Forever! Revelation 21:3 is worth reading and rereading, until its truth has gripped our imagination: "And I heard a loud voice from the throne saying, 'Now the dwelling of God is with men, and he will live with them. They will be his people, and God himself will be with them and be their God.'"

That's *redemption perfected*. We could say that it's the end of the *Epic* storyline. But for followers of Jesus Christ, it's just the beginning.

Study Guide

Icebreaker (for groups)

Describe one of your favorite endings to a book you've read or a movie you've seen. What did you like about that ending? What elements make for a great climax to a story?

1. What factors make the book of Revelation so difficult to interpret?

2. List the five main events that are described in Revelation and which culminate in *Redemption Perfected.*

3. What are five characteristics of the Great Tribulation? Once you list them, circle those that seem to be increasingly evident in our world today.

What are some practical ways in which you could prepare yourself for the possibility of living on earth through the Great Tribulation?

4. How eagerly (be honest) are you looking forward to the return of Christ? What are some good reasons to long for His appearing? (You'll find one in 2 Timothy 4:8.)

5. According to Revelation 19:11–16, 21, how will Jesus ultimately defeat His enemies? What does that tell you about Jesus?

6. Explain the *amillennial* interpretation of Revelation 20:1–4. What is one of the flaws of this interpretation?

7. What three things will Jesus Christ clearly demonstrate by reigning on this earth for a thousand years prior to establishing a new heaven and a new earth?

8. What impact does the description of the final judgment in Revelation 20:11–15 have on your life today?

Are you sure that your name is written in the *book of life*? Why or why not?

9. Read Revelation 21 and 22. Make a list of those aspects of the new heaven and new earth that you are most looking forward to.

Notes

About the Bible Savvy Series

1. Thom S. Rainer, *The Unchurched Next Door* (Grand Rapids: Zondervan, 2003), 200.

Chapter 1: Redemption Prompted (Genesis)

1. Timothy Keller, *The Prodigal God* (New York: Dutton, 2008), 46.

2. R. Kent Hughes, *Genesis: Beginning and Blessing* (Wheaton, Ill.: Crossway, 2004), 96.

Chapter 2: Redemption Prepared (Genesis–Song of Songs)

1. Tyrone Richardson, "Merry and Bright," *Baltimore Sun*, 18 December 2005, http://articles.baltimoresun.com/2005-12-18/news/0512170257_1_colby-claus-deep-calm.

2. These books are written primarily as Hebrew poetry, so some Bible experts classify the section as Books of Poetry. Because their theme is true wisdom, I will call them the Books of Wisdom.

Chapter 4: Redemption Purchased (Matthew–John)

1. "Victor Lustig," *Wikipedia*, 2011, http://en.wikipedia.org/wiki/Victor_Lustig.

2. Other claims by Jesus to deity can be found in John 10:30; 14:9; and Matthew 26:63–64.

3. Burt Constable, "Man Who Lied About $17,021 Proves Human Complexity," *Daily Herald*, 1 July 2011.

Chapter 5: Redemption Proclaimed (Acts–Jude)

1. Matthew 28:18–20; Mark 16:15; Luke 24:47–48; John 20:21–23.

2. Tom Newton Dunn, "British Government Slammed for Funding 'Invisible' Art Exhibit," *Herald Sun*, 3 December

2010, http://www.heraldsun.com.au/news/breaking-news/
british-government-slammed-for-funding-invisible-art-
exhibit/story-e6frf7jx-1225965059518.

Chapter 6: Redemption Perfected (Revelation)

1. Carol Vogel, "Reconsidered, a Met Velázquez Is Vin-
dicated," *The New York Times*, 20 December 2010, http://
www.nytimes.com/2010/12/21/arts/design/21velazquez.
html.

2. Robert Mounce, *The Book of Revelation*, The New
International Commentary on the New Testament (Grand
Rapids: Eerdmans, 1997), 168; and Grant R. Osborne, *Revelation*, Baker Exegetical Commentary on the New Testament (Grand Rapids: Baker, 2002), 310. Craig S. Keener,
in *The NIV Application Commentary: Revelation* (Grand
Rapids: Zondervan, 1999), 232, concludes "the numbers are
probably symbolic . . . [and] the 144,000 represent all those
destined for the new Jerusalem."

3. *Today in the Word*, April 1989, 27. See also George
Sweeting, *Who Said That?* (Chicago: Moody, 1995), 391.

4. David Jeremiah, *What in the World Is Going On?*
(Nashville: Nelson, 2008), 193.

5. Those who hold to a pretribulation rapture of believers conclude the Great White Throne judgment and the
judgment seat of Christ are different judgments; they cite
1 Corinthians 3:11–15 for rewards given to believers at a
separate judgment. In that case, only nonbelievers would
appear at the Great White Throne judgment.

6. Proponents of a literal, cubic-sized kingdom would
argue that just as the Holy of Holies was both a literal and
symbolic place, the millennial kingdom dimensions also can
be literal with symbolic implications. However, I still believe
the symbolic interpretation is stronger.

Bibliography

Bartholomew, Craig G. and Michael W. Goheen, *The Drama of Scripture: Finding Our Place in the Biblical Story*. Grand Rapids: Baker, 2004.

Carson, D. A. *The God Who Is There: Finding Your Place in God's Story*. Grand Rapids: Baker, 2010.

ESV Study Bible. Wheaton: Crossway, 2008.

NIV Study Bible. Grand Rapids: Zondervan, 2008.

Appendix

Your Bible's Table of Contents

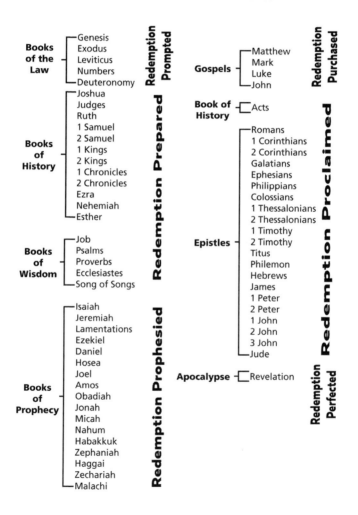

Books of the Law
- Genesis
- Exodus
- Leviticus
- Numbers
- Deuteronomy

Books of History
- Joshua
- Judges
- Ruth
- 1 Samuel
- 2 Samuel
- 1 Kings
- 2 Kings
- 1 Chronicles
- 2 Chronicles
- Ezra
- Nehemiah
- Esther

Books of Wisdom
- Job
- Psalms
- Proverbs
- Ecclesiastes
- Song of Songs

Books of Prophecy
- Isaiah
- Jeremiah
- Lamentations
- Ezekiel
- Daniel
- Hosea
- Joel
- Amos
- Obadiah
- Jonah
- Micah
- Nahum
- Habakkuk
- Zephaniah
- Haggai
- Zechariah
- Malachi

Redemption Prompted

Redemption Prepared

Redemption Prophesied

Gospels
- Matthew
- Mark
- Luke
- John

Book of History
- Acts

Epistles
- Romans
- 1 Corinthians
- 2 Corinthians
- Galatians
- Ephesians
- Philippians
- Colossians
- 1 Thessalonians
- 2 Thessalonians
- 1 Timothy
- 2 Timothy
- Titus
- Philemon
- Hebrews
- James
- 1 Peter
- 2 Peter
- 1 John
- 2 John
- 3 John
- Jude

Apocalypse
- Revelation

Redemption Purchased

Redemption Proclaimed

Redemption Perfected

More Praise for Jim Nicodem and the Bible Savvy Series

To ignite a love for the God's Word in others is the goal of any spiritual leader. Communicating God's Word is the most important of all. Pastor Jim's Bible Savvy series is the tool, the guide, and the process for worship leaders to go into deep spiritual places. His biblical scholarship, communicated with such creativity, is exactly what is needed in worship ministry today.

> Stan Endicott
> Slingshot group coach/mentor
> Worship Leader, Mariners Church, Irvine, California

Jim Nicodem leads one of America's finest churches. Jim knows how to communicate the truth of the Bible that brings historical knowledge with incredible practical application. The Bible Savvy series is the best I have ever seen. Your life and faith will be enhanced as you use and apply this material to your life.

> Jim Burns, PhD
> President, HomeWord
> Author of *Creating an Intimate Marriage* and *Confident Parenting*

Pastor Nicodem is like a championship caliber coach: he loves to teach, and he stresses that success comes from mastering the basics. The Bible Savvy series will help you correctly interpret the best Playbook ever written: the Bible. Understanding and applying its fundamentals (with the help of the Bible Savvy series) will lead one to the Ultimate Victory . . . eternity with Jesus.

> James Brown
> Host of *The NFL Today* on the CBS television network

JAMES L. NICODEM

Bible Savvy

Epic: The Storyline of the Bible unveils
the single theme that ties all of scripture
together: redemption.

Foundation: The Trustworthiness of the Bible
explains where our current bible came from
and why it can be wholly trusted.

Context: How to Understand the Bible shows
readers how to read the different parts of the
Bible as they were meant to be read and how
they fit together.

Walk: How to Apply the Bible puts the readers
increased understanding of the Bible into real
life terms and contexts.

Too many of us, regardless of our familiarity with the stories of the Bible, are blind to the story of the Bible. We miss the forest for the trees. We fail to recognize how the Bible's many individual stories fit together to tell one mega-story. The macro-story. The story of God and us.

> Phil Vischer
> Creator of Veggie Tales and What's in the Bible? video series

Jim Nicodem's purpose is to lay out, in straightforward, nontechnical language, many of the most important principles of interpretation. He does this so each person may know the foundational principles of biblical interpretation, and so understand many texts. In other words, Jim wants the church he serves, and many other churches, to be filled with men and women who will become better Bible readers.

> D.A. Carson, PhD, Research Professor of New Testament at Trinity Evangelical Divinity School,
> Author of *New Testament Commentary Survey*

As a university professor on a Christian college campus, I can tell you that biblical illiteracy is on the rise. That's why the Bible Savvy series should be a prerequisite reading for everyone. Jim Nicodem puts the cookies on the bottom shelf by making the epic story of the biblical narrative understandable and accessible. The Bible Savvy series lays out the foundation and context for God's Word and then shows us in plain language how to apply the Bible's teachings to our lives step-by-step. It's phenomenal.

> Les Parrott, PhD
> Seattle Pacific University
> Author of *You're Stronger Than You Think*

The compelling reality about the Bible is that it is full of fascinating details about God and His wise and redemptive oversight of the history of mankind. Unfortunately, the larger, more profound story often gets lost in the details. Like a master storyteller, Jim Nicodem takes us beyond the details and exposes the grand plot of Scripture. Jim's work in the Bible Savvy series will amaze many of us who have lived to master the details and will motivate all of us to stand in greater awe of the One who is navigating history to a good and glorious end.

> Joseph M. Stowell
> President, Cornerstone University

The Bible is one of the most precious possessions to a believer living in a restricted nation. I am constantly amazed by the hunger for biblical teaching expressed by those who face persecution daily. Their sacrificial passion should inspire us to rekindle our quest for biblical understanding. Jim Nicodem's Bible Savvy series is the kind of resource needed to reengage our hearts and minds with God's Word and renew a hunger for God's truth on par with our persecuted brother and sisters.

James E. Dau
President, The Voice of the Martyrs

Jim has done a masterful job in the Bible Savvy series! In these four concise books, Jim marches with clarity and skill into topics that would be difficult to tackle in a seminary classroom, much less in an American living room. And rather than a monologue, these books create a dialog among the author, the reader, their small group, and the living Word of God. These practical, approachable resources provide foundational training that is greatly needed by nearly every small group and leader I encounter.

Greg Bowman
Coauthor of *Coaching Life-Changing Small Group Leaders*
Past executive director of the Willow Creek Association

Reading the four books in the Bible Savvy series is like getting a Bible college education in a box! The Lord is calling our nation to a Bible reading revolution, and these books are an invitation to be part of it.

Hal Seed
Author of *The Bible Questions* and *The God Questions*
Lead Pastor, New Song Community Church, Oceanside, California

Living in the land of the Bible is considered a privilege by many, but the real privilege is to let the Bible become alive through us, in whatever land we may live. In the Bible Savvy series, Jim Nicodem not only helps us to understand God's plan to save us, but also His desire to change and shape us through His Word and Spirit in order to be a light in this dark world.

Rev. Azar Ajaj
Vice President and lecturer, Nazareth Evangelical Theological Seminary

To ignite a love for the God's Word in others is the goal of any spiritual leader. Communicating God's Word is the most important of all. Pastor Jim's Bible Savvy series is the tool, the guide, and the process for worship leaders to go into deep spiritual places. His biblical scholarship, communicated with such creativity, is exactly what is needed in worship ministry today.

> Stan Endicott
> Slingshot group coach/mentor
> Worship Leader, Mariners Church, Irvine, California

Jim Nicodem leads one of America's finest churches. Jim knows how to communicate the truth of the Bible that brings historical knowledge with incredible practical application. The Bible Savvy series is the best I have ever seen. Your life and faith will be enhanced as you use and apply this material to your life.

> Jim Burns, PhD
> President, HomeWord
> Author of *Creating an Intimate Marriage* and *Confident Parenting*

Pastor Nicodem is like a championship caliber coach: he loves to teach, and he stresses that success comes from mastering the basics. The Bible Savvy series will help you correctly interpret the best Playbook ever written: the Bible. Understanding and applying its fundamentals (with the help of the Bible Savvy series) will lead one to the Ultimate Victory . . . eternity with Jesus.

> James Brown
> Host of *The NFL Today* on the CBS television network

JAMES L. NICODEM

Bible Savvy

Hear from the author by
checking out the videos
on the Bible Savvy Series
with James Nicodem.

biblesavvy.com

MOODY
PUBLISHERS

Foundation
The Reliability of the Bible

James L. Nicodem

MOODY PUBLISHERS
CHICAGO

Published in association with the literary agency of Wolgemuth & Associates,
Inc.

Edited by Jim Vincent
Interior design: Ragont Design
Cover design: Smartt Guys design
Cover image: iStockphoto

Library of Congress Cataloging-in-Publication Data

Nicodem, James L., 1956-
    Foundation : the reliability of the Bible / James L. Nicodem.
      pages cm. — (The Bible savvy series)
    Includes bibliographical references.
    ISBN 978-0-8024-0634-7
    1. Bible—Evidences, authority, etc. 2. Bible—Inspiration. 3. Bible—
Canon. I. Title.
BS480.N485 2013
220.1—dc23

                                            2012044783

We hope you enjoy this book from Moody Publishers. Our goal is to
provide high-quality, thought-provoking books and products that connect
truth to your real needs and challenges. For more information on other books
and products written and produced from a biblical perspective, go to www.
moodypublishers.com or write to:

Moody Publishers
820 N. LaSalle Boulevard
Chicago, IL 60610

1 3 5 7 9 10 8 6 4 2

Printed in the United States of America

About the
Bible Savvy Series

I MET THE REAL ESTATE AGENT at my front door and invited him in. My wife and I were about to put our home on the market and I had called Jeff as a potential representative. As he sat down at our dining room table and opened his briefcase, I noticed a Bible perched on top of other papers. I asked Jeff if he was a Bible reader and he replied that he was just getting started. What had prompted his interest? He'd recently come across a list in *Success, Inc.* magazine of the most influential books recommended by business leaders. The Bible had been the most frequently mentioned book on the list. So, Jeff was going to give it a try.

My real estate agent isn't alone in his new interest in the Bible. According to a recent survey, 91 percent of those who have lately begun attending church were motivated to do so by a desire to understand what the Bible has to say to their lives.[1] That means nine of every ten visitors to church are intrigued by the Bible! But while they are curious about God's Word, they're also a bit intimidated by it. The Bible is such a daunting book, written in ancient times and addressed to

vastly different cultures. Is it really possible to draw relevant insights from it for our lives today? People are returning to church to find out.

Ironically, while an interest in Bible knowledge can be detected among those who are new to church, it seems to be on the wane among many veteran churchgoers. When my oldest daughter enrolled at a Christian college, the president of the school addressed parents on opening day. He told us that the Bible comprehension exams of each incoming class of freshmen show less and less knowledge of God's Word. And then he added: "These kids are growing up in *your* churches." Evidently, many churches are not doing a good job of teaching committed believers how to read, interpret, and apply the Bible.

The Bible Savvy series has been written to help a wide spectrum of Bible readers—from newbies to seasoned Bible study leaders—get their arms around God's Word. This multibook series covers four essential Bible-related topics that Moody Publishers has made available in one set as a comprehensive manual for understanding God's Word and putting it into practice. *Epic* is the first of the four-book series.

An added bonus to the Bible Savvy series is the Study Guide. These questions, for personal reflection and group discussion, have been crafted by a team of small-groups experts. Together they form a comprehensive study guide. The guide is also available online at *biblesavvy.com* and may be downloaded and used for personal study or reproduced for members of a small group.

Four Things You Must Know to
Get the Most Out of God's Word

The four books of the Bible Savvy series will give you a grasp of the following topics, allowing God's Word to become a rich resource in your life:

1. *The storyline of the Bible.* The Bible is actually a compilation of sixty-six books that were written over a 1,500-year period. But amazingly there is one central storyline that holds everything together. You'll trace this storyline in *Epic* from Genesis to Revelation, learning how each of the sixty-six books contributes to the overall plot.

2. *The reliability of the Bible.* How did God communicate what He wanted to say through human authors? What are the evidences that the Bible is a supernatural book? How do we know that the *right* books made it into the Bible and that the *wrong* books were kept out of it? Isn't a text that was hand-copied for hundreds of years bound to be filled with errors? *Foundation* will give you answers to questions like

these—because you won't get much out of the Bible until you're certain that you can trust it.

3. *How to understand the Bible*. People read all sorts of crazy things into the Bible, and have used it to support a wide variety of strange (and sometimes reprehensible) positions and activities. In *Context* you will learn the basic ground rules for accurately interpreting Scripture. (Yes, there are rules.)

4. *How to apply the Bible*. It's one thing to read the Bible, and it's another thing entirely to walk away from your reading with an application for your life. Even members of Bible study groups occasionally do a poor job of this. Participants leave these gatherings without a clear sense of how they're going to put God's Word into practice. *Walk* will equip you to become a Bible doer.

Do You Have Savvy?

The dictionary defines *savvy* as *practical know-how*. It is my hope and prayer that the Bible Savvy series will lead you into an experiential knowledge of God's Word that will transform your life.

Many people have contributed to my own love and understanding of the Bible over the years—as well as to the writing of this book. I owe a huge debt of gratitude to them.

Mom and Dad made God's Word central to our family life, encouraging my siblings and me to memorize big chunks of it.

When I got to high school, I was a bit turned off to church, but I started attending a youth ministry in a neighboring suburb that was led by Bill Hybels. (These were pre–Willow Creek Community Church days, when dinosaurs roamed the earth.) Bill had (and still has) an incredible ability to open the Bible, read a passage out loud, and then drive home its application to the lives of his listeners. After a year of hearing him teach God's Word in such a life-impacting way, I went away to college and decided to major in biblical studies.

Two professors (among many) fanned the flame of my love for the Bible during my college and seminary years. Dr. Gerry Hawthorne taught me Greek New Testament at Wheaton College, and there are thousands of men and women in ministry around the world today who still remember his simple-but-powerful class devotions. He'd put one verse on the chalkboard (remember chalk?) and then tease out its significance for our lives—often with tears in his eyes. Dr. D. A. Carson taught me the Bible at Trinity Evangelical Divinity School. His books (and occasional phone and email exchanges) continue to shape me today. I aspire to have even a quarter of his passion for God's Word!

After school, as I started out in youth ministry, I began listening to cassette tapes (same era as chalk) by Dr. John

MacArthur. John is internationally famous for his verse-by-verse teaching of Scripture. Although he is occasionally more adamant about certain doctrines than I am (we agree on the essentials), his love for the Bible is infectious. John has set the bar high for all pastors who want to faithfully teach their churches God's Word. As my ministry continued, I found other communicators who whet my appetite for Scripture—many of them through their books, some of them currently through their podcasts. Thank you Lee Strobel, Joe Stowell, John Ortberg, Mark Driscoll, Francis Chan, Tim Keller, and many others.

Today, my desire to get people into the Bible is fueled by the five thousand-plus eager learners whom I have the privilege of pastoring at Christ Community Church of St. Charles, Illinois, and its regional campuses. I am especially grateful for both the staff and volunteer leaders who oversee almost four hundred Community Groups that are studying God's Word. And one of those leaders, who writes incredible Bible curricula and teaches scores of Bible-hungry women, is my wife, Sue. Her devotion to Scripture is a constant inspiration to me.

Lastly, a special thanks to my faithful assistant, Angee Jenkins, who helped to edit my manuscript, track down footnotes, and protect my writing time; and to my agent, Andrew Wolgemuth, who found a great publisher in Moody to make the Bible Savvy series available to you.

Contents

To watch Jim's introduction to Foundation,
scan this QR code with your smartphone or go to
www.biblesavvy.com/video/#foundation1.

Foreword

WHEN I HEAR A SERMON or read Christian literature, my mind is programmed to take it in the information in three different ways: as a Christ-follower, as a pastor, and as a Bible professor. As a Christ-follower, I am asking, "How will these truths help me to follow Christ more closely?" As a pastor, I want to know, "How will this communicator's style bring home the important truths of Scripture to others?" As a professor, I am curious, "Has the speaker or writer done his or her homework?"

As a follower of Christ, I could tell you how the truths you learn in the following pages will give you practical guidance and insight that will motivate you to jump into the Word of God and study it more fervently.

As a pastor, I could expand on the accessibility of Jim's illustration-rich style. (It's almost as if you have an hour-long appointment with Jim at Starbucks and you've just started the conversation: "Jim, you say that the Bible is God's playbook in this game of life. Tell me, in your own words, what are the most important things I need to know about this 'playbook'?")

But I won't go into those things. Instead, I want to speak as someone who has some expertise in biblical studies. Too many well-meaning Christian writers miss the mark, either by refusing to go beyond the most basic of concepts about the Bible or, in contrast, by expounding on the backgrounds of the Bible, yet relying on bad sources. The problem with the first scenario is that it leaves far too many adults with a seven-year-old level understanding of the most important book written. The problem with the second scenario is that we are left with outdated, slightly misleading, or sometimes just flat-out wrong information.

In case you think this isn't such a big problem, think again. When as an adult you visit the doctor, you want the seven-year-old-level explanation for what ails you. You *do* want to hear your illness understood against the background of the latest medical research, all explained in layman's terms. Call it simplicity on the other side of well-researched complexity.

The beauty of this book is that it represents simplicity on the further side of the complex. If you have intellectual questions about the authority of the Bible and don't know where to begin, begin here. You won't be sorry. Jim Nicodem has done his homework.

NICHOLAS PERRIN
Professor of biblical studies, Wheaton College
Author of *Lost in Transmission: What We Can Know about the Words of Jesus*

Introduction:
A Rock-Solid Foundation

IN THE FALL OF 1970, Marshall University's football team had just lost a closely fought game to East Carolina University, 17–14. The players climbed aboard their chartered plane for the flight back to West Virginia, where family and friends waited. But they never made it home. The plane crashed and everyone on board was killed: thirty-seven football players, the coaches, team physician, booster club parents . . . everyone.

The campus community of Marshall University grieved deeply. And then they began to rebuild their football team from scratch. They had a hard time recruiting a head coach, because nobody wanted the job of leading a team that would be made up almost entirely of freshmen. But they eventually found a guy who was crazy enough to take the job. And he recruited high school seniors from around the country. The NCAA helped by giving the Thundering Herd special permission to let freshmen play on the varsity squad.[1]

So Marshall University had a coach and they had players, but they lacked one essential ingredient for building a football team: a playbook. You see, the old playbook wouldn't do. They needed a playbook that could transform a group of inexperienced freshmen into a varsity team. They needed a playbook that would be basic and uncomplicated, but effective. Somebody mentioned that a neighboring school, West Virginia University, had a basic and uncomplicated playbook. Maybe they would share it with Marshall?

Yeah, right! How many coaches would be willing to loan their playbook to another team? Well, in this particular case, West Virginia University had a generous coach who was willing to do just that. His name was Bobby Bowden and he later became famous as the "winningest coach in college football." (Bobby has also shown me great generosity by writing the foreword to my first book, *Prayer Coach*. I love that guy!) Bobby Bowden's playbook was foundational for rebuilding Marshall University's football team. It was foundational for transforming a group of raw recruits into real players.

God has a playbook. And God's playbook is foundational for transforming us into real players on His team. God's playbook is called the *Bible*. That title comes from a Greek word that means, simply, book. The Bible is God's book, and God wants us to build our lives upon it. The writer of the old hymn "How Firm a Foundation" captured this truth in the opening line of his song: "How firm a foundation, ye saints of the Lord, is laid for your faith in His excellent Word!"[2]

Back in Old Testament days, Moses reminded God's people that they were especially privileged to be the recipients of God's written Word: "What other nation is so great as to have their gods near them the way the Lord our God is near us . . . ? And what other nation is so great as to have such righteous decrees and laws as this body of laws I am setting before you today?" (Deuteronomy 4:7–8). For us, too, it's a tremendous blessing to have a book from God that can shape and direct our lives. It's a special privilege to be the people of God's book.

Of course, all this assumes that the Bible *is* God's book, that it has truly come from Him. That its claim to be His Word to us is credible. That it is free of errors that would mar its trustworthiness. Only when we are certain that the Bible is a rock-solid foundation will we be motivated to build our lives upon it.

In *Foundation* you will learn how God authored the Bible (chapter 1); protected the Bible from errors over centuries of transmission (chapter 2); reveals Himself and His will to you through the Bible (chapter 3); and expects you to saturate your life with the Bible (chapter 4).

{ **1** }

God's Autobiography

CITY RESIDENTS FOUND LITTLE comfort as they sweltered under the summer sun on August 1, 1885. But relief was on the way. Six and one-half inches of torrential rain fell on Chicago over the next twenty-four hours.

Unfortunately, this produced major flooding. Sewage from the city's 750,000 residents and runoff from the infamous stockyards washed into the Chicago River. The polluted water was then carried out into Lake Michigan. According to an exaggerated story in the *Chicago Tribune* at the time, this toxic brew was then sucked up by the intake system that provided the city with its drinking water.[1]

The *Tribune*'s story was very alarming—even if it was suspect. Chicagoans started talking about the possible outbreak of cholera, dysentery, typhoid, and other waterborne diseases. Somebody suggested, although nobody remembers *who* said it, that people were dying from these diseases.

It was eventually claimed that one out of eight Chicagoans had succumbed to the epidemic. This part of the story was repeated again and again over the following years, without any supporting evidence. Each successive retelling merely parroted the previous accounts.[2] Today those events are known as the Chicago epidemic of 1885.

In 1956, Chicago's water sanitation department actually distributed an official pamphlet describing the 1885 epidemic. It was politically motivated; the sanitation department wanted public support for projects that would upgrade Chicago's water purification system.[3] But sanitation officials knew the voters were aware of the many improvements that had already been made in this regard (such as filtration and chlorination systems), which now ensured safe drinking water. So in order to get their money, they decided to put a little scare into the local population. They printed a pamphlet that retold the story of the 1885 epidemic.

Fast-forward to recent times. In 2000 Libby Hill wrote *The Chicago River*, a history of the river's impact on the city and surrounding environs. The Northern Illinois University professor included a section on the 1885 epidemic. In her research for the book, she couldn't find any evidence for the story of a massive epidemic. In fact, Hill discovered that the death rate for 1885 was actually *lower* than for previous years. That got her thinking: If one out of eight people had died, as the epidemic story claimed, there would've been dead bodies everywhere (almost 94,000 of them)! But there weren't. And the city would've come to a grinding halt. But it hadn't.[4]

Well, it turns out that the Chicago epidemic of 1885 was a tall tale. Even the environmentalist group Friends of the Chicago River was forced to take the story off its website.[5]

Could this account serve as a metaphor for how the Bible came into existence? Is the Bible nothing more than a collection of tall tales? Have the Bible's stories been exaggerated from the beginning? Have they been stretched so that the storytellers could advance their own agenda? Has contemporary research now proven these stories to be fabrications?

Bottom line: Is the Bible reliable?

In this chapter, I will begin to answer this question (in the affirmative, of course) by making the case that the Bible has come to us from a trustworthy God. This book is, amazingly, *God's Autobiography*. And that means that it is marked by three unique, reliability-affirming characteristics—it is supernatural, inerrant, and authoritative.

A Supernatural Book

A key text for understanding the Bible's authorship is 2 Timothy 3:16. This is a verse worth memorizing. For now, I just want to roll out its opening phrase: "All Scripture is God-breathed..." What does the expression *God-breathed* mean? In the old King James Version of the Bible, the word *inspired* was used instead of *God-breathed*. Why didn't the translators of our

23

contemporary New International Version stick with *inspired*?

The NIV translators most likely dropped the word *inspired* because it wouldn't communicate to a contemporary audience what the apostle Paul meant to say when he wrote 2 Timothy 3:16. When we use the word *inspired*, we're usually referring to a person who's been emotionally or creatively moved to do something. I might say, for example: "I was inspired to clean the garage this past week." (Believe me, it would take inspiration!)

Or to use a classier example, we might say that George Frideric Handel was inspired when he composed his famous oratorio, *Messiah*. Here's a guy who wrote 260 pages of music for a complete orchestra in just twenty-four days. He didn't leave his room the entire time. He barely touched his food.[6] And when *Messiah* was first performed in 1742, it was so majestic that the King of England rose to his feet when the choir began to sing the *Hallelujah Chorus*. Yes, Handel was inspired. He was creatively moved.

But that's *not* what the apostle Paul meant to say about Scripture in 2 Timothy 3:16. The best English translation of Paul's original Greek expression is, in fact, exactly what we have in the NIV: "All Scripture is God-breathed." So, when theologians today use the old KJV word *inspired* to refer to the Bible, this is what they're talking about: the God-breathed nature of the book.

But what exactly is it about the Bible that is inspired or God-breathed? There are two mistaken notions with regard to inspiration. Some people assume that this must be a reference to the Bible's *writers*. Men like Moses and King David and the apostle Paul, who penned various books of the Bible, were inspired, right? Didn't God breathe into them some general ideas, after which they sat down and wrote out, as best they could, their particular portions of the Bible? No, that would be the first wrong notion.

The trouble with this view of inspiration is that it leaves open the possibility that these human writers might not have gotten things right. What if they misunderstood what God breathed into them to say? Or what if they didn't choose the best words to communicate these general God-given impressions to us? No, it's not enough that the *writers* themselves were inspired.

A second mistaken notion is to assume that inspiration refers to the Bible's *readers*. When you pick up the Bible and read it, God speaks to you. You, as it were, become inspired. Make sense? Some people who hold this view have gone so far as to say: "The Bible is the Word of God when it becomes the Word of God to you." Huh? What if that doesn't happen? What if you read the Bible and it doesn't feel like God is speaking to you? Is the Bible only inspired when it connects with you? Is it only inspired when you, as the *reader*, are inspired?

No. Inspiration is not about the Bible's *writers* and it's not about the Bible's *readers*. It's about the Bible's *words*. Go back to the opening phrase of 2 Timothy 3:16: "All Scripture is God-breathed." What is "God-breathed"? (Sorry to ask the obvious.) *Scripture is.* The Greek word for Scripture is *graphe*, and it means, literally, *writing*. So the writing itself, the very words that appear in print, is what God inspired. That's why theologians, when they speak of inspiration today, will often add the adjective *verbal* in front of it. "*Verbal* inspiration" clarifies the fact that God breathed out the actual words of the Bible.

WHAT GOD wanted to say got said, exactly as God wanted it said.

Why is this so important to note? Because it assures us that what God wanted to say got said, exactly as God wanted it said. Does this mean that the human writers (Moses, David, Paul, and so on) were simply secretaries, stenographers to whom God dictated His Word? Absolutely not. If you read the Bible, which is a compilation of sixty-six books, you'll quickly discover that each book reflects the vocabulary, the culture, the historical setting, and the personality of its human author.

For instance, compare Moses' laws with David's psalms, or with Paul's letters, or with Solomon's proverbs, or with Zechariah's prophecy, or with Matthew's biography of Jesus, or with Luke's history of the early church. There's a lot of variety among the books by those seven writers. That variety reflects the differences among the human authors. God didn't dictate His Word to them in some uniform fashion. However, God *did* ensure that what He wanted to say got said, exactly as He wanted it said. "All Scripture"—the writing itself, the very words that appear in print—"is God-breathed."

That makes the Bible a unique book. It's unlike any other book you can pick up at Barnes & Noble, or Amazon.com, or the public library. The Bible is *God's* Word. And because it is the Word of a supernatural God, it must be a supernatural book.

I know that sounds like an outrageous claim, especially if you are a skeptic as you read this. You probably think that I'm pretty gullible to believe that the Bible is God-breathed just because 2 Timothy 3:16 says that it's God-breathed. Well, I assure you that I have just as much of an aversion to being caught gullible as you do. I am very wary about being taken for a ride down fantasy lane.

I remember, years ago when I was a college student, taking a walk on a starry night with this good-looking girl. She began to point out constellations to me in the brightly lit sky. The Big Dipper was easy to spot. So was Orion's Belt. But as we continued to stroll, she began identifying starry configurations that I had never heard of. And when she'd ask me, "Do you see such-and-such?" I would nod my head and say uh-huh, even though I couldn't quite make out the cluster of stars that

BECAUSE IT is the Word of a supernatural God, the Bible must be a supernatural book.

she was describing. Constellation after constellation, my astronomy lesson continued. Wherever my date pointed, I would gaze and say: "Wow! That's cool!!"

About twenty minutes into the walk, an awful thought popped into my head: *What if she's making all this up?* What if she's playing a practical joke on me to see how gullible I am? What if I've been nodding my head and oohing and aahing over constellations that don't exist? What if she goes back to her dorm and tells her roommate: "You wouldn't believe the loser I suckered tonight!"

Nobody likes to be thought of as gullible . . . naïve . . . clueless . . . simpleminded. And that's why, in today's culture, it's a bit intimidating to express a belief in the Bible as God's Word; to claim that it's a *supernatural* book. No Western-civilized, college-educated, self-respecting man or woman believes that *God* authored the Bible. C'mon! Why should anybody swallow the 2 Timothy 3:16 statement that the Bible is God-breathed?

Evidence for a Supernatural Book

Very briefly, let me give you some hard evidence that points to the *supernatural* nature of the Bible. None of these proofs is conclusive in itself. But when you take them all together, they make a pretty strong case that this book has been authored by God.

Historical accuracy. When it comes to its many references to people, places, and events, the Bible is an amazingly accurate book. So say archaeologists. I'll talk more about this in the next chapter when I cover how it was determined which books to include in the Bible, because historical accuracy was a critical test that had to be passed. But let me note Luke's Gospel and the book of Acts as a quick example of the Bible getting its facts straight. Christian author and apologist Lee Strobel cites a highly esteemed archaeologist in his book *The Case for Christ*, who examined every one of Luke's references to thirty-two countries, fifty-four cities, and nine islands. And he didn't find a single mistake![7]

Fulfilled prophecy. Did you know that prophecy is fairly rare in the writings of most religions? In all the works of Buddha and Confucius there is not a single example of predictive prophecy. In the entire Quran, written by Muhammad, there's only *one* prophecy—and it's pretty general.

By way of contrast, the Bible's Old Testament alone contains over two thousand predictive prophecies. These are not vague predictions, like the kind you'd find in a fortune cookie. Many of them are very specific.

Consider just a few of the prophecies made about Jesus Christ, hundreds of years before His birth. (I refer to these prophecies, as well, in chapter 3 of *Epic* and show how they contribute to the Bible's overall storyline.) Daniel foretold the exact time of Jesus' appearing (Daniel 9:24). Micah predicted that Jesus would be born in the small village of Bethlehem (Micah 5:2). Zechariah prophesied that Jesus would enter Jerusalem triumphantly on the back of a colt, but later be betrayed for thirty pieces of silver (Zechariah 9:9; 11:12–13). Isaiah described how Jesus would be put to death alongside criminals, and yet be buried in a rich man's tomb (Isaiah 53:9). Prophecies like these surely evidence the Bible's supernatural character.

Indomitable durability. Time and again throughout history, the enemies of Christianity have attempted to undermine or even stamp out the Bible. But such efforts, though sustained, have all proven unsuccessful. My favorite anecdote in this regard concerns eighteenth-century French philosopher and skeptic Voltaire. Voltaire was a caustic critic of the Bible. He described it as a book of fairy tales that would cease to exist within a generation or two of his lifetime. It turns out that Mr. Voltaire wasn't much of a prophet. After his death, his house was purchased by a printing business that published copies of—would you believe—the Bible! Got to love God's sense of humor.

Overall consistency. Keep in mind that the Bible is actually sixty-six books in one. And yet its authors—who represent a wide variety of vocations, come from three different continents, and write over a period of fifteen hundred years—speak with remarkable harmony about *one* central theme. Imagine such a diverse collection of writers today agreeing on any topic, whether it be medicine or economics or sports or you name it.

Miraculous depictions. If the Bible is God-breathed, if it's a supernatural book, wouldn't we expect it to con-

A REASONABLE case can be made for the Bible being God-breathed based on its historical accuracy, fulfilled prophecy . . . and transformed lives.

tain stories of God's miraculous interventions in our world? And yet, ironically, this is the very thing that skeptics won't tolerate about the Bible. Thomas Jefferson is a case in point. Are you familiar with Jefferson's New Testament? Jefferson was a true child of the Enlightenment, with its emphasis on scientific investigation. If something couldn't be studied or tested in the laboratory, ol' Tom wouldn't believe it. So one day he got out his X-ACTO knife and cut out all the passages in the Gospels that describe Jesus' miracles.

Let me tell you what's so wrongheaded about Jefferson's approach. Historical events are not proven by testing them in a science lab. We verify historical events by checking out the eyewitness accounts of those events. That's how we know that George Washington crossed the Delaware River in December of 1776, and that Abraham Lincoln delivered the Gettysburg Address in November 1863, and that the Chicago Cubs won the World Series in October 1908 (as unbelievable as that last event seems). Eyewitnesses attest to each of these events. And that's how we know that Jesus did miracles: eyewitness accounts.

Transformed lives. I've been the pastor of Christ Community Church for almost thirty years. During the past three decades, I have collected several files' worth of letters from people who claim that the Bible teaching they've received from my sermons and in our community groups has changed their lives in dramatic ways. Broken marriages have been reconciled, destructive addictions have been conquered, life-purpose has been discovered, character has been reformed, difficult trials have been endured, and concern for others has been developed. And people give the credit for these positive transformations to the impact of the Bible in their lives!

Is the Bible God-breathed, as it claims to be in 2 Timothy 3:16? Is it a supernatural book? A reasonable case can be made for this position based upon the Bible's historical accuracy, fulfilled prophecy, indomitable durability, overall consistency, miraculous depictions, and transformed lives.

An Inerrant Book

What does *inerrant* mean? It means that the Bible is free from any kind of error. In the preface of a book, an author often will acknowledge all the people who helped shape that book: the mentors, the colleagues, the researchers, the editors. And then the author will make a disclaimer that goes something like this: "While I wish to thank all these people for contributing to my book, any errors that you find in these pages are entirely mine." That's a nice, generous, humble thing to say. But you won't find God saying that about His book. Why not? Because it's inerrant!

Why should you believe that the Bible is inerrant? On the basis of three testimonies. First, there is *the testimony of God's character*. The Bible repeatedly refers to God as "the God of truth" (Psalm 31:5; Isaiah 65:16). The apostle Paul tells Christ followers that God has promised us eternal life, and then Paul adds: "God . . . does not lie" (Titus 1:2). The writer of Hebrews makes this same claim even more starkly: "It is impossible for God to lie" (Hebrews 6:18). God is truthful through and through. So, when God speaks, it is reasonable to conclude that His words are true. They're inerrant. Free from any kind of error.

Psalm 119 is the longest chapter in the Bible: 176 verses. And this psalm is all about God's Word. One of the things that it repeatedly affirms about God's Word is that it's true: "Your law is true . . . All your commands are true . . . All your words are true . . ." (Psalm 119:142, 151, 160). You get the idea. Because God is the *God of truth*, because God's character is 100 percent true, God's Word, the Bible, must be true.

Here's a second reason to believe that the Bible is inerrant: *the testimony of Jesus Christ*. Jesus obviously believed that Scripture is trustworthy and true. He affirmed this in one of His prayers: "Father . . . your word is truth" (John 17:1, 17). And He constantly

JESUS BELIEVED that Scripture is trustworthy and true, and affirmed this in one of His prayers.

quoted the Old Testament to back up His teaching, beginning these citations with the words "It is written." In other words, Jesus cited Old Testament stories as if He took them at face value. Stories about Noah and the flood, the destruction of Sodom and Gomorrah, God's miraculous provision of manna in the wilderness, Jonah spending three days in the belly of a giant fish—Jesus seemed to accept all these accounts as being historically accurate.

And Jesus didn't merely believe that the Bible is true in a broad brushstroke sort of way. His position was *not*: Scripture

34

is true, generally speaking, even if some of the details are in error. No! Jesus said that not even "the smallest letter [or] the least stroke of a pen" in God's Word would disappear until it had all been fulfilled (Matthew 5:18).

A third reason to believe the Bible's inerrancy is *the testimony of logic*. This would be a good time to acknowledge that there are some Christian Bible scholars who don't care for the word *inerrant*. There are some who want us to believe that the Bible is basically trustworthy, even though it's not without error. "But that's OK," these scholars say, "because God is still able to get His message across, in spite of the errors that are sprinkled throughout Scripture." I struggle with the illogic of that perspective.

Does it make sense to you that God would speak His *truth* through statements that are occasionally *false*? (And if you point out that God speaks His truth through faulty pastors every Sunday, I would ask you how you know that these pastors are occasionally faulty. Isn't it by comparing what they say with God's faultless Word?) Furthermore, if some of what we read in the Bible is in error, who decides which statements those are? It seems to me that this position would allow us to reject portions of the Bible we don't like with a dismissive, "Oh, that's one of those errors."

I believe that the Bible is inerrant because the God of truth breathed it out, because Jesus accepted it as totally trustworthy, and because it makes logical sense that God would not leave us guessing about which parts are true and which are not. However, this doesn't mean that there aren't places in the Bible that *appear to be* in error. Let me give you several reasons why people sometimes mistakenly assume that they have found errors in the Bible.

Figures of speech are taken literally. For example, the Bible talks about "the four corners of the earth" (Revelation 7:1). Does that mean that the Bible contains scientific errors? After all, this is a description of a flat earth, right? Hardly. It's a poetic figure of speech that's not intended to be taken literally. Same thing when the Bible speaks of the sun *rising*. We all know that the sun doesn't rise. But that doesn't make the Bible wrong any more than it makes the TV weatherman wrong when he tells us the time of tomorrow's sunrise.

Narratives are not always arranged chronologically. Sometimes when the Bible tells a story, it relates the events of that story in the order in

PEOPLE SOMETIMES assume that they have found errors in the Bible when they take figures of speech literally.

which they occurred. But other times the Bible relates the events thematically or topically (e.g., lumping together several of Jesus' miracles or parables). So if one of the Gospels tells us that Jesus did things in a certain sequence, and another Gospel tells us that He did those things in a different sequence, that doesn't mean that one of the accounts is wrong. It means that one of the accounts has not been arranged in chronological order.[8]

Imprecise quotations are used. What if Matthew records that Jesus said something one way, and Mark's quote of Jesus is a little bit different. Is somebody in error? Nope. We do this all the time, don't we? We say: "My boss said . . ." or "My wife said . . ." or "My doctor said . . ." And then we give a summary, not an exact quotation, of what they said. In fact, the very next time we summarize what they said, we will probably do it a little bit differently.

Numbers are rounded off. Let me ask you a question. How old are you? On the count of three, I want you to call out your age. One . . . two . . . three! (Pause for your participation.) I bet you called out your age in a round number. I bet you said: "fifteen" or "thirty-three" or "fifty-seven." Am I right? But that's how old you were on your last birthday. That's not how old you are today. Your current age, to be precise, is a matter of years and months and days. Sometimes in the Bible, we read two different accounts of the same event, and the numbers are not exactly the same. An error? No, just rounded-off numbers.

I could add to this list of mistaken assumptions about errors in the Bible, but I think you get my point. Many of these so-called errors can be quickly straightened out with fairly simple explanations. (If there is a particular discrepancy about which you'd like some clarification, you'll probably find it covered in Norm Geisler's *When Critics Ask: A Popular Handbook on Bible Difficulties* [Baker].) Yes, I will admit that there *are* some discrepancies in Scripture that are still difficult, even impossible, to fully explain. But considering the Bible's overall track record for inerrancy, I'm prepared to give God's Word the benefit of the doubt in these cases.

An Authoritative Book

A couple of years ago, Sue and I met with our financial consultant and he suggested that we consider refinancing our mortgage. He gave us several good reasons for doing this: the low interest rates, the short amount of time it would take to recover the cost of the refinancing, and so on. In brief, our financial consultant said, "Go for it!" So we . . . didn't.

It's not that we don't trust our financial consultant. He gives great advice. But in this particular case, considering that our mortgage was almost paid off and a few other factors, we decided to sit tight. We're allowed to do that. We're not expected or required to obey everything our financial consultant says to us. He may be an expert, but he's not our final authority.

Many people respond to God's Word in a similar fashion. They treat it as if it's full of good suggestions. Kind of like the suggestions one might get from a teacher or coach or counselor or friend or investment analyst or Oprah. Please don't make the extremely dangerous mistake of dismissing God's Word as so many suggestions. God's Word is not advice—it is to be the final authority in our lives. Take a look at a story that Jesus told to illustrate this point:

" Therefore everyone who hears these words of mine and puts them into practice is like a wise man who built his house on the rock. The rain came down, the streams rose, and the winds blew and beat against that house; yet it did not fall, because it had its foundation on the rock. But everyone who hears these words of mine and does not put them into practice is like a foolish man who built his house on sand. The rain came down, the streams rose, and the winds blew and beat against that house, and it fell with a great crash."

When Jesus had finished saying these things, the crowds were amazed at his teaching, because he taught as one who had authority, and not as their teachers of the law. (Matthew 7:24–29)

Please note that both of the builders in the story represent people who have heard Jesus' teaching. They are like people who go to church and listen to sermons. The difference between the two groups is that the wise builders *do* what Jesus says to do (houses on rock) and the foolish builders *don't* (houses on sand). Are you responding to the Bible these days as if God Himself were looking you in the eye and giving you directives? Because He is. The Bible is *God's* Word. That makes it authoritative.

If God says in His book not to allow any unwholesome talk to come out of your mouth (Ephesians 4:29), then, with God's help, don't allow any unwholesome talk to come out of your mouth. Period. End of sentence. If God says in His book to abstain from sex outside of marriage (Hebrews 13:4), then don't sleep with your girlfriend, be unfaithful to your spouse, or fantasize to pornography on the Internet. It's that straightforward. If God says in His book to let go of bitterness toward those who've wronged you (Ephesians 4:31), or to return a minimal 10 percent of your income to the Lord's work (Malachi 3:10), or to honor your father and mother (Ephesians 6:1, 2), these are not optional suggestions for your consideration. This is God speaking to you. Authoritatively!

If you are ignoring God's Word, you are building your house on sand. And one day it's going to come crashing down. Let me encourage you, instead, to build your house on the rock-solid foundation of Scripture. Read the Bible daily. Join a small group and study the Bible with others. Take notes when you hear the Bible being taught at church—and don't miss a weekend service. Value the Bible's input over any advice that you get from a counselor or expert or friend. Let the Bible become your final authority.

Several months ago a husband and wife approached me after the church service, asking me to settle their dispute. The man had just lost his job. He had been an executive for a large company that was downsizing. He'd been given a very generous severance package. And that was the focus of the dispute with his wife. She felt that they should tithe on the severance (i.e., put 10 percent of it in the offering bag), since it was income the Lord had provided. And he was angry at the thought of doing any such thing. As he explained to me, executive positions are hard to find and so it would be irresponsible to give away some of the severance money that they might need to live on while he was job-hunting.

VALUE THE BIBLE'S input over any advice from an expert or friend. Let the Bible become your final authority.

The man wanted to know what I thought they should do. Even though I knew that my counsel might be suspect, since I'm the pastor of the church that would benefit from a tithe on his severance package, I still encouraged him to obey what the Bible says and return a portion of this income to the Lord. I said, "This is a time in your life when you can't afford for God to be sitting on the sidelines. You would welcome His participation by doing what His Word tells you to do."

To his credit, the guy went home and wrote out a tithe check. But that's not the end of the story. Within a week's time, four companies had called him for job interviews. He was back at work in short order. He saw that as a bit miraculous, and so did I. We both also made the connection between his submission to God's authority and God's blessing.

The Bible is *God's Autobiography*. As such, it is a supernatural, inerrant, and authoritative book. And you are a budding theologian, having just covered the critical *Doctrine of Inspiration*.

Study Guide

The *Study Guide* questions at the end of each chapter have been designed for your personal benefit. *All* questions can be used for personal study and, if you're part of a discussion group, for preparation for your group meeting. If you are part of a small group, you will find that the questions preceded by the group icon ( ) are especially useful for discussion. Your group leader can choose from among those questions when the group meets.

Icebreaker

What tall tale (i.e., frequently recounted and increasingly exaggerated personal story) has become well-known among your family or friends?

1. What is wrong with viewing the Bible's inspiration in terms of its *writers* or *readers*?

   According to 2 Timothy 3:16, what *is* it about the Bible that's inspired (i.e., God-breathed)? Practically speaking, what does this mean? How does God-*breathed* differ from God-*dictated*?

2. 🔘 Describe a situation in which your belief that the Bible is *God's* Word was called into question or ridiculed. How did you defend your position at the time (or *did* you)?

3. 🔘 List and briefly describe the six evidences that point to the supernatural character of the Bible. Which of these impresses you the most? Why?

4. Give three reasons for believing in the inerrancy of Scripture.

In what sense would refusing to believe in the Bible's inerrancy put you in a position of authority over Scripture?

5. How might you respond to someone who claims that the Bible is "full of errors"?

6. In what way(s) is the counsel of God's Word different from the counsel you receive from any other source (e.g., friend, therapist, self-help book, teacher, consultant, etc.)?

7. (icon) What is the basic difference between the guy who builds on rock and the one who builds on sand in Jesus' parable (Matthew 7:24–29)? Give some real-life examples of what could happen to you if you build on sand.

8. (icon) What step(s) might you take to ensure that you are building your life on rock?

9. (icon) Describe a time in your life (if you can) when obedience to some directive in God's Word brought you blessing.

{ 2 }

Lost in Transmission?

HAVE YOU EVER PLAYED the telephone game at a party? You know the basic setup. Everybody sits in a circle. One person is given a slip of paper with a sentence or two on it. He reads it to himself and then whispers what he's read into the ear of the person on his left. She then passes on what she thinks she's heard into the next person's ear.

Around the circle the phone message goes. By the time it reaches the last person, who completes the loop by saying the sentence out loud, it doesn't sound anything like the original statement.

Some skeptics of Christianity claim this is exactly what has happened with the transmission of the Bible. Whatever the Bible said when it was originally written was copied again and again and again over the years. And each time it was copied errors were introduced into the text. So what we read in the Bible today is a total distortion of what was originally written. Maybe you've heard this line of reasoning before.

In chapter 1, I drove home the point that the Bible is unlike any other book because its very words have been breathed out by God. Wow! But how do we know that what was breathed out by God was accurately passed along over the centuries? How do we know that it wasn't *lost in transmission* like the message that gets distorted as it goes around the circle in a game of telephone?

The Copying: *Hang Up the Phone Analogy!*

Let me begin by noting two basic problems with the telephone analogy. First, *the Bible's transmission has involved the careful copying of a written document*, not the whispered communicating of an oral message. Big difference!

To illustrate that difference, let's change the rules for the game of telephone. What if we handed out pencils and slips of paper and circulated the original message *in writing*? Each person would have to carefully copy the previous person's note before passing it on. Do you think this would improve the accuracy of the transmission? Of course it would! Well, this is how the Bible was transmitted. You say: "Well, somebody might still have become sloppy and miscopied a word." That's possible. But let me tell you how carefully the Bible was copied.

The last couple of times Sue and I were in Israel, we visited the site of the ancient Qumran community. This community thrived between 200 BC and AD 100 and it was responsible for producing the copies of the Bible that we know as the Dead Sea Scrolls. Here's what we've learned about how seriously these Bible copiers approached their task. For starters, they did their writing on specially prepared skins of clean (kosher) animals. Each skin was prepared to contain a certain number of columns. The spacing between consonants, sections, and books was precise—measured by threads. The ink had to be black and prepared according to a special recipe to ensure it would not fade.

There's more. No words could be written from memory. The transcriber had to have the manuscript he was copying right in front of him at all times. And copying the Bible was such an important task that the scribe would take a ritual bath and put on special clothes before sitting down to do it. Listen to this quotation from a first-century copier named Ishmael. He says to his fellow scribes, "Be careful in your work for it is the work of Heaven, lest you err either in leaving out or in adding one iota, and thereby cause the destruction of the whole world."[1]

No pressure, eh? You'll just destroy the world if you mess up your copying! These transcribers did their work as if the survival of the planet depended upon their accuracy. Clearly the careful copying of the written Scripture bears no resemblance to the frivolous whispering that goes on in a game of telephone.

There's a second reason why telephone is a lousy analogy for the Bible's transmission. To ensure quality control of the Bible's transmission, *copyists regularly compared manuscript copies with each other*. But this isn't how you play the game of telephone, is it?

Let's suppose there are ten people in your telephone circle. When person number five gets the message, whom does she get it from? (This is *not* a trick question.) She gets it from person number four. And that means (hang in there) that if person four miscommunicates the message, person five will pass that miscommunication on to person six. There's no way that person five can know to correct person four's error before passing on the message.

But what if we changed the rules of the game once again? What if person five is allowed to double-check the message she receives from person four, by asking persons one, two, and three for their input? Wouldn't that ensure accuracy in transmission?

That's what *does* happen today when Bible scholars reconstruct a document like the New Testament. They do it by comparing *all* the copies they have with each other. And it's estimated that there are up to 30,000 copies of the New Testament in existence. That allows for a lot of comparing!

Of course, all that comparing sometimes gives the Bible's detractors ammunition. A few years ago liberal Bible scholar

Bart Ehrman wrote a bestseller called *Misquoting Jesus*.[2] Dr. Ehrman is one of the world's leading textual critics of the New Testament. His book claims that readers can't trust the text of the New Testament today because there are between 200,000 and 400,000 variants (i.e., differences) among the manuscript copies that we have of the New Testament. Big problem, right? Dr. Ehrman thinks it is. That's why he says that any Bible you read today is most assuredly *misquoting Jesus*.

How do we respond to Ehrman? He's an expert. He's received a PhD in New Testament and teaches at a major university. He's written a popular book on this subject. Well, the best way to counter a so-called expert is with an opposing expert. And that's what Lee Strobel does in his book *The Case for the Real Jesus*. Strobel interviews Daniel Wallace on the topic of the New Testament's transmission.[3]

Dr. Wallace knows his Greek New Testament. In fact, he's written a textbook on Greek grammar that's currently being used by two-thirds of the schools that teach intermediate Greek, including Yale, Princeton, and Cambridge. Besides being a Greek expert, Wallace has studied the countless copies we have of the New Testament. He's even traveled around the world and taken more than 35,000 high-resolution digital photographs of the New Testament copies. They're posted on his website so that scholars can study them and compare them.

What does Wallace say about Ehrman's claim that there

are 200,000 to 400,000 variants among our copies of the New Testament? Wallace begins by pointing out that, since we have up to 30,000 copies of the New Testament, it's not surprising that we can find 200,000 to 400,000 variants among those copies. That averages to only ten variants per copy. Not a big deal. Furthermore, a close study of those variants reveals that between 70 percent and 80 percent of them have to do with spelling differences, often the difference of just a single letter.

UP TO 80 percent of text variants have to do with spelling differences, often the difference of just a single letter.

In addition, there are many cases in which the variant is due to the copier using a synonym. For example, one manuscript might read, "Jesus" said such and such, while other manuscripts read, "The Lord" said such and such. *Not* a huge difference. The fact is: only 1 percent of all the variants, according to Wallace, have any impact on the meaning of a text. And that impact is usually quite insignificant.

Thus the thousands of ancient copies of the New Testament that allow modern Bible scholars to compare manuscripts with each other ensure that today's New Testament is an accurate transmission of the original.

Great! But what about the copies we have of the Old

Testament? Do they also ensure an accurate transmission of the original? The answer rests in a special discovery found in several Middle East caves in 1947. That year, a shepherd boy (and subsequently archaeologists) discovered the Dead Sea Scrolls. At the time of their discovery the oldest copy we had of the Hebrew Old Testament dated back to about AD 900. But the Dead Sea Scrolls are copies of the Hebrew Old Testament that date back to 200 BC.

And you know what Bible scholars discovered when they compared the AD 900 copies with the 200 BC copies? Amazing agreement! Though these two sets of copies were separated by over a thousand years, the only variants were very minor. For example: in Isaiah 53, an important passage that prophesizes the coming of Christ and His death for our sins, there's only one word that's different between the AD 900 copies and the 200 BC copies.

Can the transmission of Old Testament manuscripts be trusted? Absolutely!

The trustworthiness of both the Old and New Testaments raises another important question, a more basic question that we now address.

The Canon: What Are the Right Books?

We've just learned that the sixty-six books of the Bible have been accurately copied over the centuries. But how do we know that scribes were copying the right books?

This question has to do with the canon of the Bible. Now, when I say *canon*, don't think boom-boom cannon—that's cannon with two *n*'s. The canon I'm talking about has only one *n*. *Canon* comes from a Greek word that means *measuring stick*. The canon of the Bible has to do with which books were accepted into the Bible (and which books were kept out). This canon was determined with the help of a measuring stick—certain standards that were used to decide which books were God-breathed and which ones were not.

Who Decides What's in and What's out?

Before we take a look at four of these standards, let me say a brief word about *who* determined the canon of the Old Testament and *who* determined the canon of the New Testament.

There are thirty-nine books in the Old Testament. The first, Genesis, was written by Moses about 1400 BC; the last, Malachi, by that prophet around 430 BC. All of the other Old Testament books were authored sometime during the thousand years between those two dates. So, how did they get collected into one volume? And who decided what was in and what was out?

Our information on the forming of the Old Testament canon is a bit sketchy, but according to Jewish tradition Ezra, a scholar and religious leader, played a huge role. Ezra helped

Israel to rebuild as a nation after many of its citizens had been released from a seventy-year Babylonian captivity. To be sure that God's people got restarted on the right foot, he put a lot of time into teaching them God's Word. But what *was* God's Word? Ezra set out to answer that question.

He pulled together a 120-person council of devout leaders, later referred to as the *Great Synagogue*. In 425 BC (just five years after Malachi completed the last book of the Old Testament), Ezra's council determined which books would comprise the Old Testament canon.

Just a footnote to this point: Even though not all Bible scholars agree that it was Ezra and his buddies who had the final say in establishing this canon, we do know that the canon must have been determined by the time of Jesus. By that time, Jesus occasionally referred to "the Scripture," indicating a standardized version of the Old Testament existed by then.

What about the New Testament canon? The New Testament is made up of twenty-seven books, beginning with the four Gospels, the biographies of Jesus. Who decided which books were in and which books were out for this portion of the Bible? And when was that decided?

Well, if you get your information from Dan Brown, the author of the best-selling mystery novel *The Da Vinci Code*[4] (which later became a Tom Hanks movie), the New Testament canon wasn't determined until AD 325 at the Council of

Nicaea. And that council was pulled together by the Roman Emperor Constantine, who was trying to unify his empire by forcing Christianity on everybody. Brown claims very conservative representatives dominated the council and chose only books for the New Testament canon that supported their narrow viewpoint that Jesus Christ was God. And they left out a lot of good stuff!

But Brown's conclusions are flagrantly wrong. For one thing, the first list we have of the New Testament's twenty-seven books dates all the way back to AD 170. That list is called the *Muratorian Fragment*. And besides the evidence of that list, historians tell us that the church was already using these particular twenty-seven books and *not* using other books, long before the Council of Nicaea met in AD 325. The only thing that this council did was to *formally* approve the twenty-seven books that the church had *informally* recognized for years as being God-breathed.

Brown also dismisses as ridiculous the belief among Christians that New Testament books are inspired by God simply because some church council included them in the canon. "C'mon!" Dan Brown would chide us: "One day Matthew's Gospel was just another ordinary biography of Jesus. And the next day it became 'inspired,' just because some church council canonized it?" But Brown is missing the point. Being canonized didn't *make* certain books inspired. Being canonized simply *recognized* these books as having been God-inspired. Do you see the difference?

Let me illustrate. Let's say I visit an antique store, buy an old painting, and take it home. When I go to reframe it, I discover another work of art on the back of it. In the corner it says: *Rembrandt*. I take it to an art dealer, an expert, and he does some tests on it after which he officially announces that my painting is indeed a Rembrandt. Here's my question: When did my

THE CHURCH councils didn't *make* the New Testament books God-inspired. They *recognized* books that were already God-inspired.

Rembrandt become a Rembrandt? When Rembrandt painted it, right? It was a Rembrandt long before that art dealer recognized it as such. It didn't take his official recognition to make it a Rembrandt!

Similarly, Ezra and his buds didn't *make* the Old Testament books that they canonized God-inspired. The church councils in AD 300-and-something didn't *make* the New Testament books that they canonized God-inspired. All that canonization did was to *recognize* which books were already God-inspired and should thus be included in the Bible, God's Holy Word.

By the way, this is the reason why the Roman Catholic

Church is mistaken to assert that church tradition is of equal or greater authority than the Bible because church tradition gave us the Bible. No it didn't! *God* gave us the Bible. Church tradition only recognized which books had been God-inspired.

The Standards: *Gotta Pass These Tests!*

So what are those standards used to decide which books are God-breathed and which ones are not? The standards to measure inspiration of the manuscripts are really four tests.

First, there's the authorship test. I'll never forget a heated exchange that took place in the vice presidential debate of 1988 between Dan Quayle (Republican) and Lloyd Bentsen (Democrat). At the time, some people considered Quayle too young and inexperienced to be the vice president. So, in an effort to address this concern, while at the same time endearing himself to voters of both parties, Senator Quayle said: "I have as much experience as Jack Kennedy did when he sought the presidency." (JFK, of course, had been a very popular president.)

Senator Bentsen, a much older man than Quayle, retorted with these stinging words: "Senator, I served with Jack Kennedy. I knew Jack Kennedy. Jack Kennedy was a friend of mine." Then Bentsen paused before delivering the zinger. "And Senator, you are *no* Jack Kennedy!"[5] Whoa! Game, set, match. Here's the point of my story. The writers of the New

Testament books were all apostles or people who were closely associated with an apostle and so they had served with Jesus, they knew Jesus, they were friends of Jesus.

Back to Dan Brown, who claims that when the church chose to make Matthew, Mark, Luke, and John the official Gospels of the New Testament, they rejected eighty-some additional biographies of Jesus. Those were equally qualified, Brown says. Grant Osborne, who has a PhD in New Testament, responds that there were only about seventeen alternative gospels around when the books of Matthew, Mark, Luke, and John were canonized. *Not* eighty![6] Brown's claim is rubbish.

Those seventeen alternative gospels can all be dated between AD 150 and 300. In other words, they were written one to three *centuries* after Jesus. This obviously means that the writers of these alternative gospels could not have been personally familiar with Jesus any more than you and I could be personally familiar with someone who lived one to three hundred years ago. (How well, for example, could you possibly know Abraham Lincoln?)

But Matthew, Mark, and John *were* deeply familiar with Jesus. Matthew and John were members of Jesus' original band of twelve disciples. Mark, although not himself a disciple, got his information about Jesus from his close friend, Peter, who was another one of the original twelve. (In 1 Peter 5:13, Peter wrote that Mark was like a son to him.) And Luke got his information about Jesus from his ministry-partner, Paul, who'd had a real-life encounter with the risen Jesus on the road to Damascus. That's why the early church considered Paul to be an official apostle, even though he'd not been one of the Twelve. So all four Gospel writers had the personal scoop on Jesus.

Take a look at what one of them, Luke, says about his credentials for writing Jesus' biography: "Many have undertaken to draw up an account of the things that have been fulfilled among us, just as they **MATTHEW, MARK, Luke, and John *were* deeply familiar with Jesus. All four had the personal scoop on Jesus.** were handed down to us by those who from the first were eyewitnesses and servants of the word" (Luke 1:1–2).

Note that Luke claims to be basing his biography of Jesus on eyewitness accounts. In fact, the word "eyewitnesses" is in the plural. Evidently, Luke not only got firsthand information about Jesus from the apostle Paul, he must have interviewed others as well. He interviewed people who had personally heard what Jesus said and seen what Jesus did.

That makes me wonder if one of those people whom Luke consulted for his biography was Mary, Jesus' earthly mother. The fact that Luke was a doctor, someone who would have had a professional interest in Mary's childbirth experience, may explain why he gives us more details about Jesus' birth than any other Gospel writer. I'm not suggesting that Luke was Mary's OB/Gyn doctor. I'm just saying that it wouldn't surprise me if he'd heard about Mary's labor and delivery from the mom herself.

So, Luke's Gospel passes the authorship test. And that's one of the reasons it was included in the New Testament, along with the Gospels of Matthew, Mark, and John. What about all the other books of the New Testament? They, too, are all tied to an apostle or to someone who was intimately familiar with Jesus. Hebrews is the only New Testament book that doesn't have a clear connection to an apostle. But for years Bible scholars associated it with the apostle Paul, which is why it initially passed the authorship test.

What's amazing about these New Testament authors is that early on their books were recognized as being on par with Old Testament Scripture. Look at what Peter says about the writings of the apostle Paul in this regard (2 Peter 3:16): "His letters [i.e., Paul's New Testament epistles] contain some things that are hard to understand, which ignorant and unstable people distort, as they do the other Scriptures." Did you catch that last phrase? Peter likens Paul's letters to Old Testament Scripture! That's more than a passing compliment. That's an incredible claim. Peter claimed Scripture status for Paul's writings.

What about the books of the Old Testament? What was the authorship test for their inclusion in

PETER LIKENS Paul's letters to Old Testament Scripture! Peter claimed Scripture status for Paul's writings.

the canon? Obviously, they weren't written by apostles, since apostles came much later. But they *were* written by prophets. Prophets were God's approved spokesmen. Moses, David, Isaiah—they were all considered prophets of one sort or another because God had put His words in their mouths. (See Exodus 4:10–12.)

I love the picturesque way that this happened in the life of Ezekiel. God appeared to Ezekiel in a vision, handed him a scroll, and told him to eat it (Ezekiel 3:3). Ezekiel records that the scroll tasted like honey to him. And when he finished the last bite, God said: "Go now to the house of Israel and speak my words to them" (v. 4). The Old Testament prophets were marked by God's *words*.

They were also marked by God's *power*. The prophets were accredited as God's spokesmen by supernatural signs that attended their ministries. All thirty-nine Old Testament books pass the *authorship test*. They were written by men who were recognized as prophets.

Second, there's the accuracy test. Back in 2004, when President George W. Bush was running for re-election, CBS News anchor Dan Rather got himself in deep weeds because of a story he aired on Bush. Reporting on the news magazine *60 Minutes*, Rather cited four memos that were supposedly written by Bush's National Guard commander back in 1972. These memos were extremely critical of Bush. They claimed that he had failed to complete his military service and that he had received special treatment because of his father's connections.

Rather made a big deal out of the authenticity of these memos. He even brought in a handwriting expert who vouched for the signature at the bottom of the notes.[7] Eventually, however, it turned out that the memos were phony—obviously phony. For starters, they had been created on Microsoft Word, not on a 1970s typewriter. (Oops!) And they had been supplied by a National Guardsman who publicly blamed President Bush for cutting his benefits. Four months later an independent panel concluded that CBS News failed to follow basic journalistic principles in the preparation and reporting of its broadcast.[8]

In the middle of this accuracy investigation came an amusing (and amazing) statement by Marian Carr Knox, the secretary to the commander of Bush's Air National Guard squadron who would have typed the documents. She told the *New York Times* she also believed the documents were fake but "the information in them is correct."[9] If you're a high school student, I don't recommend telling your history teacher, should she catch you turning in a forged research paper, "Well, the documents are fake but the information in them is accurate."

Accuracy *is* important, and the sixty-six books of the Bible had to pass the *accuracy test* in order to be included in the canon. Let's start with the Old Testament. I've already mentioned that the Old Testament's authors had to be recognized as prophets of God. And in order to be recognized as prophets of God, 100 percent of what they predicted had to come true. That's right, 100 percent! No room for one incorrect prophecy. Look at what Deuteronomy 18:21–22 says about this: "You may say to yourselves, 'How can we know when a message has not been spoken by the Lord?' If what a prophet proclaims in the name of the Lord does not take place or come true, that is a message the Lord has not spoken."

THE *ACCURACY* test was not graded on a curve. Old Testament prophets had to score 100 percent in order to pass.

So the *accuracy test* was not graded on a curve. Those who professed to be Old Testament prophets had to score 100 percent in order to pass. Let me give you a quick example of how this played out. There are over one hundred prophecies in the Old Testament concerning the ancient city of Babylon. The prophet Jeremiah predicted that one day the city's walls would be leveled and never be rebuilt. Those walls were 187 feet thick and they encircled an area of almost two hundred square miles. Amazingly, those mighty walls eventually were destroyed—even though they were stronger and longer than the Great Wall of China, which still stands today. And Babylon has never been rebuilt. Alexander the Great declared plans to do so. But Alexander died shortly after making his announcement. The Bible's prophecies were right on the money.

That shows you the accuracy of an Old Testament prophecy. But what about the basic historical episodes that the Old Testament records? Are they trustworthy? Here's an example of accurate history. Up until 1993, many so-called Old Testament scholars doubted the historicity of King David. "It's true," they said, "that the Bible has a lot to say about this King of Israel, not to mention all those psalms that he supposedly wrote. But there's never been one shred of archaeological evidence to support the fact that David ever lived." Some liberal scholars have even gone so far as to say: "David's a myth, nothing but a legendary hero." Interestingly, I recently had a discussion about the Bible with a new friend, who is a well-read skeptic, and he raised this very issue with me.

Yet in 1993 archaeologists discovered some writings that date back to the ninth century BC, shortly after David's "imaginary" reign. Those writings described a military victory of a local king over "King David of the Israelites." So much for David's mythological status. Nobody dares to say today that David never existed (except doubters who are unfamiliar with the 1993 discovery).

What about the accuracy of the New Testament writers? Let's return to Luke 1 for a moment. Luke writes, "Therefore, since I myself have carefully investigated everything from the beginning, it seemed good also to me to write an orderly account for you, most excellent Theophilus, so that you may know the certainty of the things you have been taught" (vv. 3–4).

Luke claims to have "carefully investigated everything" that he's going to write about. And he says that his Gospel is going to be an "orderly account," the facts of which his readers could be *certain*.

Did Luke pass the accuracy test? Archaeologist John McRay, author of the textbook *Archaeology and the New Testament* and a regular consultant on TV networks for stories about archaeology and the Bible, concludes, "The general consensus of both liberal and conservative scholars is that Luke is very accurate as a historian."[10]

No doubt one of those scholars alluded to by Dr. McRay is Sir William Ramsay, who concedes Luke's accuracy. Ramsay, the son of atheists, and himself at one time an atheist, had a PhD from Oxford. Ramsay gave his whole life to archaeology, setting out to disprove the Bible. He arrived in the Holy Land with the

"THE GENERAL consensus of both liberal and conservative scholars is that Luke is very accurate as a historian."

particular goal of uncovering evidence that would discredit Luke's New Testament book of Acts. After twenty-five years of investigation, he became so impressed by the accuracy of Luke that he published a work stating that this portion of New Testament history is exact, down to the minutest details. He called Luke "a historian of the first rank. . . . This author should be placed along with the very greatest historians."[11] And to top it off, Ramsay shocked the whole scholarly world by declaring himself to be . . . a Christian!

Third, there's the alignment test. Remember the standardized tests that we took in grade school? I think they were used to measure our reasoning ability. There would be a picture of four items and we were asked to identify which of the four didn't go with the others. Remember? . . . "Mittens, scarf, hammer, and boots. Which one doesn't belong?" (I hope you're not struggling with this.) One of these four things is out of alignment with the other three. If you didn't identify the out-of-alignment item as the hammer, it's amazing that you got through grade school!

What does this have to do with the Bible's canon? Simple: The canonizers tended to include books in the Bible that seemed to fit well with other books that had already been recognized as God-breathed. And they tended to exclude books from the Bible that seemed to be questionable, incomplete, or just plain weird.

A perfect example of what I'm talking about is the apocryphal books. "Apocryphal" means "hidden," because these books were considered to be hidden from acceptance by the church for centuries. They weren't considered to be God-breathed. At least, not until 1546. (I'll explain what happened in 1546 in just a moment.) The apocryphal books were all written during the period between Old Testament times and New Testament times; between 200 BC and the first century; between the days of Malachi and the days of Matthew.

Several of these books have very interesting names: Tobit, Judith, Bel and the Dragon, 1 and 2 Maccabees, the Song of Three Young Men. Some of these books give us helpful historical insights into this time period. But some contain material that just doesn't seem to align with what is taught in the rest of the Bible. And that's why they weren't considered to be God-breathed until 1546 by the Roman Catholic Church.

Do you remember what was going on in the church during 1546? The Reformation! The Roman Catholic Church was being challenged. People were leaving the church in large numbers. The problem was corruption. A lot of questionable traditions had sprung up in the church, including the sale of indulgences for the purpose of raising money for church building projects. People were objecting: "Hey, where is some of this stuff in the Bible? What's the biblical rationale for practices such as buying a deceased loved one out of purgatory? Does the Bible even mention purgatory?"

The truth was that some of the church's doctrines at the time, such as purgatory, couldn't be traced back to the Bible. At least, not back to the thirty-nine books that Ezra and company had identified hundreds of years earlier as the God-breathed Old Testament, nor to the recognized books of the New Testament. Where *did* the doctrine of purgatory come from? From 2 Maccabees, one of the apocryphal books. So in 1546, at the Council of Trent, the Roman Catholic Church decided to add the apocryphal books to the Bible.

THE APOCRYPHAL books are never quoted in the New Testament, while many of the Old Testament books are.

It's revealing to note that these books are never quoted in the New Testament, while many of the Old Testament books are. And there are only three apocryphal books that are found among the Dead Sea Scrolls, although copies of every Old Testament book except one are there (Esther). The apocryphal books don't pass the alignment test.

When it comes to the New Testament, this is why the alternative gospels (that Dan Brown loves) have been left out. There's just some weird stuff there. Now, I'm not talking about miracles, which, of course, are found in abundance in the four Gospels, written by Matthew, Mark, Luke, and John. There are instances of Jesus stilling storms, healing lepers, and feeding a crowd with five loaves and two fish. But there was an obvious purpose behind each of these miracles—to demonstrate the deity and compassion of Christ. They weren't random.

The rejected gospels, on the other hand, include stories like the one about Jesus as a toddler making birds of clay. When Jesus finished His sculpting, He clapped His hands and the clay birds flew away. What's the purpose of that random, frivolous act? Another rejected gospel, the Gospel of Peter, has Jesus stepping out of His tomb carrying the cross. (Don't ask me what the cross was doing in the tomb.) But that's not all. The cross talks! I'm not making this up.

And then there is some pretty strange teaching in these gospels-that-didn't-make-the-cut. Here are two of my favorite quotes from the Gospel of Thomas: "Blessings on the lion, if a human eats it, making the lion human. Foul is the human if a lion eats it, making the lion human."[12] Try applying that one to your life! This next one is even better:

Jesus said unto them, "When you make the two into one, and when you make the inner like the outer and the outer like the inner, and the upper like the lower, and when you make the male and female into a single one, so that the male will not be the male, nor the female be female, when you make eyes in the place of an eye, a hand in the place of a hand, a foot in the place of a foot, an image in the place of an image, then you will enter the Kingdom.[13]

Run that by me again. How does a person enter the kingdom? Crazy!

Now you understand why there was a need for an alignment test. Luke alludes to this alignment test in the very last phrase of the passage that we keep returning to in this chapter (Luke 1:1–4). Look at verse 4: "so that you may know the certainty of the things you have been taught." Luke is telling his readers that what he's about to present to them in his Gospel is going to back up the things that they have already been taught. In other words, Luke's Gospel is going to align with the rest of the Bible. Nothing weird about it.

Fourth, there's the acceptance test. I don't really need to say much about the acceptance test because nearly everything has already been said. The thirty-nine books that made it into the Bible's Old Testament canon were widely accepted by God's people. These books were found among the Dead Sea

Scrolls. They were quoted by Jesus and by the writers of the New Testament. And that can't be said for other writings, such as the apocryphal books.

Similarly, the twenty-seven books that made it into the Bible's New Testament canon were widely accepted by the church. These books weren't forced upon Christ followers by some church council that was bought and paid for by Emperor Constantine. Christ followers had already whittled down and were using the list of books that they believed were God-breathed.

Did I exhaust you with this study of the Bible's transmission? Well, I hope I also convinced you of the reliability of God's Word. That's important for our confidence and assurance for daily living. This Book can be trusted as a firm foundation for your life.

To watch Jim's midpoint comments about Foundation, scan this QR code with your smartphone or go to www.biblesavvy.com/video/#foundation2.

Study Guide

Icebreaker

Describe a favorite party or board game.

1. 👥 Why is the telephone game *not* a good analogy for how the Bible was passed down over the years?

2. Why should we *not* be alarmed by Dr. Bart Ehrman's claim that there are 200,000 to 400,000 variants in our ancient copies of the New Testament?

👥 Why do you think a book like Ehrman's *Misquoting Jesus* became a bestseller?

3. Who approved which books made it into the Old Testament and the New Testament?

4. Use the Rembrandt analogy to explain why these two councils did not *make* the approved books to be God's Word.

How does our understanding of this point impact our view of the Bible's authority?

5. List the four standards that were used in determining which books made it into the Bible and explain what is meant by each standard.

6. Next to each of standards 1–3, write out the phrase(s) from Luke 1:1–4 that supports it.

7. 🗨 Why didn't the rejected gospels (which Dan Brown is so fond of) make it into the Bible?

🗨 From what you know of Mr. Brown and his novel, why do you think he is such proponent of the rejected gospels?

8. Why would historical inaccuracies do serious damage to the Bible's credibility?

9. (•••) Several examples of how Scripture passes the accuracy test are given in *Foundation*. Pick a favorite that you'll be able to remember when the topic of the Bible's historical reliability comes up in conversation. Write it down here.

10. Why did the Roman Catholic Church add the apocryphal books to the Bible at the Council of Trent in 1546? Why don't Protestants accept these books as Scripture?

11. (•••) What did you learn in this chapter that bolsters your confidence in the Bible?

{ 3 }

The Only Way to Know

ELWOOD DOWD HAS a six-foot three-inch best friend named Harvey. Nothing unusual about that—except that Harvey is a rabbit. An *imaginary* rabbit. So goes the storyline of Mary Chase's Pulitzer Prize winning play that was later made into a Hollywood movie. Jimmy Stewart, whom everybody knows as the star of *It's a Wonderful Life*, plays the role of Dowd.

Elwood is a wealthy, forty-year-old bachelor who spends a lot of his time philosophizing about life at the local bar. His drinking buddy is a make-believe rabbit named Harvey. (We never see Harvey in the movie, although Harvey's shadow appears on the movie's promotional poster.) Elwood is good-natured and harmless. In fact, he enjoys making other people happy. Even so, his sister, Veta, tries to get Elwood committed to a sanatorium. *He's nuts!* she figures. This is where the fun begins. Staff members at the mental hospital soon come to believe in Harvey the rabbit and Veta ends up in the sanatorium.

The message of the movie is obvious: *A little bit of fantasy never hurt anybody.* In fact, if you've got an imaginary friend who positively impacts your life and the lives of others—that's great! You're not crazy. I am sure that religious skeptics would apply a message like this to a belief in God. They view God as a fantasy, along the same lines as Harvey, the six-foot-tall rabbit. Go ahead and believe in him if that gets you through the day. But he's not *real.* Or is he?

The Bible argues that God *is* real and that He has revealed Himself to us in its pages. The Bible claims to be the definitive source of information about God. While it is not our only source of information about Him, it is the only way to know Him deeply and personally. The Bible is where we go to learn about God's attributes, His plan of salvation, and His will for our lives. That is the focus of this chapter—what theologians refer to as the *Doctrine of Revelation.*

God's Attributes

A while back I was shopping at the grocery store when I ran into a woman whom I'd seen at one of our church's special events. A friend had brought her to Christ Community. When I inquired as to whether she'd enjoyed her visit, she responded enthusiastically with "I loved it!" So I asked her if she had any plans to return for one of our regular weekend services. Very politely, she declined, saying: "My husband and I have our own ideas about God." Although I hear lines like this all the time, they always leave me shaking my head.

"I have my own ideas about God." Is that allowed? Are we permitted to make up whatever we want to about God? Does God then become, in reality, what we imagine Him to be? This approach to God strikes me as so ridiculous that I want to shake people by the shoulders and declare: "You can't do that!" (So far, I've been able to suppress this impulse.) What makes people think that they can base their knowledge of God on their own ideas? Would you want people to come by their knowledge of *you* in this way?

Imagine this: You're at work, and you overhear two people talking in the office cafeteria. To your surprise, they're talking about you. Your ears prick up the moment you hear your name. They mention certain personality traits of yours, your likes and dislikes, your vocational goals, the causes that you're passionate about. But here's what's weird about the information they're throwing around—you've never talked with either one of them. They're making all this stuff up. They didn't get their insights about you from *you*. Wouldn't that drive you crazy?

People do that all the time with God. They surmise what He's like. One of the best-selling novels of recent years is *The Shack*. It's the account of a grieving dad who encounters God after his daughter has been murdered. The triune God appears in the book as a large African woman with a great sense

of humor (God the Father), a laid-back handyman who likes
to skip stones (God the Son), and a slight, young Asian woman (God the Spirit).

The author of this novel, in numerous interviews, has said
that this is just his way of communicating what *he* thinks God
is like. And millions of people who have read *The Shack* believe that they've gained a greater understanding of who God
is through the book. I contend that this is sheer nonsense. We
don't get to know God through *speculation* (whether that of
a best-selling author or our own). The only way to truly know
Him is through *revelation*—His disclosure of Himself to us.

There are two major sources of this revelation. They are
vividly described in Psalm 19. C. S. Lewis, who taught literature at both Oxford and Cambridge, called this psalm "the
greatest poem in the Psalter and one of the greatest lyrics in
the world."[1] Take a look at the opening nine verses of Psalm
19 and see if you can identify the two major ways by which
God reveals Himself to us:

> The heavens declare the glory of God; the skies
>   proclaim the work of his hands.
> Day after day they pour forth speech; night after night
>   they display knowledge.
> There is no speech or language where their voice is not
>   heard.

Their voice goes out into all the earth, their words to the
ends of the world.

In the heavens he has pitched a tent for the sun,
which is like a bridegroom coming forth from his
pavilion, like a champion rejoicing to run his course.
It rises at one end of the heavens and makes its circuit
to the other; nothing is hidden from its heat.

The law of the Lord is perfect, reviving the soul.
The statutes of the Lord are trustworthy, making wise
the simple.
The precepts of the Lord are right, giving joy to the
heart.
The commands of the Lord are radiant, giving light to
the eyes.
The fear of the Lord is pure, enduring forever.
The ordinances of the Lord are sure and altogether
righteous.

King David, the author of Psalm 19, begins his poem in
praise of how God reveals Himself to us in creation. David is
especially interested in what the sky has to say, whether it's
the stars that shine at night or the sun that blazes during the
day. These aspects of creation have a voice of their own. Just

look at all the verbs that David uses to describe creation's effort to communicate with us about God: *declare; proclaim; pour forth speech; display knowledge.*

The apostle Paul, no doubt with the opening lines of Psalm 19 running through his mind, makes a similar statement about the way in which creation reveals God to us: "What may be known about God is plain to them, because God has made it plain to them. For since the creation of the world God's invisible qualities—his eternal power and divine nature—have been clearly seen, being understood from what has been made" (Romans 1:19–20).

CERTAIN ATTRIBUTES of God are revealed to us when we walk outside and look up at the sky (or at the oceans, the mountains, the flowers).

So, according to Paul, certain attributes of God, such as His *eternal power* and His *divine nature*, are revealed to us when we walk outside and look up at the sky (or at the birds, the oceans, the mountains, the flowers, or anything else that God has made). This is a wonderful truth. But it comes to us with a caveat. It is possible to gaze at the stars on a clear summer night and not conclude anything at all about God. Lots of people do this. Many are able to enjoy the stars, in fact, who deny the very existence of God. That is because creation speaks to us in a somewhat subtle voice. And even when her voice *is* heard, the information she gives us about God is not very specific. The attributes of His that she declares are rather generic.

If we are to know God in an intimate fashion, we need a revelation from Him that is more specific. Let me illustrate the value of a more explicit disclosure. Suppose that you're walking down a deserted beach one day. You see countless patterns in the sand that have been made by waves, by wind, by debris, and by sand crabs. But suddenly you come across some writing. It says: "Jason loves Lauren." You would immediately conclude a couple of things from that inscription. Not only would you deduce that a young man named Jason had recently been on this stretch of the beach (because there is no way that such writing got there by chance), you would also know something very particular about Jason: *he's wild about Lauren!*

God wants to disclose particulars about Himself to us. How does He do this? Let's go back to Psalm 19 and take a closer look at the second half of David's poem. After declaring that creation reveals God to us in broad brushstrokes, David makes a sharp right turn and begins to talk about a second, more specific form of revelation: God's Word. David's move from creation to Scripture is so abrupt that various liberal Bible scholars surmise that this psalm must actually be a compilation of two different poems, which some editor clumsily put together. But such reasoning totally misses the fact that there is a unifying, main point to Psalm 19. The main point is that God reveals Himself to us.

This revelation takes two forms, described in the two halves of Psalm 19. The first is creation. The second is the Bible, referred to by David as *laws, statutes, precepts, commands,* and *ordinances*. These two forms of revelation are closely tied together in David's psalm. While creation's sun, for example, is known for giving light to the world and sustaining physical life (v. 6), so God's Word is capable of *giving light to the eyes* (v. 8) and *reviving the soul* (v. 7).

GOD USES A second form of revelation . . . because it takes words to convey specifics.

Theologians are fond of speaking of creation as God's *general* revelation and of Scripture as God's *special* revelation. Another way that it has been put is that creation is the "Big Book" about God and the Bible is the "Little Book" (little in size, that is, not in terms of all it communicates). Why is a second form of revelation necessary? Because it takes words to convey specifics. Without God's written Word, we'd be left with only the general impressions about God that are observable in nature. It is worth noting that David uses the *generic* name for God (Hebrew *El,* from *Elohim*) in the first half of his psalm when he's talking about creation's revelation, but switches to the *personal* name for God (Hebrew *Yahweh*) when he turns to Scripture's revelation.

Words convey personal details. Just as the writing in the sand told us that *Jason loves Lauren*, so the Bible tells us that God loves us—something that we would not have been able to deduce from creation alone. And love is not the only attribute of God that we find in the Bible. There are over 250 names, titles, and character traits in Scripture that describe God. Over 250! (In my first book, *Prayer Coach*, I include this list as an appendix so that readers can be specific when praising God in prayer.) If we want to know God—really know God—then we must make it our goal to discover all that He reveals about Himself in His Word.

God's Salvation

My good friend Nick Perrin is a New Testament scholar. Nick sure didn't see his vocation coming as he was growing up. Raised in a family of agnostics, none of the Perrins ever entered a church. But his mom and dad were very smart and wanted Nick to be very smart, so they sent him to a New England prep school during his high school years. Nick discovered he was pretty good at languages, taking Latin for four years.

In the summer before his senior year, he decided to try his hand at Greek. (Isn't this what all high school students do during their summer break?) He bought a Greek grammar book and began to master the basic rules. Once he had these under his belt, he looked for something to translate. The school was holding a used book sale, and Nick managed to pick up a copy of the Greek New Testament. He began in the Gospel of Mark, slowly translating one word at a time. In spite of the tediousness of the process, Nick became enthralled with the person of Jesus Christ. Shortly thereafter, he became a Christian. And years later, Nick Perrin is now a New Testament scholar. (By the way, I borrowed the title for the previous chapter, *Lost in Transmission?* from a book that Nick wrote on the same subject.[2] His writing is extremely engaging and I would highly recommend his book to those who want more information about how God has safeguarded the Bible from errors over the centuries of its transmission.)

There are many people like Nick, who have come to faith in Jesus Christ by simply reading the Bible. Mark Driscoll is another intriguing example. Mark was raised in a home behind a strip club in a rough neighborhood near Seattle. In his youth, he attended a Roman Catholic church where he served as an altar boy. But he gave up on "religion" as he got older. One day, as a college student, he picked up a Bible and started reading Paul's epistle of Romans. Gradually he began to understand the difference between religion and a personal relationship with Christ. Five years after surrendering his life to Jesus, Mark began Mars Hill Church where thousands of people now worship in Seattle and at satellite churches.

You get the idea. God uses His Word to point people to the salvation that is

GOD USES His Word to point people to the salvation that is found in His Son.

found in His Son, Jesus Christ. This is how Timothy, to whom Paul wrote two New Testament epistles, came to faith. Paul reminds Timothy of "how from infancy you have known the holy Scriptures, which are able to make you wise for salvation through faith in Christ Jesus" (2 Timothy 3:15). The backstory is that Timothy was raised in a home where his dad was probably not a believer, but his mom and grandmother were. (See Acts 16:1 and 2 Timothy 1:5.) It's not hard to imagine Timothy's mom, Eunice, faithfully sharing the good news of Jesus with her son by reading the Bible to him.

Keep in mind that the Bible in Timothy's home would have been just the Old Testament. And yet there was plenty of information in this BC-dated book about a coming Savior. The Old Testament describes this Savior as a descendant of Eve (i.e., a human) who would defeat Satan, as a descendant of Abraham who would bring blessing to all peoples, as a prophet who would be greater than Moses, as a king who would reign on David's throne, and as a sacrificial lamb who would pay the penalty for people's sins with His death. This Savior turned out to be Jesus, as Timothy's mom would have explained to her son.

The Old Testament pointed so clearly to Jesus that Jesus Himself cited verses from it as proof that He was God's promised Savior. He told one group of religious listeners: "You diligently study the Scriptures because you think that by them you possess eternal life. These are the Scriptures that testify about me" (John 5:39).

On another occasion, shortly after Jesus' resurrection, He spoke with a couple of followers who were disillusioned by His crucifixion and not yet aware that He'd risen from the dead (nor that it was the resurrected Jesus who was speaking to them). Jesus "said to them, 'How foolish you are, and how slow of heart to believe all that the prophets have spoken! Did not the Christ have to suffer these things and then enter his glory?' And beginning with Moses and all the Prophets, he explained to them what was said in all the Scriptures concerning himself" (Luke 24:25–27).

Paul too used the Old Testament to point people to Christ. In city after city that he visited, he made a beeline for the local synagogue where "he reasoned with them from the Scriptures, explaining and proving that the Christ had to suffer and rise from the dead" (Acts 17:2–3). Paul proclaimed Jesus to be this Christ.

When Paul was later on trial for his faith before King Agrippa, he again referred to the Old Testament, declaring: "I am saying nothing beyond what the prophets and Moses said would happen—that the Christ would suffer and, as the first to rise from the dead, would proclaim light to his own people and to the Gentiles" (Acts 26:22–23). Even in Paul's final incarceration, "from morning till evening he explained and declared to them [i.e., large numbers of visitors] the kingdom of God and tried to convince them about Jesus from the Law of Moses and from the Prophets" (Acts 28:23).

The Bible, Old Testament as well as New, reveals to us God's Savior and His plan of salvation. Without the Bible we would be spiritually lost. Consider some of the specific truths that God's Word spells out regarding our need for salvation, truths without which we wouldn't have a clue about how to begin a relationship with God.

Sin's Consequences

For starters, the Bible explains that we have a very serious problem: *sin*. And our sin keeps a Holy God at a great distance. "For all have sinned and fall short of the glory of God" (Romans 3:23). "Your iniquities have separated you from your God; your sins have hidden his face from you, so that he will not hear" (Isaiah 59:2).

All this talk about sin, of course, raises the question: What is sin? Without a definition of such, we might be able to convince ourselves that we're not really that bad. That our own wrongdoing is the insignificant, harmless, garden variety kind. Here again, the Bible proves indispensable, because it spells out God's moral laws, which we regularly transgress, thus becoming clearly guilty of sin. As the apostle Paul says in Romans 7:7, he would not have known that coveting was a sin unless God's law had identified it as such. So the Bible defines sin before warning us that sin alienates us from God.

Unfortunately, the bad news gets worse. The Bible tells us that if something is not done about our sinful alienation from God, we will suffer the consequences of death. "The wages of sin is death. . . . The soul who sins is the one who will die . . . You will die in your sin" (Romans 6:23; Ezekiel 18:4; John 8:21). And as the Bible talks about death as a consequence for our sins, it presents a picture that includes spiritual, physical, and eternal death (see Ephesians 2:1 and 1 John 5:11–12.) Without God's Word, we would be naïve to this dreadful danger.

The Bible's Good News

Thankfully, the Bible also tells us that we can be rescued from our awful predicament. Jesus Christ, God's Son, was sent to earth to bear the penalty that our sins deserved. He suffered death on our behalf:

> For Christ died for sins once for all, the righteous for the unrighteous, to bring you to God. (1 Peter 3:18)

God demonstrates his own love for us in this: While we were still sinners, Christ died for us. (Romans 5:8)

He was pierced for our transgressions, he was crushed for our iniquities; the punishment that brought us peace was upon him, and by his wounds we are healed. We all, like sheep, have gone astray, each of us has turned to his own way; and the Lord has laid on him the iniquity of us all. (Isaiah 53:5–6)

This is good news. The best news in the world! But knowing all this, we would still be spiritually lost if it were not explained to us how we could tap into what Christ has done. How do we access the salvation that He purchased on the cross? Does God give it as a reward to those who measure up to a certain standard, or who live by the Golden Rule, or who go to church and participate in religious rituals, or who stay out of deep moral weeds? No! Once again, the Bible comes through with the necessary information, explaining that salvation is not acquired through personal efforts but by putting our faith in Jesus Christ as Savior and Lord:

For it is by grace you have been saved, through faith— and this not from yourselves, it is the gift of God—not by works, so that no one can boast. (Ephesians 2:8–9)

However, to the man who does not work but trusts God who justifies the wicked, his faith is credited as righteousness. (Romans 4:5)

If you confess with your mouth, "Jesus is Lord," and believe in your heart that God raised him from the dead, you will be saved. For it is with your heart that you believe and are justified, and it is with your mouth that you confess and are saved. (Romans 10:9–10)

I [Jesus] tell you the truth, whoever hears my word and believes him who sent me has eternal life and will not be condemned; he has crossed over from death to life. (John 5:24)

Clearly the Bible plays an indispensable role in revealing God's salvation to us. There is no way that we could figure out how to be saved without the input and clear direction of God's Word. That's why I wince every time I hear someone who is attempting to present God's offer of salvation to others but who is not using a generous amount of Scripture to do so.

Thirty years ago as a youth pastor, I brought a special speaker to a junior high retreat, a former Air Force pilot during the Vietnam War. For forty-five minutes on the first night he regaled us with stories about the dangerous missions he had flown. A hundred middle schoolers, jacked up on Mountain Dew and s'mores, listened spellbound to these tales of adventure.

At the end of his talk, the heroic pilot abruptly asked the students to bow their heads and raise their hands if they wanted to begin a relationship with Jesus Christ. Scores of hands punched the air. But afterward I quickly learned that most of these kids had no idea what they were signing up for. They just wanted to experience some of the same excitement that the speaker had radiated.

People don't come to Christ for salvation—not genuinely—simply on the basis of having heard someone's moving story. Nor do vague invitations to "become a follower of Jesus" or "experience God's love and forgiveness" result in true conversions if they are not preceded by a thorough, biblical explanation of what salvation is all about. Without the Bible, we would be left in the fog regarding God's salvation.

WITHOUT THE Bible, we would be left in the fog regarding God's salvation.

This is why it's so important, when talking with others who are investigating the faith, to use a tool that explains salvation with a generous supply of Scripture verses. I personally like to scribble out a diagram, affectionately dubbed "The Bridge Illustration" by those who use it, on any available scrap of paper or napkin. It pictorially shows how we are separated from God by the chasm of our sins; none of our personal efforts to traverse the chasm work; Christ's cross bridged the chasm; and we can move across that bridge by putting our faith in Christ. These truths are all backed up with Bible verses, such as the ones that I quoted above.

I know that a tool like "The Bridge" strikes some people as being a bit canned. But I can tell you, from my own experience, that it's been immeasurably helpful in explaining God's plan of salvation to my friends. In fact, I know of at least two guys, now Christ followers, who still carry around in their wallets the copy of this diagram that I sketched for them on a napkin in some coffee shop years ago. Because it led them to salvation! (And if you are artistically challenged, don't feel like you need to be able to draw a diagram. Just start using one of the many small booklets, such as Billy Graham's *Steps to Peace with God* or the Navigators' "The Bridge to Life" illustration,[3] that explains salvation in simple terms to seekers with the help of Bible verses.)

God's Will

Some time ago, the title of a book by a well-known Christian author and speaker caught my eye. It promised to teach readers "the best question" that they could ever ask themselves when facing big decisions. To be honest, I initially tried to find out what the magic question was without buying the book. I skimmed the back cover, the introduction, and the first couple of chapters in search of it. But this writer did a pretty good job of hiding the question so that people like me would be forced to fork out the money for the book and read it cover to cover.

I'm going to do you a huge favor and give you that question for free. Here it is: *What is the wise thing to do?* I think that's a fantastic question to ask ourselves when trying to determine what direction to take as we stand at a crossroads. But there's one basic problem we're going to face in trying to use it. The question assumes that we're wise enough to figure out what the wise thing to do is.

You may have to read that last sentence a few times in order to catch its point. Maybe this would help. Imagine that you're stuck while taking a multiple-choice test at school. Would it be beneficial to ask yourself: *What's the smart answer to this question?* Wouldn't you have to *be* smart in order to know which answer is the smart one?

How do we become wise in the first place, so that when we ask ourselves, *What is the wise thing to do?* we will be able to answer our own question? Unfortunately, although the author of the book told his readers to address their concerns to God and fully submit to His leading—good advice—he didn't provide much instruction beyond that about how to become a wise person.

But, good thing for us, the apostle Paul explains how ordinary people can acquire indispensable savvy. Look at what Paul writes, just after reminding Timothy that it was the Bible that first introduced him to God's salvation: "All Scripture is God-breathed and is useful for teaching, rebuking, correcting and training in righteousness, so that the man of God may be thoroughly equipped for every good work" (2 Timothy 3:16–17).

If this passage sounds familiar, it's because in chapter 1 we camped out on it when we considered the inspiration of Scripture. The Bible is a supernatural book, you'll recall, because it is *God-breathed*. But having made this point, Paul now tells us what it means, practically speaking, for our lives. Paul informs us how to put the Bible to good use in our daily experience. Note carefully the four gerunds (*-ing* words) in verse 16: *teaching, rebuking, correcting,* and *training.*

Bible scholars tell us that these four action words fall into two neat categories. The first two action words describe the Bible's impact on our beliefs. It *teaches* us sound doctrine (i.e., truths about God and His ways) and it *rebukes* any erroneous thinking of ours. The second two words address the Bible's impact on our behavior. The Bible *corrects* any misconduct and *trains* us to act in a God-pleasing manner. The end result of all this input from God's Word is that we are "equipped for every good work."

This is the recipe for becoming a wise person that we've been looking for! The Bible is able to shape our beliefs and our **THE BIBLE is able to shape our beliefs and our behaviors so that we become wise people.**

behaviors so that we become people whose lives are marked by fruitful service to God—wise people. And wise people are able to make wise decisions. They are able to answer the question: *What is the wise thing to do?*

Sometimes the answer to that question will be explicit in the Bible. Some verse will very directly say, regarding the decision you are facing, *Do this* or *Don't do that*. But even when the Bible does not clearly address the specifics of your situation, it will still prepare you to make a wise decision by making you a wise person.

Should you put your aging parent in a nursing home? There's no verse in the Bible that says yes or no to that. What should your major be in college? There's no verse that says *biology* or *literature* or *business*. Should you take the job transfer that offers more money but requires relocating your family to a new city? There's no verse that says to stay put or move to Denver. However, if you are saturating your life with God's Word, you will be able to make wise decisions in cases like these because you will be a wise person.

The key is to saturate your life with God's Word. Begin

now. Don't wait until you're staring an important but daunting decision in the face. You won't be able to become wise in that instant. You will already be wise or not be wise, depending on how much time you've been investing in your Bible. I think it was the great nineteenth-century preacher Charles Spurgeon who said that we should immerse ourselves in Scripture until our blood becomes *bibline*. I like that.

At the end of a recent football season, my Chicago Bears were embroiled in an intense play-off game. Unfortunately, our starting quarterback was injured and had to be replaced by his backup. It got worse. The second string quarterback got hurt and had to be replaced by our third-stringer. As the camera zoomed in on this guy just before he left the bench to jog onto the football field, he was frantically studying the playbook! I laughed out loud and shouted at my TV screen: "It's too late, pal. Game on! If you don't know the plays by now, you're in a heap of trouble!"

The same thing could be said of our personal lives. If we're suddenly faced with a big decision and desperately want to know God's will for our lives, frantically flipping through the Bible for explicit directions will probably not yield favorable results. However, if we are becoming wise people by constant exposure to God's Word, we will most likely make wise decisions.

As noted in this chapter, the Bible *reveals* to us God's

attributes, God's salvation, and God's will. This is a summary of what theologians are referring to when they talk about the doctrine of *revelation*.

Study Guide

Icebreaker

What guidelines do you think people should follow when providing information about themselves on Facebook? Is social media a good tool for getting to know other people? Why or why not?

1. When it comes to knowing who God is, what's the difference between *speculation* and *revelation*?

   Why is "I have my own ideas about God" such a ridiculous statement?

2. What are the two main sources of revelation about God? Why is the second source necessary?

What would you say to the guy who doesn't think that listening to a preacher in a church on Sunday is necessary since he can connect with God out in nature on his bass boat?

3. What specific truths about salvation are important for a spiritual seeker to understand? Next to each truth put a Bible verse or two that affirms that truth.

4. What is the danger in not using Scripture when presenting the gospel to someone?

5. Have you found a booklet that has helped you communicate God's plan of salvation to others? If yes, what do you like about it? If no, how could you get your hands on such a resource this week?

 What are the benefits and liabilities of using a tool like this?

6. Why is it *not* helpful to ask yourself the question, *What is the wise thing to do?* when trying to make an important decision?

7. How does the Bible equip you to make wise decisions?

What is a big decision that you are currently faced with? What Bible verses (that you can think of) might help you with this decision—either by speaking to it directly, or by laying out principles for you to consider?

8. What specific steps could you take to ensure that you are moving in the direction of becoming Bible-wise?

{ 4 }

Get a Grip

ACCORDING TO A RECENT study by the U.S. Department of Education, almost half of all American adults have difficulty reading. To be exact, 43 percent are reading at a "basic" or "below basic" level.[1] "Basic" means that these adults could find their favorite sitcom listed in *TV Guide* but would have trouble reading the newspaper. The newspaper!

Reading is becoming a lost art for many people—especially young people. Less than one-third of thirteen-year-olds read on a daily basis, a 14 percent decline from twenty years ago.[2] Fifteen- to twenty-four-year-olds spend about seven minutes of their daily leisure time reading. That's less time than it takes them to pick up a latte at Starbucks.[3]

So what is everybody doing with the time that people used to invest in reading? You could probably guess the correct answer to that question, right? Those fifteen- to twenty-four-year-olds who read for a whopping seven minutes each day are watching two hours of TV. And television is only the tip of the iceberg when it comes to media distractions. Let's scroll through a few more of the alternatives to books.

There's the iPod (or similar mp3 players). Four of every five teens (79 percent) own one.[4] Apple sold more than 100 million iPods in the first five years.[5] There is the cell phone— not just for calling but for texting and tweeting. I recently read in my news magazine an article entitled "The Twitter Revolution." The second line of the article asked the question: "Is Twitter a breakthrough in personal communication or a colossal waste of time?"[6] Well, if it's a colossal waste of time, there are a lot of time-wasters out there, from the president of the United States to Martha Stewart. Everybody's tweeting!

Another big distraction from traditional reading is the Internet. In his book *The Shallows: What the Internet Is Doing to Our Brains*, technology writer Nicholas Carr concludes the Internet is making us stupid. He's got scientific research to back him up.[7] Studies show that jamming our brains with all sorts of data, from pop-up windows to hyperlinks, causes our memories to malfunction. We don't retain *anything*. What's the antidote? Carr says that reading books stretches our minds and improves our memories.

Still another alternative to reading good books is Facebook. One of every twelve people on the planet has a Facebook account today. At one point, an average of 700,000 new accounts were opened every day,[8] which is why *Time* magazine named Mark Zuckerberg, Facebook's founder, its "Person of the Year" in 2010. By fall 2012, Facebook announced they had more than one billion people who logged in each month.[9] How much time do you spend Facebooking these days?

Why am I making a big deal about the way in which modern media are minimizing the time that we spend reading good books? Because God's primary way of communicating with us is through a book—the Bible. If we are not voracious readers of God's book, our relationship with God and our spiritual growth are going to be seriously stunted. Which is why I am going to challenge you in this chapter to get into the Bible. Don't wait for the movie!

How to Get the Bible into Our Lives

Thus far in *Foundation* we have focused on how *God* authored the Bible, how *God* protected the accurate transmission of the Bible over hundreds of years, and how *God* reveals Himself and His will for our lives through the Bible. Do you see a pattern in these topics? The spotlight has been on God. We've been studying *His* role in the communication process. But now we're going to focus on *our* responsibility. How do we take full advantage of this book that God has given us? How do we get the Bible into our lives?

Reading is obviously a big part of it, because books

107

require reading. But we're going to look at three additional activities, besides reading, that will enable us to *get a grip* on the Bible. And speaking of getting a grip on the Bible, here's a little experiment. Of course, you'll need your own Bible to participate in this exercise. First, hold your Bible with your thumb and one finger. Not too hard to do, eh? OK, now I want you to hold your Bible with two fingers. That's better, but it's still not much of a grip, is it? It would be easy for the Bible to slip out of your grasp. Now try a three-finger grip . . . a four-finger grip.

It doesn't feel like you've got a really firm grip on your Bible until you're holding it with your thumb and all four fingers, right? What's my point? I'm about to give you five activities that will enable you to get a firm grip on God's book, the Bible. Don't settle for one or two of these activities. Begin, as soon as possible, to practice all five. (By the way, I learned the importance of these five activities years ago from the Navigators ministry. They specialize in getting people into God's Word and are known for their diagram of a five-finger grip on the Bible.[10])

Get a Grip on Scripture by Hearing

We're going to pitch our tents in Nehemiah 8 in this chapter, so you might want to open your Bible to that passage. The year is about 430 BC, and God's people have recently returned from seventy years of captivity in Babylon. Their country is a mess. The walls of their capital city, Jerusalem, and their once-beautiful temple are both heaps of rubble. The people are demoralized. They fully realize that the reason for their years of exile was because they'd wandered from God. So they want to be sure that this doesn't happen again.

How could they get their lives turned around and on the right track? Instinctively they know that it's time to start listening to God. They are eager to *hear* God's Word. So they call on their spiritual leader, a guy named Ezra, to read God's book to them.

Remember Ezra? In chapter 2 we described how Ezra and 120 of his buds—a group later referred to as the *Great Synagogue*—determined which thirty-nine books made it into the Old Testament. Now let's read what happened as God's people gather to hear the Bible read by Ezra upon their return from exile:

> All the people assembled as one man in the square before the Water Gate. They told Ezra the scribe to bring out the Book of the Law of Moses, which the Lord had commanded for Israel.
>
> So on the first day of the seventh month Ezra the priest brought the Law before the assembly, which was made up of men and women and all who were able to

understand. He read it aloud from daybreak till noon as he faced the square before the Water Gate in the presence of the men, women and others who could understand. And all the people listened attentively to the Book of the Law.

Ezra the scribe stood on a high wooden platform built for the occasion. . . . Ezra opened the book. All the people could see him because he was standing above them; and as he opened it, the people all stood up. Ezra praised the Lord, the great God; and all the people lifted their hands and responded, "Amen! Amen!" Then they bowed down and worshiped the Lord with their faces to the ground.

The Levites . . . instructed the people in the Law while the people were standing there. They read from the Book of the Law of God, making it clear and giving the meaning so that the people could understand what was being read. (Nehemiah 8:1–8)

Wow! These people really wanted to *hear* God's Word. The opening verses tell us that *everybody* gathered to listen—men, women, and children who were old enough to understand. And they listened, Scripture says, "from daybreak till noon" (v. 3). What is that, about five to six hours? All that time they listened "attentively" (circle the word "attentively" in your Bible). Please note, too, the reverent way in which they listened. We're told that they bowed down and worshiped God before listening to Ezra read from God's book; then they stood to their feet and remained standing the entire time that they listened. That's reverence!

One last observation, here: Ezra and his Levite pals (all members of the priesthood) didn't just *read* the Bible to God's people. They *explained* it. The leaders were "making it clear and giving the meaning so that the people could understand what was being read." So, the people weren't just hearing Bible-*reading*, they were hearing Bible-*teaching*.

How do we become people of God's book? How do we begin to get a grip on the Bible? For starters, we must *hear* God's Word taught. Let me give you a few tips with respect to *hearing* God's Word.

First, listen with regularity. This was the top priority of the early church. Acts 2 tells us that after Jesus rose from the dead and ascended back to heaven, Peter stood up in Jerusalem and preached a sermon about Jesus. Three thousand people responded, repenting of their sins and putting their faith in Christ (v. 41). What did they do next? These brand-new Christ followers immediately "devoted themselves to the apostles' teaching" (v. 42). The word *devoted* means to do something with regularity and determination, to stick to it. What were they sticking to? Listening to their spiritual leaders teach them God's Word.

Is this something that you're devoted to? Making it to church one or two weekends a month is not devotion. If you are new to attending church, a couple of times a month may seem like a huge commitment. But it's not enough to give you a firm grip on God's Word. You'll end up missing a good deal of what your pastor is teaching. Make it your goal to

LISTEN WITH regularity, discernment, a pen in hand . . . and with the aim of putting what you hear into practice.

listen with regularity by getting to church every weekend. And on the rare occasion that you have to miss, listen to the teaching online if your church has a website that offers downloadable sermons.

Second, listen with discernment. I always cringe when I hear a sermon that is Bible-lite. You know what I mean by Bible-lite? Bible-lite sermons are constructed like skyscrapers (sorry about the coming pun): one story on top of another. Unfortunately, people love this kind of sermon, because it's funny, it's entertaining, it's emotionally moving. But it won't strengthen your grip on God's Word.

Make sure that you are attending a church whose pastor preaches sermons that are rooted in and filled with Scripture. At our church, my main points typically come out of one central Bible passage. Occasionally, when I'm delivering a topical message, I'll switch texts from point to point. But my goal is always to leave listeners impressed with God's Word, not with me as a communicator. A preacher's stories won't change your life long-term. Only God's Word will. So, listen with discernment.

Third, listen with a pen in hand. Communication experts tell us that we remember, at best, only 10 percent of what we hear. I hate that statistic, because I spend twenty to twenty-five hours a week preparing a sermon that people are going to *listen* to. And they're only going to remember 10 percent of it? How discouraging!

I know that I speak for all pastors when I say: Please, please, pretty please with sugar on top, pick up a pen and write down something as you're listening to a sermon. You'll get a better grip on God's Word by doing so. And you'll make your pastor's day! (Just a side note here: If you use a phone-app or e-reader for your Bible, don't let that keep you from writing something down. Either take notes on your phone/e-reader or use a pen and paper to record your insights.)

Fourth, listen with the aim of putting what you hear into practice. I was tuned in to a Christian radio station the other day—something I don't do a lot of—and a woman called in to express her gratitude for being able to listen to preachers all day long on that station. I immediately thought to myself: *How could she possibly put that much Bible teaching into practice?* She needs to turn her radio off! And if it sounds like I'm being too hard on her, James 1:22 puts it even more bluntly: "Do not merely listen to the word, and so deceive yourselves. Do what it says."

The ultimate aim of hearing God's Word is not Bible-*listening*; the ultimate aim is Bible-*doing*. That's one of the reasons that I gravitate toward teaching the Bible in topical series at my church. Now, from time to time someone will ask me why I don't do more "expository" teaching:

JAMES 1:22 puts it bluntly: "Do not merely listen to the word. . . . Do what it says."

starting with the first verse of a book of the Bible and working my way through that book, verse after verse after verse. An occasional critic will even go so far as to suggest that a topical approach is for beginners, while a verse-by-verse approach is for mature believers.

Really? I usually ask that critic if Jesus was a topical preacher or a verse-by-verse guy. You see, Jesus could have gone through the Old Testament verse-by-verse, but that's not what you'll find in the Gospel accounts of His teaching, such as His famous Sermon on the Mount (Matthew 5–7). Jesus went from topic to topic.

The reason that I often teach God's Word topically (although we occasionally go through an entire book of the

Bible) is that it forces people to hear something again and again until they put it into practice. It may be four straight sermons on *prayer*, or three in a row on *wise money management*, or a five-part series on *parenting*—all rooted in Scripture. I intend to drive my listeners crazy until they *do* something with what they're hearing from God's Word. Make sense?

By the way, it's not my intention to disparage expository, verse-by-verse sermons. If that's your pastor's approach, great! I just want you to know that topical preaching can also be soundly biblical and have a major impact on listeners.

Get a Grip on Scripture by Reading

I'm a big fan of classical music. One of my favorite composers is Joseph Haydn, who wrote over a hundred symphonies during the eighteenth century. Recently I went to Amazon.com to purchase a good biography on Haydn. Their top recommendation was a book published back in 1904. Fortunately, I was able to track down a used copy of that book. And when it arrived in the mail, I was pumped.

You book lovers can appreciate this: I love the look, the feel, the smell of an old book. And I thought to myself: *People have been reading this very book for over a hundred years—since 1904.* Well . . . not exactly. As I began to read the book myself, I quickly discovered that about a third of the pages weren't even cut; they were still stuck together. I had to slice them apart in order to keep on reading. That means that while someone had *owned* this book for over a hundred years, nobody had actually *read* it!

If your Bible is still open to Nehemiah 8, circle the word "read" in verse 3: "[Ezra] read it [God's Word] aloud" to the people "from daybreak till noon." Now, go down to verse 8 and circle the same word: Ezra's buddies "read from the Book of the Law of God, making it clear."

Why did the people need Ezra and his coleaders to read the Bible aloud? Why didn't the people just read it for themselves? Well, besides the possibly that some of them were illiterate, they didn't have a personal copy of the Book of the Law. That's why they asked Ezra to break out *his* copy of the Scriptures and bring it to the town square (v. 1). He was the only guy who had a Bible (probably a leather-bound, gold-edged study Bible with a concordance and maps).

That's the same reason why the apostle Paul told a young pastor he was mentoring, Timothy, to devote himself to the public reading of Scripture (1 Timothy 4:13). The people in Timothy's church had no opportunity to read Scripture for themselves. But that's not true of us, is it? According to a recent poll, 95 percent of Christians say that they have a Bible in the house. In fact, those who identify themselves as "active" Christians have an average of six Bibles in the house! And 98 percent of those active Christians say that they actually *read* the Bible.[11]

That's the good news. But then the pollster asked a question that revealed some not-so-good news. How often do you read the Bible? Among those calling themselves active Christians, slightly more than one-third (35 percent) responded they read the Bible daily. Yet 19 percent read their Bible just two or three times a week. And 37 percent—almost four in ten active Christans—admit they read the Bible just one time a week or less.[12] Is it possible to be an "active" follower of Jesus Christ while ignoring His Word?

> **ACCORDING TO one poll, among active Christians only 35 percent responded that they read the Bible daily.**

If you're not yet a regular Bible reader, let me give you a few quick tips to get you started. Perhaps you've heard similar advice before. But as I noted earlier, I like to stay on a topic until people either *do* something about it or I drive them crazy!

First, *get yourself a solid study Bible.* There are several good ones available, but I personally like the *NIV* (New International Version) *Study Bible*, the work of a team of evangelical Hebrew and Greek scholars, and all the wonderful explanatory footnotes in the *NIV Study Bible*. Evidently, I'm not the only fan of the *NIV Study Bible*. There are more than seven million copies in print!

Second, *pick up a Bible reading schedule.* You'll find a read-through-the-Bible-in-four-years schedule online at *www.biblesavvy.com.* I prefer this pace over one-year reading plans, which *may* give you a complete read-through in twelve months, but often will leave you falling behind and unable to finish in one year. More on the advantages of the four-year plan appear in *Walk* (book four of the Bible Savvy series), where we delve into the topic of Bible application.

Third, *choose a time and a place for daily Bible reading.* If you're like me, it may be best to do your reading first thing in the morning. Otherwise, once the day gets going it's almost impossible to stop everything and carve out a niche of time for Bible reading. Where's the best place to do it? I have a friend who arrives at work early and sits in his truck in the parking lot to read his Bible. Other friends do it on the treadmill, or

READ WHEN you don't feel like it and when other distractions are pulling you to put your Bible down.

at a corner table at Starbucks, or in their favorite chair in the family room—wherever there's a little bit of privacy and a good chance of developing a habit.

Fourth, *just do it!* Read when you don't feel like it. Read when the reading schedule's chapter for the day is in the book of Ezekiel and you have a hard time figuring out how to apply it to your life. Read when other distractions are pulling you to put your Bible down and pay attention to them. A lot of people find it helpful to make it a rule not to engage in any other leisure activity until they've read God's Word for the day. No newspaper reading, no Facebooking, no eating breakfast, no working out, no texting a friend—nothing before the Bible.

Not too long ago, I received an email from someone who has been attending our church for a few years. He wrote about how both his relationship with God and his marriage have begun to blossom. And then he explained how all that got started. He'd heard me challenge everybody to buy an *NIV Study Bible*, pick up a reading schedule, and get after it. So he did. This is what he wrote in his email to me:

"I changed my schedule in the mornings, started waking up 30 minutes earlier and would take that time to read from the Bible. Since then I've done pretty well at reading at least 5 times a week. Sure, I slipped here and there . . . but each time I rededicated myself."

Now, read the close of his email: "This morning I finished the Bible, cover to cover. This was very important to me, because I stopped messing around and really started to dig into Christianity and the Word of God. I began to become much more engaged with the sermons, because I had either already read the Bible texts or would be reading them soon. . . . God willing, I will continue reading and learning from His Word my whole life. By my calculations, I should be able to read through the whole thing another 25 times minimum. It's made a real difference in my life."

This guy not only encouraged his pastor but also laid down a solid foundation for himself by reading through the entire Bible.

Get a Grip on Scripture by Studying

Let's go back to Nehemiah 8 and look again at the closing verse of our passage (v. 8). God's people were not merely hearing the Bible and reading the Bible. They were digging into it. Their leaders were explaining the Bible's meaning to them, helping them to understand the text and apply it to their lives.

I've got good news for you. You can do this for yourself these days. I'm not suggesting that you don't need the regular input of a Bible-teaching pastor. I've already covered the importance of that. I'm just challenging you to do your own study as well, with the assistance of a good study Bible that will explain difficult passages and with the camaraderie of a small group. (I hope your church offers small groups that meet to discuss and apply Scripture.)

Studying the Bible is not an option for genuine Christ followers. God expects us to become expert handlers of His Word.

That requires going beyond merely reading the text. It

entails drilling down into specific verses, looking up the cross-references that your study Bible supplies, and recording your insights and applications in a journal or filling in the study guide that your small group is using.

As the apostle Paul puts it, "Do your best to present yourself to God as one approved, a workman who does not need to be ashamed and who correctly handles the word of truth" (2 Timothy 2:15). Are you becoming skilled at handling God's Word? It doesn't happen overnight. It doesn't happen without effort. It doesn't happen without studying.

We may be tempted to object, "I don't have that kind of time." Or, "I never was very good in school." Or, "This sounds like Christianity 501, but I'm content with 101 or 201." But shouldn't we be so hungry for God's Word that we push past excuses like these?

Allow me to embarrass all of us for just a moment by comparing our sometimes meager appetite for the Bible with the ravenous hunger for it in other parts of the world. Here are a couple of quick snapshots I want you to look at. The first snapshot is from my most recent *Voice of the Martyrs* news magazine. (*VOM* is an organization that supports persecuted Christ followers around the world.) It's a picture of Ahmed, a truck driver in Egypt. Ahmed has been repeatedly arrested and tortured by the Egyptian secret police. Why? Because Ahmed is a Christ follower.

But worse than that, Ahmed has supplied Bibles to a group of forty-two former Muslims who have become Christ followers. And these men were not just Muslims—they were members of a radical group called the Muslim Brotherhood. Ahmed has refused to tell the Egyptian secret police where these guys are hiding—even though they hung him upside down and beat him.[13]

But Ahmed did tell *VOM* that the last time he'd visited his new Christian friends they'd just finished going through the Bible for the eighth time. The eighth time! How many of us have been through it once?

The second snapshot is a group picture described in Charles Colson's book *The Faith*. It's a pretty big group. It's the church in China. Back in 1949, Mao Tse-tung began to systematically persecute these believers. Anyone caught in possession of a Bible was tortured or thrown into prison. Or just plain executed.

In spite of that threat, Christ followers have been hand copying the Bible so that they can read and study it on their own. And if an underground church is fortunate enough to have its own copy of the Bible, it's usually broken up into a number of portions and distributed among the church's members. That way, if any of their houses are raided by the secret police and one portion of the Bible is confiscated, they won't lose the whole thing.

Christ followers have even dug up the graves of believers who died before Mao came to power, because there is often a Bible in the coffin. Anything to get a Bible that can be read and studied. When Mao began to persecute the church in 1949, there were four million Christ followers in China. Now, there are an estimated 80 million or more.[14]

After looking at snapshots like these, any excuses we offer for not studying the Bible on our own and in small groups sound pretty lame.

Get a Grip on Scripture by Memorizing and Meditating

My older sister, Kathy, has a master's degree in piano performance. When I was growing up, I was subjected to hearing her practice four to five hours every day. During her high school years, she won several prestigious piano competitions. I can still hum the melodies of the pieces that she played in those contests because she rehearsed them again and again and again.

Interestingly, the very first thing that Kathy would do when she was learning a piece was to memorize it. That's a twist, isn't it? Most of us who grew up taking piano lessons only memorized pieces after we'd worked on them for weeks and weeks. But if you're a pro, you memorize the piece first and *then* you start working on it. You don't set the tempos, add the dynamics, or shape the phrases until you know the piece by heart.

This is very similar to how we should approach memorizing and meditating on God's Word. If we would first *memorize* a Bible verse or two, we could then go to work on that text. We could *meditate* on it, which simply means to turn it over and over in our minds, squeezing insights out of it, reflecting on what it teaches us about God, and considering ways it might be applied in our lives.

So memorizing and meditating go together. First we memorize, then we meditate on what's been memorized. Interestingly, the Bible doesn't even bother to use the word *memorize.* Not because memorizing God's Word is unimportant but because meditating (a word the Bible *does* use frequently) presupposes memorizing.

Of course, another reason the Bible doesn't bother to use the word *memorize* is because there are many colorful expressions that it employs in place of that word. Moses tells us, for example, to bind God's Word on our foreheads (Deuteronomy 6:8). The psalmist encourages us to hide God's Word in our hearts (Psalm 119:11). The prophet Ezekiel says that he ate God's Word and it was sweet to his taste (Ezekiel 3:3). Jesus asks us to allow His words to remain in us, like branches remain in a vine (John 15:7). The apostle Paul writes: "Let the word of Christ dwell in you"; that is, let it set up residency in your life (Colossians 3:16). All of these pictures suggest that we should be memorizing Scripture, even if the word *memorize* is never used.

But memorizing verses from the Bible still sounds like a daunting task, doesn't it? Some of us complain that we have lousy memories. But that isn't true. We've memorized all sorts of things: our social security number; the words to the "Star Spangled Banner"; the birthdays of family members; our bike lock combination; the name of our kindergarten teacher. (My teacher's name was Mrs. Polkinghorn. How cool a name is that for a kindergarten teacher?)

There's nothing wrong with our memories. And there's nothing more important to memorize than God's Word. Let me tell you three benefits that you'll experience when you memorize portions of the Bible. These three benefits are mentioned in the opening three verses of Psalm 1:

> Blessed is the man who does not walk in the counsel
>   of the wicked or stand in the way of sinners
>   or sit in the seat of mockers.
> But his delight is in the law of the Lord,
>   and on his law he meditates day and night.
> He is like a tree planted by streams of water,
>   which yields its fruit in season and whose leaf
>   does not wither.
> Whatever he does prospers.

The first benefit of memorizing is *the Bible will become portable*. In the middle of this passage, the psalmist describes a person who is able to meditate on God's Word *day and night*. Let me point out the obvious. In order to meditate on God's Word *day and night*, you either have to have a copy of the Bible constantly open in front of you (along with a flashlight if it's the middle of the night), or you have to know portions of the Bible by memory, right?

When you know portions of the Bible by memory, you can take the Bible with you wherever you go. You can pull out a key verse when you're offering counsel to a friend, or when you're praising God on a starry night, or when you're wrestling with a difficult decision, or when you're passing time while washing the dishes. The Bible will become portable.

WHEN WE memorize Scripture, the Bible becomes portable, preventive, and productive in our lives.

The second benefit of memorizing is *the Bible will become preventive*. Look again at the opening verse of Psalm 1. The psalmist warns us not to get sucked into temptation. We've got to resist: the counsel of the wicked, the way of sinners, and the seat of mockers. How do we do that? The answer is in verse 2: by *meditating* on the Bible (i.e., those verses that we've memorized).

Psalm 119:11 puts it this way: "I have hidden your word

in my heart that I might not sin against you." When we know verses from the Bible by memory, the Holy Spirit has something to bring to our minds when we're facing temptation. This is how Jesus defended Himself when Satan tempted Him in the wilderness. Satan threw three different temptations at Jesus (Matthew 4) and Jesus fought back with three different Scripture verses, each of them from the book of Deuteronomy. Deuteronomy! When was the last time we even *read* Deuteronomy, much less *memorized* portions of it?

The apostle Paul warns us that the Devil and his evil cohorts are constantly scheming against us. How are we to protect ourselves against their attacks? Paul tells us that God has given us six pieces of spiritual armor that must be put on every day. (See Ephesians 6:10-17.) The last piece of armor on the list is "the sword of the Spirit, which is the word of God." Perhaps if we would memorize some *preventive* Bible verses, we would lose fewer battles with Satan.

SATAN THREW three different temptations at Jesus, who fought back with three different Scripture verses.

The final benefit of memorizing is *the Bible will become productive.* The last verse in the Psalm 1 passage paints a great picture of a person who memorizes and meditates on God's Word: he or she is a fruitful tree, never withering, always prospering. Does that describe your life? It could, if you are willing to invest some time in memorizing Scripture, which could then be brought to mind throughout the day.

How to Memorize Scripture

Let me get real practical. Sometimes we just need a few simple how-tos to get us started down the path of a new behavior. Here are four basic tips that will help you develop the habit of memorizing the Bible.

Tip 1: Record a text. Pick out a Bible verse (or verses) that you'd like to memorize and write it down on a 3 x 5 card. It might be a verse about God that moves you, or speaks of some character virtue that you'd like to develop, or that sums up what you recently learned in a sermon or small group lesson—whatever. You might even decide to start with an entire chapter of the Bible, like Psalm 1. (It's only six verses long.) Write out the verses of that chapter on some 3 x 5 cards.

Joe White is a former college football coach, the director of a premier youth sports camp, and a parenting expert. Dr. White raised four outstanding boys of his own. And before they were given the car keys for the first time as teenagers, they had to recite the entire New Testament book of Philippians! (That's four chapters; 104 verses.) Joe says that Bible memorization was the greatest shaping influence in his sons' lives.[15]

When people ask Joe where to begin memorizing the Bible, he always responds: "With verse 1." "Verse 1 of what?" people want to know. "Verse 1 of your favorite chapter" is Joe's reply. "But then what?" they ask. "Well, then you go on to verse 2." So what are you waiting for? Record a text.

Tip 2: Repeat one line at a time. You've heard the expression "rote memory"? The word *rote* suggests the use of routine or repetition. There's really no trick to memorizing a Bible verse other than to repeat the first line of it again and again and again, until you can say it without looking at it. And then you move on to the second line. It's a good idea to start your memorizing with the reference. That way you'll remember where to find the verse in the Bible, even if you forget the verse itself.

Tip 3: Recruit a partner. Every week hundreds of grade school children attend our church's Awana program. In addition to participating in lots of fun and games, these kids are learning scores of Bible verses by heart. This necessitates that moms and dads listen to their recitations during the week. So, from time to time I challenge the parents in our congregation to occasionally turn the tables at home and ask their children to listen to the Bible verses that mom and dad are memorizing. Of course, that assumes that mom and dad *are* memorizing Bible verses. What a great example to set for the kids!

Sue and I are almost always working on some Bible

memory project together. John 15, Isaiah 40, Romans 8, and various psalms are some of the favorite passages that we've committed to memory. It's wonderful, on a long car ride or walk along the river, to review these portions of God's Word with each other.

At this writing my mom is eighty-five years old and still memorizing the Bible! Last January she called from Florida, where my parents winter, to tell me that she was working on Romans 8 (all thirty-nine verses) and hoped to quote it to me when she returned home in April. Then she threw down the gauntlet, challenging me to be able to recite it with her at that time.

Tip 4: Recite word-perfect. When you're reviewing your verses with your partner, ask to be corrected if you don't recite the verses word-perfect. This isn't because you want to be a perfectionist. It's because it's easier to memorize something if you repeat it the same way every time.

Well, that concludes my tips for memorizing the Bible. I hope you'll put into practice what you learned in this chapter. My prayer is that you'll *Get a Grip* on God's Word by hearing, reading, studying, memorizing, and meditating. At the risk of mixing my metaphors, let me add that it takes getting a grip on God's Word in order for it to become a rock-solid *foundation* for your life.

Study Guide

Icebreaker

What media-related activity is most likely to keep you from reading good books?

1. Read Nehemiah 8:1–8 and note anything that strikes you about the way in which these people listened to God's Word.

2. (•••) Which of the four Bible-hearing tips would be most helpful if you put it into practice? Why?

3. (•••) How many Bibles are there in your home (guesstimate)? How many days a week (be honest) do you sit down and read the Bible? If you read it less than three times a week, what keeps you from being a more consistent reader? If you

read it three or more times a week, what has helped this become your regular habit?

What is (or would be) the best time of the day and location for you to read the Bible? Why?

4. How does *studying* the Bible differ from merely *reading* it?

5. What are the benefits of studying the Bible with a group of people?

6. What is the relationship between *memorizing* and *meditating on* the Bible?

What are some good reasons for you to memorize portions of the Bible? (If you have already become a Bible-memorizer, feel free to add your own reasons to the three that are mentioned in *Foundation.*)

7. Choose a text to memorize and write it out on a 3 x 5 card. What passage did you choose, and why?

8. 🗩 Do a quick review of *Foundation* and write out your best takeaway from each of the four chapters.

"God's Autobiography"

"Lost in Transmission?"

"The Only Way to Know"

"Get a Grip"

Notes

About the Bible Savvy Series

1. Thom S. Rainer, *The Unchurched Next Door* (Grand Rapids: Zondervan, 2003), 200.

Introduction: A Rock-Solid Foundation

1. "Plane Crash Devastates Marshall University," This Day in History, http://www.history.com/this-day-in-history/plane-crash-devastates-marshall-university.

2. George Keith, "How Firm a Foundation," *Inspiring Hymns* (Grand Rapids: Zondervan, 1968), in public domain.

Chapter 1: God's Autobiography (Doctrine of Inspiration)

1. Libby Hill, "How Did an 1885 Flood of Little Consequence Become an Epidemic that 'Killed' 90,000 Chicagoans?" *Chicago Tribune*, 29 July 2007, 16 ff.; see also http://faculty.ccc.edu/jtassin/geology201/homework/Chicagogeo/cholera.htm.

2. Ibid. The *Chicago Tribune* corrected the story in 2005 and published Hill's article "How Did an 1885 Flood of Little Consequence Become an Epidemic?" in 2007, but later in 2007 it reverted to the erroneous statistic that one of every eight Chicagoans died in the alleged epidemic. See "Corrections and Clarifications," *Chicago Tribune*, 29 September 2005, http://articles.chicagotribune.com/2005-09-29/news/0509290134_1_section-epidemic-incorrect-first; and "Chicago's Legendary Epidemic," *Chicago Tribune*, 22 August 2007, http://articles.chicagotribune.com/2007-08-22/news/0708210481_1_cholera-epidemic-chicago-river-metropolitan-water-reclamation-district.

3. Hill, "How Did an 1885 Flood of Little Consequence Become an Epidemic?"

4. Ibid. See also Libby Hill, *The Chicago River: A Natural and Unnatural History* (Chicago: Lake Claremont Press, 2000), 116–17.

5. Ibid.

6. John Kandell, "The Glorious History of Handel's Messiah, *Smithsonian*, December 2009, http://www.smithsonianmag.com/arts-culture/The-Glorious-History-of-Handels-Messiah.html#ixzz28FotSiRc; also "Handel's 'Messiah' Inspires Listeners, Transcends Time," CBN News, broadcast 16 December 2011, http://www.cbn.com/cbnnews/us/2011/December/Handels-Messiah-Inspires-Listeners-Transcends-Time/.

7. Lee Strobel, *The Case for Christ* (Grand Rapids: Zondervan, 1998), 98.

8. For example, both Matthew and Luke tell the story of Satan tempting Jesus in the desert. Both describe the same three enticements, but they differ on the order in which the temptations were presented. A closer inspection of the two texts reveals that Matthew is following a chronological order (indicated by his use of words like "then" and "again"), while Luke is tying the temptations together without any reference to a time continuum. So Matthew tells us that Satan's second temptation was to entice Jesus to hurl Himself from the pinnacle of the temple, but Luke treats this as the third and final temptation—perhaps because it's the most climactic of the three (cf. Matthew 4:1–11; Luke 4:1–13).

Chapter 2: *Lost in Transmission?* (History of the Canon)

1. Nathan Ausubel, "Sofer," *The Book of Jewish Knowledge* (New York: Crown, 1964), 420. An *iota* is the nearest Greek equivalent to the Hebrew *yodh*, the smallest letter of the Hebrew alphabet.

2. Bart Ehrman, *Misquoting Jesus: The Story Behind Who Changed the Bible and Why* (New York: HarperOne, 2007).

3. Lee Strobel, *The Case for the Real Jesus* (Grand Rapids: Zondervan, 2007), 69–99.

4. Dan Brown, *The Da Vinci Code* (New York: Anchor, 2009).

5. Liz Halloran, "Lloyd Bentsen to Dan Quayle: 'Senator, You Are No Jack Kennedy,'" *US News*, 17 January 2008, http://www.usnews.com/news/articles/2008/01/17/the-mother-of-all-put-downs.

6. Grant Osborne, "Decoding the DaVinci Code," *Trinity Magazine*, Fall 2004, 20.

7. Rebecca Leung, "New Questions on Bush Guard Duty," *CBS News*, 11 February 2009; the transcript of the 8 September 2004 broadcast on *60 Minutes* can be found at http://www.cbsnews.com//2100-500164_162-641984.html.

8. Ibid.

9. Maureen Balleza and Kate Zernike, "Memos on Bush Are Fake but Accurate, Typist Says," *New York Times*, 15 September 2004; http://www.nytimes.com/2004/09/15/politics/campaign/15guard.html.

10. As quoted in Lee Strobel, *The Case for Christ* (Grand Rapids: Zondervan, 1998), 97.

11. William M. Ramsay, *The Bearing of Recent Discovery on the Trustworthiness of the New Testament* (Grand Rapids: Baker, 1953), http://www.blueletterbible.org/faq/don_stewart/stewart.cfm?id=804; http://www.bibleevidences.com/archeology.htm.

12. Gospel of Thomas 7:1–2, as cited in Ron Cameron, *The Other Gospels: Non-Canonical Gospel Texts* (Westminster Press, 1982), 26.

13. Gospel of Thomas 22:4–7, quoted in ibid., 28.

Chapter 3: The Only Way to Know (Doctrine of Revelation)

1. C. S. Lewis, *Reflections on the Psalms* (New York: Harcourt, Brace, World, 1958), 63.

2. Nicholas Perrin, *Lost in Transmission?* (Nashville: Nelson, 2009).

3. See http://www.Navigators.org/resources/shared/tools/bridge.pdf for a copy of the Navigators' illustration of the bridge, complete with tips, text, and Bible verses for using the bridge as an evangelistic tool.

Chapter 4: Get a Grip (Means of Learning)

1. Chart, "Percentage of Adults in Each Prose, Document, and Quantitative Literacy Level: 1992 and 2003," in National Assessment of Adult Literacy, 2003, http://nces.ed.gov/naal/kf_demographics.asp. The survey, published by the Institute of Education Sciences, shows 43 percent of adults read prose at "basic" or "below basic" levels.

2. "To Read or Not to Read," Research Report #47, National Endowment for the Arts, Washington, D.C., November 2007, 7.

3. Ibid., 9.

4. Amanda Lenhart et al., "Teens, Social Networking, Mobile, Generations, Blogs, Web 2.0: Social Media and Young Adults," Pew Internet and American Life Project, 3 February 2010, http://pewinternet.org/Reports/2010/Social-Media-and-Young-Adults.aspx.

5. "100 Million iPods Sold," Apple Inc., 9 April 2007.

6. "The Twitter Revolution," *The Week*, 23 April 2009, at http://theweek.com/article/index/95694/the-twitter-revolution.

7. "Review: *The Shallows: What the Internet Is Doing to Our Brains*," *The Week*, 18 June 2010, 24.

8. During midyear 2009, according to a report by Facebook's Inside Facebook: Justin Smith, "Facebook Now Growing by over 700,000 Users a Day, and New Engagement Stats," 2 July 2009, at http://www.insidefacbook.com/2009/07/02/facebook-now-growing-by-over-700000-users-a-day-updated-engagement-stats/.

9. Barbara Ortutay, "Facebook Now Home to 1 Billion Monthly Users," *Businessweek*, 4 October 2012, at http://www.businessweek.com/ap/2012-10-04/facebook-tops-1-billion-users.

10. For more information on what the Navigators calls "The Word Hand," see http://www.navigators.org/us/resources/illustrations/items/The%20Word%20Hand.

11. Sam O'Neal, "American Christians and Bible Reading," *Christianity Today*, Spring 2009, R7.

12. Ibid., R9.

13. Tom White, "Loving the Ugliest," *VOM Magazine*, January 2011.

14. Charles Colson, *The Faith* (Grand Rapids: Zondervan, 2008), 44.

15. Joe White, *Faith Training* (Carol Stream, Ill.: Tyndale, 1994), 54.

Bibliography

Geisler, Norman and Thomas Howe. *When Critics Ask: A Popular Handbook on Bible Difficulties*. Wheaton: Victor Books, 1992.

Keller, Timothy. *The Reason for God*. New York: Riverhead Trade, 2009.

Perrin, Nicholas. *Lost in Transmission?* Nashville: Nelson, 2009.

Strobel, Lee. *The Case for Christ*. Grand Rapids: Zondervan, 1998.

———. *The Case for the Real Jesus*. Grand Rapids: Zondervan, 2007.

Wright, Christopher. *The God I Don't Understand*. Grand Rapids: Zondervan, 2008.

JAMES L. NICODEM

Bible Savvy

Epic: The Storyline of the Bible unveils
the single theme that ties all of scripture
together: redemption.

Foundation: The Trustworthiness of the Bible
explains where our current bible came from
and why it can be wholly trusted.

Context: How to Understand the Bible shows
readers how to read the different parts of the
Bible as they were meant to be read and how
they fit together.

Walk: How to Apply the Bible puts the readers
increased understanding of the Bible into real
life terms and contexts.

Too many of us, regardless of our familiarity with the stories of the Bible, are blind to the story of the Bible. We miss the forest for the trees. We fail to recognize how the Bible's many individual stories fit together to tell one mega-story. The macro-story. The story of God and us.

Phil Vischer
Creator of Veggie Tales and What's in the Bible? video series

As a university professor on a Christian college campus, I can tell you that biblical illiteracy is on the rise. That's why the Bible Savvy series should be a prerequisite reading for everyone. Jim Nicodem puts the cookies on the bottom shelf by making the epic story of the biblical narrative understandable and accessible. The Bible Savvy series lays out the foundation and context for God's Word and then shows us in plain language how to apply the Bible's teachings to our lives step-by-step. It's phenomenal.

Les Parrott, PhD
Seattle Pacific University
Author of *You're Stronger Than You Think*

The compelling reality about the Bible is that it is full of fascinating details about God and His wise and redemptive oversight of the history of mankind. Unfortunately, the larger, more profound story often gets lost in the details. Like a master storyteller, Jim Nicodem takes us beyond the details and exposes the grand plot of Scripture. Jim's work in the Bible Savvy series will amaze many of us who have lived to master the details and will motivate all of us to stand in greater awe of the One who is navigating history to a good and glorious end.

Joseph M. Stowell
President, Cornerstone University

The Bible is one of the most precious possessions to a believer living in a restricted nation. I am constantly amazed by the hunger for biblical teaching expressed by those who face persecution daily. Their sacrificial passion should inspire us to rekindle our quest for biblical understanding. Jim Nicodem's Bible Savvy series is the kind of resource needed to reengage our hearts and minds with God's Word, and renew a hunger for God's truth on par with our persecuted brother and sisters.

James E. Dau
President, The Voice of the Martyrs

Jim has done a masterful job in the Bible Savvy series! In these four concise books, Jim marches with clarity and skill into topics that would be difficult to tackle in a seminary classroom, much less in an American living room. And rather than a monologue, these books create a dialog among the author, the reader, their small group, and the living Word of God. These practical, approachable resources provide foundational training that is greatly needed by nearly every small group and leader I encounter.

Greg Bowman
Coauthor of *Coaching Life-Changing Small Group Leaders*
Past executive director of the Willow Creek Association

Reading the four books in the Bible Savvy series is like getting a Bible college education in a box! The Lord is calling our nation to a Bible reading revolution, and these books are an invitation to be part of it.

Hal Seed
Author of *The Bible Questions* and *The God Questions*
Lead Pastor, New Song Community Church, Oceanside, California

Living in the land of the Bible is considered a privilege by many, but the real privilege is to let the Bible become alive through us, in whatever land we may live. In the Bible Savvy series, Jim Nicodem not only helps us to understand God's plan to save us, but also His desire to change and shape us through His Word and Spirit in order to be a light in this dark world.

Rev. Azar Ajaj
Vice President and lecturer, Nazareth Evangelical Theological Seminary

To ignite a love for the God's Word in others is the goal of any spiritual leader. Communicating God's Word is the most important of all. Pastor Jim's Bible Savvy series is the tool, the guide, and the process for worship leaders to go into deep spiritual places. His biblical scholarship, communicated with such creativity, is exactly what is needed in worship ministry today.

> Stan Endicott
> Slingshot group coach/mentor
> Worship Leader, Mariners Church, Irvine, California

Jim Nicodem leads one of America's finest churches. Jim knows how to communicate the truth of the Bible that brings historical knowledge with incredible practical application. The Bible Savvy series is the best I have ever seen. Your life and faith will be enhanced as you use and apply this material to your life.

> Jim Burns, PhD
> President, HomeWord
> Author of *Creating an Intimate Marriage* and
> *Confident Parenting*

Pastor Nicodem is like a championship caliber coach: he loves to teach, and he stresses that success comes from mastering the basics. The Bible Savvy series will help you correctly interpret the best Playbook ever written: the Bible. Understanding and applying its fundamentals (with the help of the Bible Savvy series) will lead one to the Ultimate Victory . . . eternity with Jesus.

> James Brown
> Host of *The NFL Today* on the CBS television network

JAMES L. NICODEM

Bible Savvy

Hear from the author by
checking out the videos
on the Bible Savvy Series
with James Nicodem.

biblesavvy.com

MOODY
PUBLISHERS

Context

How to Understand the Bible

James L. Nicodem

MOODY PUBLISHERS

CHICAGO

All Scripture quotations are taken from the *Holy Bible, New International Version*®, NIV®. Copyright © 1973, 1978, 1984 by Biblica, Inc.™ Used by permission of Zondervan. All rights reserved worldwide.

Scripture quotations marked AMP are taken from *The Amplified Bible*. Copyright © 1965, 1987 by The Zondervan Corporation. *The Amplified New Testament* copyright © 1958, 1987 by The Lockman Foundation. Used by permission.

Published in association with the literary agency of Wolgemuth & Associates, Inc.

Edited by Jim Vincent
Interior design: Ragont Design
Cover design: Smartt Guys design
Cover image: Thomas Northcut

Library of Congress Cataloging-in-Publication Data

Nicodem, James L., 1956-
    Context : how to understand the Bible / James L. Nicodem.
        pages cm. — (The Bible savvy series)
    Includes bibliographical references.
    ISBN 978-0-8024-0635-4
    1. Bible—Introductions. I. Title.
BS475.3.N53 2013
220.6'1—dc23
                                        2012047218

We hope you enjoy this book from Moody Publishers. Our goal is to provide high-quality, thought-provoking books and products that connect truth to your real needs and challenges. For more information on other books and products written and produced from a biblical perspective, go to www.moodypublishers.com or write to:

Moody Publishers
820 N. LaSalle Boulevard
Chicago, IL 60610

3 5 7 9 10 8 6 4

About the
Bible Savvy Series

I MET THE REAL ESTATE AGENT at my front door and invited him in. My wife and I were about to put our home on the market and I had called Jeff as a potential representative. As he sat down at our dining room table and opened his briefcase, I noticed a Bible perched on top of other papers. I asked Jeff if he was a Bible reader and he replied that he was just getting started. What had prompted his interest? He'd recently come across a list in *Success, Inc.* magazine of the most influential books recommended by business leaders. The Bible had been the most frequently mentioned book on the list. So, Jeff was going to give it a try.

My real estate agent isn't alone in his new interest in the Bible. According to a recent survey, 91 percent of those who have lately begun attending church were motivated to do so by a desire to understand what the Bible has to say to their lives.[1] That means nine of every ten visitors to church are intrigued by the Bible! But while they are curious about God's Word, they're also a bit intimidated by it. The Bible is such a daunting book, written in ancient times and addressed to

vastly different cultures. Is it really possible to draw relevant insights from it for our lives today? People are returning to church to find out.

Ironically, while an interest in Bible knowledge can be detected among those who are new to church, it seems to be on the wane among many veteran churchgoers. When my oldest daughter enrolled at a Christian college, the president of the school addressed parents on opening day. He told us that the Bible comprehension exams of each incoming class of freshmen show less and less knowledge of God's Word. And then he added: "These kids are growing up in *your* churches." Evidently, many churches are not doing a good job of teaching committed believers how to read, interpret, and apply the Bible.

The Bible Savvy series has been written to help a wide spectrum of Bible readers—from newbies to seasoned Bible study leaders—get their arms around God's Word. This multi-book series covers four essential Bible-related topics that Moody Publishers has made available in one set as a comprehensive manual for understanding God's Word and putting it into practice. *Context* is the third of the four-book series.

An added bonus to the Bible Savvy series is the Study Guide that follows every chapter of each book. These questions for personal reflection and group discussion have been crafted by a team of small-groups experts. The Study Guide is also available online at biblesavvy.com and may be downloaded and used for personal study or reproduced for members of a small group.

Four Things You Must Know to
Get the Most out of God's Word

The four books of the Bible Savvy series will give you a grasp of the following topics, allowing God's Word to become a rich resource in your life:

1. *The storyline of the Bible.* The Bible is actually a compilation of sixty-six books that were written over a 1,500-year period. But amazingly there is one central storyline that holds everything together. You'll trace this storyline in *Epic* from Genesis to Revelation, learning how each of the sixty-six books contributes to the overall plot.

2. *The reliability of the Bible.* How did God communicate what He wanted to say through human authors? What are the evidences that the Bible is a supernatural book? How do we know that the *right* books made it into the Bible and that the *wrong* books were kept out of it? Isn't a text that was hand-copied for hundreds of years bound to be filled with errors? *Foundation* will give you answers to questions

like these—because you won't get much out of the Bible until you're certain that you can trust it.

3. *How to understand the Bible*. People read all sorts of crazy things into the Bible, and have used it to support a wide variety of strange (and sometimes reprehensible) positions and activities. In *Context* you will learn the basic ground rules for accurately interpreting Scripture. (Yes, there are rules.)

4. *How to apply the Bible*. It's one thing to read the Bible, and it's another thing entirely to walk away from your reading with an application for your life. Even members of Bible study groups occasionally do a poor job of this. Participants leave these gatherings without a clear sense of how they're going to put God's Word into practice. *Walk* will equip you to become a Bible doer.

Do You Have Savvy?

The dictionary defines *savvy* as *practical know-how*. It is my hope and prayer that the Bible Savvy series will lead you into an experiential knowledge of God's Word that will transform your life.

Many people have contributed to my own love and understanding of the Bible over the years—as well as to the writing of this book. I owe a huge debt of gratitude to them.

Mom and Dad made God's Word central to our family life, encouraging my siblings and me to memorize big chunks of it.

When I got to high school, I was a bit turned off to church, but I started attending a youth ministry in a neighboring suburb that was led by Bill Hybels. (These were pre–Willow Creek Community Church days, when dinosaurs roamed the earth.) Bill had (and still has) an incredible ability to open the Bible, read a passage out loud, and then drive home its application to the lives of his listeners. After a year of hearing him teach God's Word in such a life-impacting way, I went away to college and decided to major in biblical studies.

Two professors (among many) fanned the flame of my love for the Bible during my college and seminary years. Dr. Gerry Hawthorne taught me Greek New Testament at Wheaton College, and there are thousands of men and women in ministry around the world today who still remember his simple-but-powerful class devotions. He'd put one verse on the chalkboard (remember chalk?) and then tease out its significance for our lives—often with tears in his eyes. Dr. D. A. Carson taught me the Bible at Trinity Evangelical Divinity School. His books (and occasional phone and email exchanges) continue to shape me today. I aspire to have even a quarter of his passion for God's Word!

After school, as I started out in youth ministry, I began listening to cassette tapes (same era as chalk) by Dr. John

MacArthur. John is internationally famous for his verse-by-verse teaching of Scripture. Although he is occasionally more adamant about certain doctrines than I am (we agree on the essentials), his love for the Bible is infectious. John has set the bar high for all pastors who want to faithfully teach their churches God's Word. As my ministry has continued, I have found other communicators who whet my appetite for Scripture—many of them through their books, some of them currently through their podcasts. Thank you Lee Strobel, Joe Stowell, John Ortberg, Mark Driscoll, Francis Chan, Tim Keller, and many others.

Today, my desire to get people into the Bible is fueled by the five thousand-plus eager learners whom I have the privilege of pastoring at Christ Community Church of St. Charles, Illinois, and its regional campuses. I am especially grateful for both the staff and volunteer leaders who oversee almost four hundred Community Groups that are studying God's Word. And one of those leaders, who writes incredible Bible curricula and teaches scores of Bible-hungry women, is my wife, Sue. Her devotion to Scripture is a constant inspiration to me.

Lastly, a special thanks to my faithful assistant, Angee Jenkins, who helped to edit my manuscript, track down footnotes, and protect my writing time; and to my agent, Andrew Wolgemuth, who found a great publisher in Moody to make the Bible Savvy series available to you.

*To watch Jim's introduction to Context,
scan this QR code with your smartphone or go to
www.biblesavvy.com/video/#context1.*

Contents

Foreword

THE BIBLE CLEARLY says, "There is no God." That's an exact quotation from the Bible. Of course, including a wee bit more of the context reverses one's understanding: "The fool says in his heart, 'There is no God'" (Psalm 14:1). Paying attention to the immediate context makes all the difference.

This example, of course, is too easy. Sometimes contexts reach beyond a verse or a paragraph or a chapter. Sometimes they extend to an entire biblical book or to an author like Paul—or even to the entire canon of Scripture. To be sensitive to the context demands alertness not only to words and sentences, but to the diverse literary forms of Scripture.

Now, some people are better readers than others. They instinctively uncover the plot of a narrative, listen carefully for the characterizations of people mentioned in the text, pick up on repeated topics, and think carefully about words. They may not know much about rules of interpretation; they are simply good readers. But *all* readers—better readers and poorer readers—will benefit from some introductory exposure to how literature *works*, including biblical literature. And which of us would not want to become better, more accurate, more attentive readers of God's most holy Word?

God in His wisdom has not only given us Scripture, but He has ordained that there be pastor/teachers in the church. Such pastors are more gifted than many others at understanding Scripture and explaining it to others. They have a peculiar function within the body: they are like stomachs that take in nourishment and distribute it to the rest of the body.

So think of Jim Nicodem as a stomach. As a pastor, what Jim does in this short book is something a little more and a little less than simply explain Scripture in order to nourish the body. Although he provides many examples that actually do explain this or that passage of Scripture, his purpose is to lay out, in straightforward, nontechnical language, many of the most important principles of interpretation. He does this so each person may know the foundational principles of biblical interpretation, and so understand many texts. In other words, Jim wants the church he serves, and many other churches, to be filled with men and women who will become better Bible readers. If you think your way carefully through this book, Jim's high goal will be amply realized.

> D. A. CARSON, PhD
> Research Professor of New Testament
> Trinity Evangelical Divinity School
> Author of *New Testament Commentary Survey*

Introduction:
Fitting the Pieces Together

JIGSAW PUZZLES are a popular holiday diversion in my home. After a big meal with family and friends, our guests will fan out into different rooms to read, talk, nap, or watch a ball game. But inevitably a card table will be set up in the living room, a lamp will be plugged in nearby for greater illumination, and the thousand pieces of a jigsaw puzzle are dumped out for assembly.

There are usually a few diehards in the group who stay at it from beginning to end. But almost everybody contributes at some point—grandparents, teenagers, ball game watchers on commercial breaks. It's irresistible. You can't stop at the table for even a minute without picking up a piece and trying to put it in its proper spot. And when our puzzles are completed, we coat their surfaces with a transparent glue (Mod Podge, if you're interested) and hang them on the walls of our downstairs playroom as decorations.

As a person who knows something about puzzles, I can tell you that an indispensable aid to putting one together is the top of the box that it comes in. That's where the picture is. The picture lets you know what your final product is supposed to look like. A giant cheeseburger? A bouquet of flowers? A Norman Rockwell painting? A panoramic view of the Grand Canyon?

More importantly, the picture gives you clues about where to place each puzzle piece that you hold in your hand. Is it blue? Then it's probably part of the sky in the upper right portion of the puzzle. Does it have letters on it? Then it must belong to the sign on the side of the building that's in the puzzle's center.

I would never try putting a puzzle together without looking at the box top. Any puzzle assembler needs to know the overall picture. Unfortunately, this is not how many people approach the Bible. They read it in bits and pieces, without reference to its big picture. They have no idea how it all fits together. They're unfamiliar with the larger context of a particular passage that they're looking at. And this makes it difficult to understand that passage correctly.

Context (the third book in the Bible Savvy series) will equip you to interpret God's Word with accuracy. The key to the process is understanding the Bible's big picture. We're going to look at that big picture from four vantage points. We'll be considering the Bible's historical, literary, theological, and immediate settings. Don't be intimidated by these four categories. You will fully understand what is meant by each and how they can help you better understand the Bible by the time you're done reading the following pages.

{ 1 }
The Historical Setting

I WAS A BIBLICAL STUDIES major in college. One of my favorite professors taught me Old Testament and Hebrew. He was a very dignified, articulate, God-fearing man. He kind of reminded me of an ancient prophet. One Sunday I stopped by his house to drop something off and his wife was getting their six-year-old son, Scotty, ready for church in another room.

In the middle of my conversation with this professor, we heard Scotty scream at the top of his lungs: "I don't want to go to church! You can't make me go to church! I HATE CHURCH!!" The face of my very dignified, articulate, God-fearing professor turned beet-red with embarrassment. But he very quietly said to me: "You must understand the *context* of that outburst. You see, Scotty has just been pulled from the sandbox."

Ahhh! "You must understand the context." That also happens to be the most important rule for interpreting the Bible. *You must understand the context.* Have you ever heard a skeptic complain, "Oh, people can make the Bible say whatever they want it to say"? That skeptic is absolutely right. People *can* make the Bible say whatever they want it to say—*if* they take Bible verses out of context. But that's a violation of the number one ground rule for interpreting the Bible.

There are ground rules for interpreting the Bible? Yes, there are ground rules for interpreting *any* piece of serious writing, whether it's the Bible, Shakespeare's plays, Robert Frost's poems, or Jane Austen's novels. Interpreting great literature requires ground rules. The ground rules for interpreting the Bible are called *hermeneutics*.

Herman who? *Hermeneutics* is a Greek word. If you know your Greek mythology, you probably recall that Hermes was the messenger god. He was responsible for conveying information from the gods to humans. So, hermeneutics refers to the ground rules that must be followed in order to ensure that the Word of God, the Bible, is accurately understood by us.

Context is really just a short course in hermeneutics. No matter what your current level of Bible understanding, you need hermeneutics. If you're not yet a Bible reader because you're put off by a book that's set in cultures so vastly different from your own, you need hermeneutics. If you regularly read the Bible but come across passages that leave you asking, "What in the world does this mean?" you need hermeneutics. If you want to hear God speak to you through the Bible but you're not always certain if you're reading His thoughts *out* of the text or your own thoughts *into* the text (you see the difference?), you need hermeneutics. If you belong to a Bible study group in which there are occasionally as many interpretations of a passage as there are participants around the table, you need hermeneutics.

Hermeneutics are the basic ground rules for interpreting the Bible. And all of the ground rules are founded on one important principle: *You must understand the context*. There are four kinds of context that we'll be considering in this section, the first of which is the Bible's historical setting. If we want to interpret the Bible correctly, we have to pay attention to the historical background of every passage we turn to. How do we do that? Let me spell it out in the form of three directives.

Pursue the Objective Facts

Some time ago, I read a book review of a new biography on the life of Ronald Reagan. According to the reviewer this biography contains a lot of fabricated information; the author has made up details about Ronald Reagan's life that are not completely true. However, the reviewer quickly added, the book tells a really good story and is well worth reading. I thought: *Huh? Who wants to read a biography that's not grounded on historical facts?*

Did you know that Christianity is unique among the world's religions in that it is grounded on historical facts? These facts are objective and verifiable. Take away the facts and the Christian faith crumbles. What *are* the facts? Well, according to the Bible's record, Jesus Christ, God's eternal Son, came to earth as a human being. He did miracles that provided evidence of His deity. Then He died on a cross to pay the penalty for our sins. And three days later He rose from the dead, proving that His sacrifice was effective and that He has the power to give people new and eternal life.

Take away these objective facts and there's not much left of the Christian faith. But that's not true of other world religions. Buddhism, for example, doesn't depend upon the historicity of its founder. It doesn't revolve around the life of *The Buddha*, Siddhartha Gautama, in 500 BC. It revolves around a set of teachings referred to as the Eightfold Path that will lead you to nirvana.

The same is true of Hinduism. Objective facts about Vishnu aren't important. Religious ideas are what hold Hinduism together. The same is true of Islam. Even though we know a lot about the actual life of Muhammad, Islam isn't built on the historical events of Muhammad's life. It's built on the Five Pillars of Faith as revealed in the Quran.

Christianity is the only major world religion that stakes its existence on objective facts. The apostle Paul drove home this point when he summarized the basic content of his teaching in the following verses:

Now, brothers, I want to remind you of the gospel I preached to you, which you received and on which you have taken your stand. By this gospel you are saved, if you hold firmly to the word I preached to you. Otherwise, you have believed in vain.

For what I received I passed on to you as of first importance: that Christ died for our sins according to the Scriptures, that he was buried, that he was raised on the third day according to the Scriptures, and that he appeared to Peter, and then to the Twelve. After that, he appeared to more than five hundred of the brothers at the same time, most of whom are still living, though some have fallen asleep. (1 Corinthians 15:1–6)

What does the apostle Paul say is the core of the Christian faith that he preaches? Christianity is grounded on certain objective facts: that Jesus died for our sins and was buried; that He rose again on the third day; and that scores of eyewitnesses actually saw all this! Take away those historical events and you lose the gospel, the good news of the faith. Take away those objective facts and "you [Christians] have believed in vain" (v. 2).

I heard about a very liberal theologian who was asked the question, "What if it could be proven beyond the shadow of a doubt that Jesus did *not* rise from the dead? What if Jesus'

bones were discovered—verifiably—in a first-century tomb?"
His reply: "That wouldn't make any difference to *my* faith. I
would still believe that the spirit of Jesus is alive today."

What do you think about that theologian's response? I'll
tell you what the apostle Paul would think about it. If we
drop down to verse 14 of the passage we just read (1 Corinthians 15), Paul says: "And if Christ has not been raised, our
preaching is useless and so is your faith." Genuine Christianity rests on objective facts.

Now, why am I making such a big deal about this point?
What does this have to do with how we approach the task of
understanding the Bible? Here's the reason for the big deal.
The Bible's message is wrapped up in objective facts. If we
want to interpret that message correctly, then we need to
understand those objective facts. We need to understand the
historical setting of whatever Bible passage we're looking at.

Are you following me? The Bible is *not* a Magic 8 Ball.
Remember those? (Mattel, the toymaker, is still making
them.) They were originally designed back in 1950 by a guy
whose mother was a psychic. You ask the liquid-filled Magic
8 Ball a yes-or-no question, then you turn it upside down and
an answer floats to the surface. The answer may be: *Outlook
good;* or *Don't count on it;* or *Reply hazy, try again.*

Some people do this with the Bible. They open it to a random passage, hoping that it will speak directly to their lives,

without any consideration of the historical facts behind that passage. If they open, for example, to the New Testament epistle of Colossians, they don't care *who* the Colossians were or *why* the apostle Paul was writing this letter to them. They just want a Magic 8 Ball message for *their* lives. If they open to the Old Testament book of Esther, they don't care *when* this story took place or *what* was going on in Esther's life at the time. They just want to know: What is this passage saying to *me*?

SOME PEOPLE open the Bible to a random passage, hoping it will speak directly. They just want a Magic 8 Ball message for *their* lives.

R.C. Sproul, a well-known theologian and author, tells an amusing story from his days of teaching at a Christian college.[1] One of his female students, a senior, found herself approaching graduation with no man in her life. Many of her friends had serious boyfriends or even fiancés.

So this young woman prayed for a guy. Then she got out her Bible and opened it at random to Zechariah 9:9: "Rejoice greatly, O Daughter of Zion! Shout, Daughter of Jerusalem! See, your king comes to you, gentle and riding on a donkey."

Now, if you know the objective facts behind this verse, you realize that it was written about 500 BC as a prophecy concerning a coming Savior; a prophecy that Jesus later fulfilled when He rode into Jerusalem on a donkey at the beginning of Holy Week. But this college senior interpreted Zechariah 9:9 as God's promise to provide her with a Prince Charming, even if he showed up on a donkey instead of on a white charger.

This is not good Bible interpretation (as I hope you already concluded). The historical setting of the passage we're reading matters. We must pursue the objective facts.

Cross the Cultural Rivers

One of my favorite *Far Side* cartoons shows a guy lecturing his dog. In the first of two panels, the guy says: "OK, Ginger! I've had it! You stay out of the garbage! Understand, Ginger? Stay out of the garbage or else!" The caption under this first panel reads: *What People Say.* The caption under the second panel reads: *What Dogs Hear.* What does Ginger hear? The thought bubble above her head says: "Blah, blah, blah, blah . . ." In case you missed the point of the joke, there's a formidable communication barrier between people and dogs.

There's even a formidable communication barrier between people when two groups of humans come from vastly different cultures. Have you ever experienced that? Have you ever tried to explain American football to a Brazilian friend, or been greeted with a bear hug by a Russian coworker whom you hardly knew? Or maybe you've been on one of your church's short-term mission trips to Haiti, Czech Republic, or Bangladesh. And you couldn't understand the language or the local customs.

One of my first mission trips, years ago, was to Amsterdam. Our Dutch hosts welcomed us with a meal. There was a milk bottle on the table that I assumed contained . . . well . . . milk. But as I poured it into my glass, it came out thick and lumpy. I just assumed that the milk wasn't homogenized and that the cream had floated to the top of the bottle. Well, I didn't want to pour it back, so I just drank it. Wow, was it sour!

Afterwards, one of the Dutch hosts asked me, "Is it the custom to *drink* yogurt in America?"

I quickly stammered, "Oh, yeah! Yogurt . . . of course. Love to drink that stuff."

As you read the Bible and *pursue the objective facts* that make up the historical setting of the passage you're looking at, you will also need to *cross some cultural rivers*. What I mean by that is: you will have to travel from *your* side of the river (a twenty-first-century, Western, technological society) to the *other* side of the river. If you're reading, let's say, the Old Testament book of Proverbs, the other side of the river is a tenth-century BC, Middle Eastern, agrarian society. If you're reading the New Testament epistle of 1 Corinthians, it's a first-century AD, Greco-Roman, urban society.

If you don't cross these cultural rivers, you won't understand much of what you read. For example, let's say that you're reading the Book of Ruth. Ruth is a destitute young widow. But she has a relative named Boaz who wants to help her out. Boaz wants to buy Ruth a piece of property, a place to live. Ruth 4:7 tells us that the guy who sells Boaz the property seals the contract by handing Boaz his sandal.

Now, that makes absolute sense to you, right? I mean, when you purchased *your* home and you went to the closing, didn't the seller hand you his shoe to seal the deal? He didn't? So, what's up with this sandal-passing business? In Ruth's day, this was the way for the seller to say: "The property that I used to walk on as my own now belongs to you." Pretty cool, eh?

We just crossed a cultural river. And we'll have to cross cultural rivers every time we pick up our Bibles, if we want to understand what we read, because we live in a time and place that's vastly different from Bible times and places. Now, you may be thinking, *But I could never do what you just did. That bit about handing over the sandal was amazing. How did you come up with that? Do they teach you that stuff at seminary? Was that from one of your doctoral courses?*

No, I think it was from a footnote in a study Bible. Most study Bibles have an introduction to every book of the Bible that explains the book's historical setting. A study Bible also has countless footnotes on every page that explain cultural phenomena. Think of a study Bible as a bridge that will enable you to cross cultural rivers. I recommend the *NIV Study Bible* for its wonderful explanatory footnotes. (The *ESV Study Bible* is a close runner-up.)

Ask the Journalistic Questions

I remember taking a class in journalism back in high school. And the teacher drilled into us that every good reporter relentlessly asks the five "w" questions: *Who? What? When? Where? Why?*

These are also good questions to ask whenever we read the Bible. Let me show you how this works. I'll ask each of the "w" questions for a couple of Bible passages. You'll quickly see how the answers to these questions help us interpret the passages.

Who Questions. We'll begin with the Ninevites. Here's a simple but key *who* question to ask: Who were these people that God asked the prophet Jonah to go and preach to? You probably remember certain aspects of this story. Take a look at the opening verses of Jonah:

The word of the Lord came to Jonah son of Amittai: "Go to the great city of Nineveh and preach against it, because its wickedness has come up before me."

But Jonah ran away from the Lord and headed for Tarshish. He went down to Joppa, where he found a ship bound for that port. After paying the fare, he went aboard and sailed for Tarshish to flee from the Lord. (Jonah 1:1–3)

Now, it's never a good idea to try and run away from God. You can run, as the saying goes, but you can't hide. Jonah was eventually thrown overboard and ended up in the belly of a giant fish. That's when he decided that obeying God would probably be a good thing to do. So, the fish chucked him up and Jonah reluctantly fulfilled his mission. He preached to the Ninevites.

So, *who* were these guys? Why was Jonah so intent on staying miles away from them? If you don't know the answer to that question, you might assume that Jonah was just being rebellious. He rejected God's assignment because he thought he had better things to do with his time. Was that it? No. Jonah didn't want to go to Nineveh because he hated and feared its inhabitants. And we won't understand Jonah's hatred and fear toward them until we know *who* they were.

Unfortunately, the Bible passage we're looking at doesn't give us any details about the Ninevites. But here's the scoop— and it's information that I picked up from the *NIV Study Bible*'s introduction to the book of Jonah. Nineveh was the capital city of ancient Assyria. Assyria was the superpower of Jonah's day and the Assyrians were notorious for the brutal way in which they treated the people they conquered. Sometimes they beheaded their victims and stacked up the heads in piles. Other times they impaled their captives on stakes. Or they skinned them alive.

So, if *you* were Jonah and God sent you to the Ninevites, wouldn't you jump on a ship in the opposite direction? You can see how knowing the *who* of a Bible passage enables us to better interpret the text.

KNOWING THE *who* of a Bible passage enables us to better interpret the text.

Let's try another *who* question. Who were the recipients of 1 Corinthians 13, the apostle Paul's famous "love chapter"? I'm sure you've come across the words of this text before. They're often read at weddings. Or they're painted on wall plaques. It's a nice, sweet passage on love. Probably written to a nice, sweet group of people, right? Wrong!

The Corinthians may have been Christ followers, but they were arrogant, divisive, gnarly Christ followers—which is why the apostle Paul had to lecture them on the topic of love. First Corinthians 13 is not meant to be nice and sweet. It's meant to be in-your-face and tail-kicking. And now that you know that little bit of historical background, open your Bible and read verses 1–8 of that passage. I'm sure you'll see the text with new eyes.

What Questions. Reading the Bible will raise all sorts of *what* questions in your mind. For example, you're reading

Psalm 1 and you come to verse 4, where the psalmist describes those who don't meditate on and follow God's Word as *chaff*. Is that bad? Depends on the answer to the question: What is chaff?

Well, *chaff* is the thin, outer husk that surrounds a kernel of wheat. And in the ancient world, farmers would thresh their wheat by beating it up into the air—preferably on a day with a strong breeze. The hard kernels of wheat would fall to the ground and be gathered up. But the thin, outer husks, the useless *chaff*, would blow away. So, if you're not spending daily time in God's Word, the psalmist is warning you that you're wasting your life. Your life is just blowing away.

Here's another *what* question from a different passage: What is a firstborn? You say, "Now that's an easy one. A firstborn is the *first* one *born* into a family." Well, your definition creates a huge theological problem for Christians. You see, the apostle Paul refers to Jesus Christ as the *firstborn* over all creation (Colossians 1:15). According to your definition, Paul would be saying that God gave birth to Christ before He created everything else. But Christians believe that Christ is the *eternal* Son of God. He had no beginning. Maybe we'd better reconsider our definition of *firstborn*.

Let me tell you what's meant by this word. Sometimes the Bible uses *firstborn* to indicate a person's prominence. In the ancient world, a firstborn son was the heir to his father's fortune. He held a place of honor in the family. He had special rights and privileges. So the expression *firstborn* came to be used as a synonym for

> SOMETIMES THE Bible uses *firstborn* to indicate a person's prominence.

most prominent one. That's why Psalm 89:27 refers to David as Israel's *firstborn* king. Now, we know that David wasn't the very first king of Israel. Saul was. But David was Israel's *greatest* king.

So when Colossians 1:15 calls Christ "the firstborn over all creation," it doesn't mean that He was the first created being, or that God gave birth to Him at some point in the past. It means that Christ reigns supreme over everything!

When Questions. Let's try a *when* question: When did the apostle Paul write the epistle of Philippians? Before I answer that question, let me tell you why it matters. The theme of Philippians is *joy.* Paul uses that word again and again and again in this New Testament letter. This is an amazing theme considering that Paul wrote Philippians *when* he was in jail! Not only that, he was in jail on trumped-up charges. I don't know about you, but I'm much more willing to listen to what a guy has to say about joy if he is joyful himself, even in the most adverse circumstances.

Here's another *when* question: When did Ruth live? In the most basic terms, that question is answered in the very first verse of the Old Testament book of Ruth. This is how Ruth 1:1 begins: "In the days when the judges ruled . . ." You say, "Big deal!" Well, let me tell you why it *was* a big deal. I referred to Ruth's story earlier in this chapter. She was the destitute young widow for whom

RUTH WAS a very godly, virtuous woman. But she didn't live in a godly, virtuous culture.

Boaz bought some property. Ruth was also a very godly, virtuous woman. But she didn't live in a godly, virtuous culture.

Ruth lived *in the days when the judges ruled*. The judges were the guys who led Israel before Israel had kings. And it was a dark era in Israel's history. In fact, the closing verse of the Old Testament book of Judges describes what that period was like with these words: "In those days Israel had no king; everyone did as he saw fit" (Judges 21:25). That's the world in which godly, virtuous Ruth lived. Have you ever complained about how hard it is to live a Christ-honoring life in a contemporary world that's irreverent, materialistic, violent, and sex-crazed? Meet Ruth—she can be a role model for you!

Just a footnote to this point about *when* questions. In *Epic*, the first book in the Bible Savvy series, I traced the storyline of the Bible from the beginning of creation (Genesis) to the eternal new heaven and new earth (Revelation). Once you learn that storyline you'll be able to place people and events in their appropriate historical settings as you come across them in your Bible reading.

When did Noah build his ark? *When* did Abraham and Sarah have a miracle son? *When* did Solomon rule over Israel? *When* did Ezekiel prophesy? *When* did Peter walk on water? *When* did Stephen get stoned to death? *When* did Timothy pastor a church? Can you place these events on a timeline? Did you know that I arranged the people just mentioned in chronological order? You would if you knew the Bible's storyline.

Where Questions. I'll just give you one *where* question: Where was Laodicea? The quick answer is that the city of Laodicea was located in a region which is part of modern-day Turkey. It was the site of a first-century church. This was one of seven churches to whom the apostle John penned letters, as recorded in Revelation 2 and 3.

John told the church at Laodicea that the risen and exalted Christ had a special message for them. The message was this (and I'll just paraphrase it for you): "Stop being spiritually lukewarm—or I'll spit you out of my mouth." That's not the sort of message that you want to hear from the risen and exalted Christ!

Here's the interesting thing about the language that Christ uses. Laodicea had a problem with its drinking water. The local river was muddy, so drinking water had to be brought in by an aqueduct. The water originated from a nice, cool spring five miles away, but by the time it traveled all the way to Laodicea it was tepid and unappetizing. One sip and you'd want to spit it out. So, because of *where* they lived, the Christians in Laodicea got Jesus' point when He warned them to stop being spiritually lukewarm.

The Bible raises a lot of *where* questions. It's extremely helpful to find out about places like the city of Jericho . . . the empire of Babylon . . . the Sea of Galilee . . . the church in Ephesus.

Why Questions. I could come up with a bazillion *why* questions to be asked as the Bible is read. But I'll give you just one example so you can understand what I'm talking about: Why did Elijah confront the false prophets of the pagan god, Baal, on Mt. Carmel? (You can read about this showdown in 1 Kings 18:16–40.)

Do you know this story? God's people had defected. Many of them had begun worshiping Baal. So God sent His prophet Elijah to duke it out with Baal's representatives. Elijah challenged them to a duel. These were his terms. Elijah said (my summary), "Meet me at the top of Mt. Carmel. I'll build an altar to my God. You build an altar to Baal. Then we'll both call upon our respective gods to send fire from heaven and consume the sacrifices on our altars. Whichever god answers is the one true God!"

Whoa! That was putting it all on the line. But *why* did

Elijah choose Mt. Carmel as the location for this heavyweight bout? Because Mt. Carmel was considered to be the dwelling place of Baal. In other words, Elijah was purposefully giving Baal home-field advantage. And that made the victory even bigger and better when Elijah's God was the only one who sent fire from heaven.

If we'll learn to ask *who, what, when, where,* and *why* questions as we read the Bible, we'll be amazed at how much more understandable and impactful God's Word becomes.

The overarching ground rule for interpreting the Bible is this: *You must understand the context.* In this chapter we covered the first of four kinds of context: the Bible's historical setting. How do we get a handle on this when reading Scripture? We *pursue the objective facts, cross the cultural rivers,* and *ask the journalistic questions.*

Sounds like work. Is it worth the effort? It is, if we want to hear God speak to us!

Study Guide
The Historical Setting

The *Study Guide* questions at the end of each chapter have been designed for your personal benefit. *All* questions can be used for personal study and, if you're part of a discussion group, for preparation for your group meeting. If you are part of a small group, you will find that the questions preceded by the group icon ( ) are especially useful for discussion. Your group leader can choose from among those questions when the group meets.

Icebreakers

Do you enjoy putting jigsaw puzzles together? Why or why not? Describe a key event or circumstance in your past that would provide others with some context for understanding who you are today.

1. What is hermeneutics? Why is it important for a proper understanding of the Bible? What is the most basic ground rule of Bible interpretation?

2. How does Christianity differ from most other major world religions when it comes to objective facts? What bearing does this have on how we interpret the Bible?

3. Have you ever traveled or lived in a foreign culture? If so, describe a few of the differences between that culture and your own.

   Why is it important to *cross the cultural rivers* when reading the Bible? (Or, what might happen if you don't cross the cultural rivers when reading the Bible?) What resource(s) will help you understand the culture of whatever Bible passage you're reading?

4. What are the five *journalistic questions* that should be asked of every Bible passage?

   For items 5–8, answer the expanded journalistic questions that are asked of each Bible text. Then you will have the opportunity to craft some journalistic questions of your own—and answer them—for a final passage.

Context

5. (icon) Read Leviticus 16; then answer the following questions:

Who was Aaron (i.e., what unique role did he play in ancient Israel and what were the responsibilities of that role)?

What was the Most Holy Place—and *what* was so special about it?

When was Aaron allowed into the Most Holy Place? What is meant by the name given to this annual day?

Where was the live goat sent and what was the significance of that destination?

Why was the Day of Atonement to be a day of rest, when no work was done? (Hint: What does this say about the contribution that God expects from people in order for them to be forgiven?)

6. Read Joshua 3.

   Who was Joshua?

   What would be significant about crossing the Jordan River at flood-stage?

   When did this event take place in the history of ancient Israel?

   Where were Joshua and God's people headed?

   Why were the priests, who were carrying the ark of the covenant, the first ones to step into the water?

7. Read Luke 15:11–32.

   Who were the three major players in Jesus' parable—and *who* did each of them represent?

What was especially distasteful about the younger son's plunge to pig level? *What* was especially meaningful about the father's gift to this son upon the boy's return?

When did Jesus tell this parable (i.e., what occasioned it)?

Where did the father see the returning son—and what does that tell you about this dad?

Why was the older brother angry? *Why* had he been missing out on the blessings of his father's house?

8. Read 2 Corinthians 8:1–15.
   Who were the Macedonian believers and how did they differ from the Corinthians?

What was Paul collecting money for?

When did Paul first raise the issue of giving toward this project with the Corinthians and what does that say about his bringing the subject up again in this letter?

Where did Paul draw the Corinthians' attention for an example of supreme generosity?

Why were the Corinthians not in a generous mood?

Now that you've gotten the hang of answering some journalistic questions, it's time for you to craft a few of your own. Create a who, what, when, where, and why question for the following passage. Then answer your questions.

9. 🫂 Read Ruth 3.

Who (somebody other than Ruth, since her profile has already been covered in this chapter) . . .

What . . .

When . . .

Where . . .

Why . . .

10. What did you learn from this exercise about the importance of understanding a Bible passage's *historical setting*?

The Literary Setting

HOW WELL DO YOU know the field of sports? Here's a little sports trivia quiz: ten questions. Lock in your answers as you go. I'll give you the correct answers at the end of the quiz so that you can see how well you did.

In which sport would you:

1. Use a mashie or niblick?
2. Stand at a silly point?
3. Dial 8?
4. Throw stones at houses?
5. Do an eggbeater?
6. Employ the O'Brien shift?
7. Go 5 hole?
8. Use a box-and-one defense?
9. Make a nutmeg pass?
10. Be penalized for a crackback?

How did you do? You can match your answers with the following key and give yourself a grade. No cheating by changing your answers as you go. (None of this, "Oh yeah, that's what I really meant to say . . .")

1. *Golf.* The irons were called mashies and niblicks before Spalding Sporting Goods started naming them by number back in the 1930s.
2. *Cricket.* The fielding position closest to the batter is called a silly point. Maybe because you would be knocked silly if the batter hit you with his bat?
3. *Baseball.* Dial 8 is baseball slang for hitting a home run. Before 1970 that was the number you had to dial from a hotel phone in order to make a long distance call.
4. *Curling.* Don't ask me to explain throwing stones at houses (although I'm told the stone is the forty-two-pound disk you slide along the ice). I have serious reservations about even considering curling a sport.
5. *Water polo.* Because it's against the rules to go underwater in this sport (and drowning is strictly off-limits), players have to kick their legs in a circular motion like eggbeaters to stay afloat.
6. *Shot put.* O'Brien was a famous shot-putter and the first guy to face the back of the circle and do a 180-degree spin before releasing the shot.
7. *Ice hockey.* There are four corners of a net to aim at when you're shooting the puck. But the fifth target is

to go for the hole right between the goalie's legs.

8. *Basketball*. This is when four players set up a zone defense while the fifth player goes man-to-man (or woman-to-woman, as the case may be) with his opponent.

9. *Soccer*. Passing or dribbling the ball between the opposing player's legs is a nutmeg. The Australians call it a "nuttie." Enough said.

10. *Football*. This is an illegal block. One blocker more than two yards laterally from the incoming defensive player goes in motion and hits him below the waist. The defensive guy doesn't see the blocker coming and risks a major injury. You can understand why it's called a crackback!

Here's the point I want to make with this trivia quiz: All the answers come from the same world—the world of athletics. We're not talking about art or science or business or food here. We're talking about sports. However, even though all these activities are in the same category—sports—they're not at all alike. In fact, they're played by very different rules. If you sack the quarterback on a football field, for example, that's a good thing. But if you sack an opposing player on a basketball court, it's a technical foul. The same field of sports—but different rules.

The Literary Genre and
Rules of Interpretation

Well, that's how it is with the Bible. You may be used to looking at the Bible as a single volume, but it's actually made up of sixty-six books. And while all of those books belong to the same Bible, each one must be read according to its own rules of interpretation. In the last chapter you learned that the rules for interpreting the Bible are called *hermeneutics* and that the mother of all rules is: *You must understand the context.*

There are four contexts to be considered. The first is the historical setting of whatever Bible passage you happen to be reading. The second context, which is the focus of this chapter, is the literary setting. The books of the Bible represent a wide variety of literary genres. Genres is just a fancy word for *kinds.* As you read the Bible, you'll come across the following genres: laws, narratives (stories), poetry, proverbs, prophecies, epistles (letters), gospels (biographies), parables . . . and more. Some Bible books are just one genre; others may have two or more genres.

Each one of these literary genres must be interpreted according to its own rules. We're going to look at six of these genres and learn two or three rules for interpreting each of them. This is not a chapter to be read once and then set on a shelf. You'll want to keep a bookmark in these pages so that you can refer to them again and again, reminding yourself of the various rules that apply to whatever genre of biblical literature you're reading at the time.

How to Interpret Laws

There are over six hundred laws in the Bible, and all of them are found in books two through five of the Old Testament (Exodus through Deuteronomy). If you read *Epic*, you covered these books as you traced the Bible's storyline from beginning to end. You might remember that the biblical laws fall into three major categories.

There are *moral* laws that help God's people of every era determine right from wrong. There are *ceremonial* laws that enabled Old Testament believers to maintain a proper relationship with God. (Many of these laws had to do with priests, sacrifices, and the temple.) And, finally, there are *civil* laws that were used to govern the nation of Israel.

As you're reading through the opening books of the Old Testament and you come across one of these laws, the first rule for correctly interpreting it is this: *Determine whether the law is moral, ceremonial, or civil.*

Why is that important? Because only the moral laws are *directly* applicable to our lives today. (I'll say a word about laws that are *indirectly* applicable in a moment.) The moral laws are timeless. That's *not* the case with the other two kinds of laws. Ceremonial laws have been fulfilled by Jesus Christ, who is now our high priest, our sacrifice for sins, and the One who makes us into a temple for the Holy Spirit. And **ONLY THE moral laws *directly* apply to our lives today. The moral laws are timeless.** civil laws, strictly speaking, were for regulating community life in ancient Israel.

Let's practice distinguishing between different kinds of laws by sampling a chapter from the book of Leviticus. You may want to turn in your Bible to Leviticus 19, since we'll be looking at a variety of laws in this chapter. First, let's look at verse 18: "Do not seek revenge or bear a grudge against one of your people, but love your neighbor as yourself. I am the Lord."

OK, which kind of law is this: moral, ceremonial, or civil? It's obviously a moral law, which means it's still in force today. It prohibits revenge-seeking and grudge-holding. Are you mad at somebody? Are you determined to give them the same bad treatment they've given you? God's law says, "Stop it! Ask God to help you love that person."

But now look at the very next verse: "Keep my decrees. Do not mate different kinds of animals. Do not plant your field with two kinds of seed. Do not wear clothing woven of two kinds of material" (v. 19).

What do you think? Which kind of law are these? Do

they sound like moral laws to you? No, they're actually ceremonial laws. Let me explain why. When we traced the Bible's storyline in *Epic*, through the *Books of the Law*, I pointed out that God chose the nation of Israel for a special purpose. They were to be a blessing to all other nations by lighting the way to the one true God. This was their mission. They were set apart for this unique purpose.

Do you recall how God helped them remember that they were set apart and different from everybody else? God gave them ceremonial laws like the ones you just read in Leviticus 19:19. Laws that commanded them to separate different kinds of animals or seeds or fabrics (i.e., just as God had separated them from other people). These laws are not for us today. It's OK to plant carrots alongside tomatoes in your vegetable garden. It's OK to wear the blouse that blends cotton and rayon. (Just make sure it goes with the rest of your outfit. You don't want to break any *fashion* laws!)

So, *the first rule for interpreting an Old Testament law is to determine whether the law is moral, ceremonial, or civil.* And, by the way, this rule will come in handy when defending God's Word against various social critics today. Gay activists, for example, will often argue: "Sure, there's an Old Testament law that prohibits homosexuality. But there's also a law that prohibits cooking a young goat in its mother's milk. C'mon! Neither one of these laws makes any sense in today's culture."

That argument stems from bad hermeneutics. It misinterprets the Bible. The Old Testament law that prohibits homosexuality is a moral law, which means it's timeless. Still applicable today. But the law that prohibits cooking a young goat in its mother's milk is ceremonial. It describes a common idolatrous ritual that was practiced by the nations surrounding Israel, which is why God commanded His Old Testament people to steer clear of it. But this is hardly a practice we have to worry about today.

Now, let me throw in one disclaimer with regard to this first rule for interpreting an Old Testament law: It won't always be obvious whether a law is moral, ceremonial, or civil. (Sorry.) We've been sampling laws from Leviticus 19. Here's one more from that chapter: "Do not cut your bodies for the dead or put tattoo marks on yourselves. I am the Lord" (v. 28).

I get asked about tattoos all the time. Does this verse apply to us today or not? Either way, it's not my intention to make you uncomfortable if you already have a tattoo. Chances are, you didn't even know about this verse before you got the tat. So, what are we to make of this Old Testament law?

Bible scholars hold two very different interpretations of this prohibition against tattoos. Some say that the tattoos in Leviticus 19:28 were part of a pagan grieving ritual in Old Testament times. That would make this a ceremonial law, prohibiting participation in this ancient pagan ritual. So it would no longer be applicable. But other Bible experts say that this law fits with a broader biblical theme: we have been made in the image of God and so we shouldn't deliberately do anything that mars our body. That would make this a moral law. It's still valid today.

Which is it: moral or ceremonial? Well, if you already have—or would like to get—a tattoo, you'll probably nonchalantly dismiss this law as ceremonial. But if you favor caution, you might want to interpret this as a moral law and stay out of tattoo parlors. (How's that for dodging the issue and remaining friends with all my readers?)

Here's *the second rule for interpreting the Bible's laws: Look for the principle behind the law.* Most moral laws are pretty straightforward. The principle is obvious. It's clear what God wants you to do—or *not* do. But sometimes the principle is buried beneath the cultural trappings of Bible times and you'll have to dig it out in order to apply it to contemporary life. Let's take another look at Leviticus 19: "When you reap the harvest of your land, do not reap to the very edges of your field or gather the gleanings of your harvest. Do not go over your vineyard a second time or pick up the grapes that have fallen. Leave them for the poor and the alien. I am the Lord your God" (vv. 9–10).

How do you apply these laws to your life if you're not a Bible-times farmer or vineyard owner? Well, you *look for the principle behind the law.* What's the principle here? God commands us to provide food for the poor. That's something every one of us can do today by dropping off canned goods at the local food pantry, or by contributing to our church's special offering for disaster relief, or by some other means.

Now, let me point out something interesting about these laws regarding food for the poor that we've just looked at. They're actually *civil* laws. They had to do with the governing of society in ancient Israel. They comprised ancient Israel's welfare system. But didn't I previously make the point that we don't have to obey the Old Testament's civil laws? Didn't I say that they're not for us today? Only the moral laws are applicable, right? Generally speaking, that's correct. But here's an interesting insight. When we discover the principle behind a law, even the civil and ceremonial laws become *indirectly* applicable to our lives.

WHEN WE discover the principle behind a law, even the civil and ceremonial laws become *indirectly* applicable to our lives.

I've just given you an example of what the principle behind a *civil* law looks like (i.e., provide food for the poor). Let me do the same thing with a *ceremonial* law. The book of Leviticus has several chapters of laws that deal with the treatment of infectious skin diseases. When you read these laws for the first time, you're liable to think, *This is gross stuff. What is it doing in the Bible? And what significance could these laws possibly have for me?*

Well, these were ceremonial laws, part of Israel's religious life. So, on the one hand, we could dismiss them as no longer applicable today. But on the other hand, there's a principle behind these laws that *is* applicable to our lives. At a deeper level, the skin disease laws are a reminder to stay away from sinful behaviors that would compromise a readiness to be used by God. God wants His people to be set apart from sin so that they're primed to carry out their special mission.

Keep that principle in mind the next time you read about skin rashes or leprosy in Leviticus. Say to yourself: "God wants me to deal with sin in my life as seriously as I'd deal with a gross or deadly disease. Then I'll be spiritually prepared to point others to Him." Get it?

So, for good biblical interpretation (hermeneutics), remember and practice the two rules for interpreting Old Testament laws: (1) Determine whether the law is moral, civil, or ceremonial; and (2) look for the principle behind the law.

How to Interpret Narratives

Narratives are stories. Over one-third of the Bible comes to us in this form. All of the Old Testament's *Books of History* (from Joshua to Esther) are collections of narratives. So are the New Testament's Gospels and book of Acts. I wonder if God teaches us through narratives because He knows that nobody can resist a good story. Young and old, educated and uneducated, Easterners and Westerners—we all love stories.

The Bible is full of engaging stories: Israel crossing the Red Sea on *terra firma*; Samson falling for a hairdresser by the name of Delilah; David taking down the giant Goliath with a slingshot; Jonah being swallowed—and later chucked up—by a giant fish; Jesus multiplying a boy's brown-bag lunch to feed thousands; Peter being sprung from jail by an angel. And none of these Bible's stories is made up. They're all true. They describe a supernatural God intervening in the lives of ordinary people.

Let me give you two rules for interpreting narratives. First, *summarize the theme (or major lesson) of the story.* Unfortunately, the Bible doesn't do this for us. At least, not explicitly. The narratives don't conclude with the words: "And so, the moral of this story is . . ." Have you ever read a story that ends like that?

I'll tell you a quick one. It's about a guy named Benny. (No, this isn't in the Bible, so don't start flipping through the pages to find it there.)

Benny was out exploring ancient ruins one day and he came across a Grecian urn. When he wiped off the urn with his handkerchief, a genie appeared. But this wasn't a nice genie offering Benny three wishes. This was a genie who was ticked off at having been disturbed. So, she put a curse on Benny. (I can't believe I'm telling you this story.) She said, "You must never shave, for on the day that you shave I'll turn *you* into an urn." So Benny never put a razor to his face.

But eventually Benny's beard got so long and straggly and itchy that he just had to shave it off. The minute he finished the job the genie appeared and—*poof*—she turned Benny into an urn. And so, the moral of this story is (can you guess?): *A Benny shaved is a Benny urned!*

OK, OK. That was pretty lame. But I want to illustrate the fact that—contrary to how Benny's story concluded—the Bible's stories rarely come right out at the end and tell us the moral, the theme, the major lesson of the story. It's our job to figure it out. And the reason that it's a good idea to try figuring it out is that this exercise keeps us from misinterpreting the *details* of the story. I've heard some pretty whacked-out interpretations that people have pulled out of Bible narratives because they've read way too much into a minor detail or two.

What is the theme of the *whole* story? Why do you think God included this story in His Book? And here's something else to keep in mind while you're

THE REAL HERO of every narrative in Scripture is *God*. Reflect on what *God* is up to in the Bible story.

trying to sum up the theme of a story. Remember that the real hero of every narrative in Scripture is *God*. So reflect on what *God* is up to in the Bible stories you read.

For example, Genesis 39 relates the story of Joseph and Mrs. Potiphar. Mrs. Potiphar was the wife of Joseph's boss and she had the hots for Joey. She tried to seduce him. One day she grabbed Joey by his coat and said: "Come to bed with me!" (I'm not making any of this up. It's all in Genesis 39, as well as in the popular musical *Joseph and the Amazing Technicolor Dreamcoat*. Go, Donny Osmond!) Do you know what Joseph did? He left his coat in Mrs. Potiphar's hand and ran out of the house.

An obvious theme (major lesson) that we could take away from this story is that we should flee (i.e., run away as far and fast as possible) from sexual temptations. That works. But there's a bigger theme behind *that* theme. Joseph wasn't the only hero in the story. What about *God*? If you go back and read Genesis 39 in context, you'll discover that God was watching over Joseph's life every step of the way because He had big plans for the young man. Joseph eventually became Pharaoh's second-in-command and was given the job of overseeing a famine-relief program. Among those he was able to feed were his very own brothers, thus keeping his family alive. And hundreds of years later that family line produced a descendant named *Jesus*!

That's the really big theme behind the Joseph and Mrs. Potiphar story. If God had not rescued Joseph from this lady's sexual advances, Jesus' ancestors would have starved to death. There would have been no family line stretching to Jesus. I've heard a friend of mine, who's a brilliant Bible scholar, put it this way: "*God* enabled Joseph to keep his pants zipped up so that *God* could later give the world a Savior." A bit crudely put? Perhaps. But you won't forget *that* theme.

Here's a second rule for interpreting narratives: *Decide what's descriptive and what's prescriptive.* Some details of Bible stories are merely *descriptive.* They give us the particulars of what happened. They are not meant to be a pattern for our lives. But other details of Bible stories are *prescriptive.* God is indeed saying to us readers today, "This is how I want you to respond in similar situations."

How can we tell the difference between what is *descriptive* and what is *prescriptive*? Very simply, the *prescriptive* parts of a story will always be backed up by non-narrative, directive passages in other parts of the Bible. Let me illustrate what I'm talking about with a couple of Bible stories. I'll go back to the Joseph and Mrs. Potiphar story for my first example. Was Joseph's running away from sexual temptation *descriptive* or *prescriptive*? In other words, are we being told something that's just part of *that* particular story (*descriptive*) or is God saying to us: "I want you to do the same thing that Joseph did when you're faced with sexual temptation" (*prescriptive*)?

I think Joseph's behavior is *prescriptive*. Why do I say that? Because there are a number of non-narrative, directive passages in the Bible where we're told to run away from sexual temptation. Proverbs 5:8 cautions guys to keep their distance from tempting women. The apostle Paul warns Timothy to "flee the evil desires of youth" (2 Timothy 2:22). So Joseph's 100-yard dash in the opposite direction of sexual allurement is *prescriptive* for all of us.

> **JOSEPH'S 100-yard dash from sexual allurement is *prescriptive* for all of us.**

Let's try another story—the story of the Holy Spirit's outpouring on first-century believers (Acts 2). This event takes place fifty days after Jesus' resurrection and return to heaven. The disciples are waiting in Jerusalem for the Holy Spirit, whom Jesus had promised to send them. Suddenly, the Spirit shows up and fills them and they begin to speak in different languages (literally, *other tongues*). Is this experience of tongues *descriptive* or *prescriptive*?

Some Christ followers (usually my charismatic or Pentecostal brothers and sisters) say: "It's prescriptive. We should all speak in tongues, once we've put our trust in Jesus and He's filled us with the Holy Spirit." But wait a minute! The Acts 2 account also says that flames of fire appeared over the heads of those that the Holy Spirit filled. Should we also expect flames of fire over *our* heads? (I don't know too many people who believe *that*!)

No, I think that this is a *descriptive* passage. This is what happened to Jesus' original followers. But it's not *prescriptive*. There are no non-narrative Scripture passages telling us that we *must* speak in tongues as a sign of the Holy Spirit's filling. That doesn't mean that I don't believe in the filling of the Spirit or the *gift* of tongues. I do! The apostle Paul talks about this gift at length in 1 Corinthians 12 and 14. Some Christ followers obviously have it. But the gift of tongues is never spoken of in the Bible as a *must* for every believer today.

So two rules prevail for interpreting narratives: 1. Summarize the theme (or major lesson) of the story. 2. Decide what's descriptive and what's prescriptive.

How to Interpret Poetry

I owe my marriage to poetry. When I was a junior in college, I wrote Sue a proposal poem and set it to music. Then I sang it to her, accompanied by my guitar, under a shady tree on campus.

Between the second and third verse of the song, I pulled out a ring box and handed it to Sue. By the time I was done with verse three and the chorus, she was mine. She didn't stand a chance against my poetry. Poetry is powerful stuff!

Poetry makes up over one-third of the Bible. There are entire Bible books that come to us in this form: Job, Psalms, Proverbs, Song of Songs, and Lamentations. Many of the *Books of Prophecy* are also filled with poetry.

Here are three quick rules for interpreting Bible poetry. I mostly have in mind here the poetry in the book of Psalms. In fact, if your Bible is still within reach, you may want to turn to Psalm 51. We'll be applying rule one to the opening verses of this psalm:

> Have mercy on me, O God,
>   according to your unfailing love;
>   according to your great compassion
> blot out my transgressions.
> Wash away all my iniquity
> and cleanse me from my sin.
>
> For I know my transgressions,
> and my sin is always before me. (vv. 1–3)

Rule number one is to *note the historical background.* Do you know the historical background of this poem of confession? (In the case of this psalm, the header before verse 1 gives it away.) King David had an affair. He got his neighbor Bathsheba pregnant. And Bathsheba's husband was one of David's most loyal soldiers, a guy named Uriah. Do you recall how David dealt with his sin? Initially, he tried to cover it up. He instructed one of his generals to abandon Uriah in battle. After Uriah was killed, David married the widow, which made it appear as if Bathsheba's pregnancy was on the up and up.

All his tracks covered, right? Not from God's eyes. God sent a prophet, Nathan, to deal with David. It was a pretty intense toe-to-toe confrontation. (You can read about it in 2 Samuel 12:1–13.) But David finally broke and Psalm 51 is his prayer of confession. This poem marks the beginning of a long road back. Just knowing the historical background to Psalm 51 increases your understanding of the poem immeasurably, doesn't it?

There's a historical background to be discovered for many of the psalms. There's also a *historical background* to Song of Songs (King Solomon's love poem), the poetic messages of the prophets, and to most of the poetry you'll find in the Bible. Check it out.

Here's a second rule for interpreting Bible poetry: *Unpack the figurative language.* The language of poetry is colorful and highly emotional. Many of the words and expressions are meant to be understood *figuratively*, not *literally*. The poet is painting word pictures.

Let's go back to David's confession of sin in Psalm 51. Look at verse 7: "Cleanse me with hyssop, and I will be clean; wash me, and I will be whiter than snow." What does David mean by that phrase, *cleanse me with hyssop*? Here's the scoop: hyssop is a tall reedy plant, with a head of bushy leaves. It looks like a giant paintbrush. And that's one of the most notable ways it was used in Bible times.

Do you remember the story of Israel's deliverance from slavery in Egypt? Pharaoh needed some convincing to let God's people go. So, God sent an angel of death to slay all the firstborn humans and animals in Egypt. But God's people were spared, having identified their homes by covering the doorframes with the blood of a sacrificed goat or sheep. The angel of death passed over these places (which is why this event has been celebrated ever since as *Passover*). What role did hyssop play in this story?

HYSSOP BECAME associated with God's mercy—the turning aside of God's judgment.

Hyssop was the giant paintbrush that God's people used to spread the blood on their doorframes. As a result, hyssop became associated with God's mercy—the turning aside of God's judgment.

Now do you see the tremendous significance behind David's prayer? "Cleanse me with hyssop, and I will be clean." David was pleading with God for forgiveness based upon the shed blood of sacrifices. We voice a similar prayer today when we ask God to forgive us because of Christ's death on the cross. If we've put our trust in Jesus Christ, His blood has been applied to our lives, causing God's judgment to pass over us. (Interestingly, the only mention of hyssop in the New Testament is when a sponge full of wine vinegar was extended to Jesus as He hung upon the cross.)

You'll find a lot of *figurative* language in the Psalms whose meaning will have to be unpacked. In the familiar Psalm 23, as another example, David describes God as his shepherd and himself as a sheep that longs to "lie down in green pastures" and be led "beside quiet waters" (v. 2). Doesn't that sound refreshing to you? Sounds good to me! In Psalm 116, David cries out: "The cords of death entangled me" (v. 3). That, too, is poetic language. David wasn't *literally* tied up with ropes. He just felt like his troubles were wrapped around him and pulling him into a dark pit. Ever felt that way?

We all express ourselves, from time to time, with *figurative language*. When you exclaim, "I could strangle that guy who cut me off in traffic," I hope you're not *literally* contemplating murder. When you say, "I bombed that chemistry test," I'm guessing you didn't bring explosives to school. Bible poetry uses colorful, highly emotional *figurative* language. Sometimes it's dark. Sometimes it's rich and inspiring. Savor it. Meditate on what it's saying.

One final rule for interpreting Bible poetry: *Look for truths about God*. This is especially applicable when you're reading Psalms. In the Bible as a whole, we find over 250 names and titles and attributes that describe God. The book of Psalms is a gold mine for those descriptors. You can't read a single psalm without learning a ton about God.

BIBLE POETRY uses highly emotional figurative language. Sometimes it's dark. Sometimes it's rich and inspiring.

So, try reading the psalms out loud and stopping every time you come across one of God's names, titles, or attributes. Take a moment to praise God for what that particular word or expression tells you about Him. In fact, you could do this with every bit of poetry that you come across in Scripture—even the passages where the prophets are denouncing other nations for their brutality against Israel. Note what those poems teach you about *God*, then praise and worship Him along those lines.

So here are the three rules for interpreting Bible poetry: 1. Note the historical background. 2. Unpack the figurative language. 3. Look for truths about God.

How to Interpret the Proverbs

When you're reading the Old Testament book of Proverbs, there is just one key rule to follow: *Remember that proverbs are not absolute promises but statements about how life usually works.* Why don't you turn in your Bible to the book of Proverbs and we'll take a look at several examples of what I'm talking about.

> Honor the Lord with your wealth,
> with the firstfruits of all your crops;
> then your barns will be filled to overflowing,
> and your vats will brim over with new wine.
> (Proverbs 3:9–10)

This proverb encourages us to tithe—to give God the *firstfruits* (the first 10 percent) of our income. If we'll do this, God will see to it that we prosper. Is this an *absolute promise?* Is tithing a sure way to grow rich? Will people who give to the Lord never lose their jobs? No. But, generally speaking (*generally speaking* is the operative phrase), tithers will experience God's blessing on their lives in a variety of ways (e.g., answers to prayer, intimacy with God, freedom from worry.).

Now consider this verse from Proverbs 15:1: "A gentle answer turns away wrath, but a harsh word stirs up anger." If we put this proverb into practice, will 100 percent of the people who argue with us calm down? No. Some of them will still lose it. But, generally speaking, a gentle answer is a good way for us to resolve a conflict.

Here's the advice of Proverbs 22:6: "Train a child in the

way he should go, and when he is old he will not turn from it."
So if we raise our kids in a godly home environment, they'll
never rebel, right? Well, I've known some great parents whose
kids wandered far from God and some of those kids never
came back. If this proverb is an *absolute promise*, then those
parents must have somehow messed up in their child-raising.
Because if they hadn't messed up, their kids would still be
walking with God. No! This is not an absolute promise. It's
a statement of how life usually works. If we'll invest time and
effort in the spiritual training of our children, moms and dads,
most often it will pay off in their lives.

Next, let's look at two verses from Proverbs 26 that, at
first glance, may seem to contradict each other. Beginning
with verse 4, we're told how to answer a fool: "Do not answer
a fool according to his folly, or you will be like him yourself."
If we interpreted this verse as an *absolute*, we would never
ever respond to someone who's acting like a jerk toward us.
We would always just ignore him, refusing to stoop to his
level.

However, look at the very next verse of Proverbs 26: "Answer a fool according to his folly, or he will be wise in his own
eyes" (v. 5).

What is this verse saying? Evidently, it's sometimes wise
to *ignore* a fool (v. 4) and it's sometimes wise to *correct* a fool
(v. 5). If either of these proverbs were applied in an *absolute*

manner, it would cancel out the other one. No. They are both examples of *how life usually works* and the reader should apply whichever one seems most appropriate in a given situation.

One footnote to this rule for interpreting proverbs: Always keep in mind that the power for putting the proverbs into practice has to come from God. These are not just *self-*help principles. Proverbs isn't like a *self-*improvement book that you order through Amazon.com. You can't do it by yourself. A relationship with God is required if you want to benefit from the Bible's proverbs. The Holy Spirit must be living in your life.

Years ago, my dad taught a Bible study for businessmen in Chicago's Loop. He used Proverbs as his curriculum because there's a lot of good counsel regarding wise business practices in this Old Testament book. Some of the guys who attended his Bible study weren't Christ followers. They were just attracted to the group by the helpful content of the study. So, it was important for my dad to regularly remind them: "You won't really benefit from this stuff until you put your trust in Christ and begin a relationship with God. Then God's Spirit will empower you to live wisely."

Here's the single rule for interpreting proverbs: Remember that proverbs are not absolute promises but statements about how life usually works.

Interpreting Prophecy

As I pointed out when tracing the Bible's storyline in *Epic*, there are more Bible books that fall into the *prophecy* category than any other. Sixteen of the Old Testament books are prophetic, written by four major prophets (so called because they wrote *longer* books) and twelve minor prophets (so called because they wrote *shorter* books). Only one book of the New Testament, Revelation, is predominantly prophetic. But there are scores of prophetic passages in other New Testament books as well.

Please remember that much of what you read in the Old Testament *Books of Prophecy* has very little to do with predicting the future. The vast majority of what the prophets have written simply confronts sin in people's lives and urges them (and us) to turn back to God. The confronting sin portions of Bible prophecy are fairly straightforward, so I won't take any time to explain how to interpret those passages.

But let me give you a couple of rules for interpreting prophecies that have to do with predicting the future. First, *distinguish between what has already been fulfilled and what—as yet—is unfulfilled.* Let's suppose that an Old Testament prophet told God's people in 750 BC about something that would happen in the future. And let's suppose that what he predicted actually came true 150 years later. Question: Would the fulfillment of that prediction be in *our* future? (This is not a trick question.)

No. The fulfillment of that prediction would be history for us. It would have come true in 600 BC (if we've done the math correctly). Are you following this? Why is this an important point? Because we often assume—wrongly—that Old Testament prophecies about future events have to do with events in *our* future. We're looking *ahead* to see their fulfillment. But we should look *behind* because many of these predictive prophecies have to do with events that have already taken place.

This means that it's important to know our Bible history. Knowing Bible history will enable you—when you're reading in Isaiah or Daniel or Amos—to distinguish between what has already been fulfilled and what—as yet—is unfulfilled. Where do you go to learn about Bible history? By now you probably know my standard answer to that question. Pick up *a study Bible* (I recommend the NIV) and read the Old Testament *Books of Prophecy* with the aid of all those helpful historical introductions and footnotes.

KNOW BIBLE history to distinguish between what has been fulfilled and what—as yet—is unfulfilled.

Here's a second rule for interpreting prophecy: *Distinguish between figurative descriptions and literal descriptions.* This rule is especially important to keep in mind when you're reading the New Testament book of Revelation.

Will the Antichrist—that despotic ruler who takes over the world in the end times—*literally* have ten crowned horns on seven heads, as described in Revelation 13:1? I don't think so. As I explained when I covered the Revelation portion of the Bible's storyline in *Epic*, this is a *figurative* description of a leader who will have a vast amount of political and military power.

Will the capital city of the eternal new earth *literally* measure 12,000 stadia long (roughly 1,400 miles) by 12,000 stadia wide by 12,000 stadia high, as described in Revelation 21:16? I doubt it. I think that's a *figurative* description of a city, which is cube-shaped because a cube represents the presence of a triune God (Father, Son, and Spirit).

Bible prophecy teachers, who speak on Christian radio stations and write bestselling books, are frequently guilty of providing us with way too many *literal* details that they've drawn out of very *figurative* prophetic passages. Be careful of these experts! Most often they don't even agree with each other in their interpretations.

Again, distinguish between figurative descriptions and literal descriptions. Granted, sometimes you won't be able to resolve whether a description is figurative or literal. Let me give you the biggest example of this dilemma in the Bible. There are many Old Testament prophetic passages that talk about a future day when God will restore the nation of Israel to a place of prominence in the world. Now, there are two *huge* schools of interpretation with regard to these prophecies.

One school says that they're to be taken quite literally. In fact, the re-creation of Israel as a nation-state in 1948 may be the beginning of the fulfillment of these prophecies, so say the Bible scholars who belong to the *literal* school.

But another school of Bible scholars interprets these prophecies about Israel figuratively. Its members point out that the New Testament speaks of Christ followers as "the Israel of God" (Galatians 6:16), heirs of the promises that were made to Abraham (Galatians 3:14, 29). So all the Old Testament prophecies that have to do with Israel's future should now be applied to the church, the corporate body of Christ followers.

This *figurative* school of interpretation teaches, for example, that chapters 40 through 48 of Ezekiel, describing a future temple in Jerusalem, are not about an actual building that's eventually going to replace the current Dome of the Rock. Ezekiel was describing a group of people who would become a temple for the Holy Spirit. Who would that be? Us! Followers of Jesus Christ.

I'm not going to resolve the debate between these two schools in this book. I'm just trying to make you aware of the challenge and the need to distinguish between figurative descriptions and literal descriptions when interpreting Bible prophecy. So hold your conclusions humbly and loosely.

What are the two rules for interpreting prophecy? First, distinguish between what has already been fulfilled and what—as yet—is unfulfilled. Second, distinguish between figurative descriptions and literal descriptions.

Interpreting the Epistles

There are twenty-one epistles in the New Testament, thirteen of them written by the apostle Paul. Many readers find these letters to be among the easiest portions of the Bible to interpret and apply because their teaching is so direct and because they're written to fellow Christ followers (not citizens of ancient Israel). We'll still need a few rules, however, to ensure accuracy when interpreting epistles.

The first rule is a drum that I keep beating and beating: *Discover the historical background.* This applies to whatever epistle you're reading. (And should I say *consult your study Bible* one more time?) Bible scholars sometimes refer to the New Testament epistles as *occasional* letters because the writing of each of them was *occasioned* by certain circumstances. It helps if you know those circumstances. Otherwise, it will be difficult to interpret the epistles.

Imagine this: You take a letter out of your mailbox and,

without looking at the front of the envelope, you tear it open and begin to read it. Unfortunately, the mailman has delivered the letter to the wrong house. It belongs to your neighbor. It's been written by a friend of his, who immediately launches into a lengthy discussion of circumstances that you know nothing about.

What are your chances of accurately interpreting that letter? (Not that you *should* be interpreting the letter, since you're reading your neighbor's private correspondence. Put it back in the envelope.)

Here's an example from a New Testament epistle that will illustrate the importance of *discovering the historical background* of whatever passage you're reading. Let's say that you pick up the apostle Paul's first letter to the Corinthians and you begin reading at chapter seven. In the opening verse of this chapter, Paul writes: "It is good for a man not to marry" (1 Corinthians 7:1).

So Paul is down on marriage, eh? He must be a big fan of celibacy. Whoa! Not so fast! This is the same Paul who wrote to the Ephesians that marriage is a model of Christ's relationship with His followers (i.e., the church). That doesn't sound like someone who wants to discourage people from getting married, does it?

Seems like a real disconnect, right? Well, knowing the historical background to Paul's first letter to the Corinthians helps make sense of what's happening. The letter's recipients were falling prey to all sorts of sexual immorality. People in the church were even rationalizing liaisons with prostitutes. One church member was having an affair with his stepmother—and nobody seemed to think it was a big deal.

In that sort of an environment, it was appropriate for Paul to raise a yellow flag for those who were considering marriage. The Corinthians needed some basic teaching on God's standards for sexual expression before they sent out any wedding invitations. That's why Paul wrote to them, "It is good for a man not to marry."

The second rule for interpreting the epistles: *Read the epistle in its entirety before trying to interpret parts of it.* Isn't that how we usually read a letter that somebody has sent to us?

When I was a college student, I fell in love with Sue. And shortly thereafter I took a job in Europe for the summer. We'd write each other several times a week, four to five pages at a shot. (No such thing as international cell phones or Skype back then! This was just a few years after the Pony Express quit operating.)

Whenever I got a letter from Sue that summer, I would immediately stick it in the back pocket of my jeans, and pull it out in fifteen-minute intervals to read it. The first time I pulled it out, I would randomly read the fifth paragraph on the third page. Then I'd put the letter back in my pocket.

Later, I'd pull it out again and choose the second paragraph on the first page. Put the letter away. Pull it out later and read the seventh paragraph on the fifth page.

Are you buying my story? Of course not! Nobody reads a letter like that. The first time through you read it from beginning to end. Now, you may go back later many times to a favorite paragraph or two—but only after you've read that letter in its entirety.

That's how to read a New Testament epistle: *not* in bits and pieces (at least, not initially) but *in its entirety.* Then you can go back and take it apart, a paragraph or a chapter at a time.

Here's the third rule in interpreting a portion of a Bible epistle: *Summarize the main point of the passage.* I've already mentioned this rule for other types of Bible literature, so I won't elaborate on it here. Let me note again, however, that the reason people often misinterpret the Bible is because they tend to pull out minor details and then blow them out of proportion. The easiest way to avoid making this mistake is to evaluate each passage you read as a whole.

You've probably heard the saying: *I can't see the forest for the trees.* This can happen to you when you're reading the

READ A NEW Testament epistle not in bits and pieces (at least, not initially) but *in its entirety*.

Bible. You can stand with your nose so close to the individual trees that you miss the overall forest. Step back from specific verses and *summarize the main point of the* (entire) *passage.*

Once more, the three rules for interpreting epistles are: 1. Discover the historical background. 2. Read the epistle in its entirety before trying to interpret its parts. 3. Summarize the main point of the passage.

Put It All Together

Are you ever going to remember all the rules that were spelled out in this chapter? Not right away. But if you'll put a bookmark in these pages, pull out the rules each time you begin reading a new book of the Bible, and review the two or three rules that apply to that book's *literary* setting, over time you will gain a greater and greater understanding of God's Word.

It's kind of like taking golf lessons. The instructor adjusts your stance, messes with your grip, reminds you to keep your head down, shows you how to address the ball, explains the importance of a smooth backswing, warns you to follow through, follow through, follow through. And then he says: "OK, let's see you put it all together."

Seems impossible!! And all those instructions are just for your tee shot. What about your irons in the fairway? (Your mashie and your niblick?) What about your chip shots to the green? What about your putting?

You'll catch on—if you'll just stick with it. And once you catch on, golfing will be a joy (well, sometimes). Let me tell you, there's no greater joy than learning to skillfully interpret God's Holy Word so that the Bible begins to transform your life.

To watch Jim's midpoint comments about Context, scan this QR code with your smartphone or go to www.biblesavvy.com/video/#context2.

Study Guide
The Literary Setting

Icebreaker

What genre of literature do you enjoy the most—and why?

1. Although baseball, football, and basketball all come from the world of sports, they are played by very different rules. What does this analogy teach us about interpreting the Bible?

2. Why is it bad hermeneutics to dismiss the Old Testament law that prohibits homosexuality on the basis that some other laws are obviously obsolete?

3. Read the fourth commandment in Exodus 20:8–10. This is a difficult law to categorize because it seems to qualify as two different kinds of law. Which two? (Pick from *moral*, *ceremonial*, and *civil*.) Explain your answer. (Romans 4:5 may help you identify one of the categories.)

(icon) What principle(s) do you see behind this law (i.e., how is it applicable today)?

4. Read the brief story in Matthew 8:5–13. What is the overall theme of this narrative? Which elements of the story seem to be *descriptive* and which ones are *prescriptive*?

5. Many of David's psalms praise God for delivering him from his enemies. What are some of the probable backstories to these psalms of deliverance? (If you're unfamiliar with the Old Testament, take a look at 1 Samuel 17:32–50, 1 Samuel 18:6–11, and 2 Samuel 15:1–14.)

(icon) How does knowing the backstories to David's psalms of deliverance help you apply these psalms to your own life?

6. Isaiah 55:1–3 is an example of the poetry that can be found in the *Books of Prophecy.* Explain the figurative language in these verses. (What are the *wine, milk,* and *bread* that Isaiah is referring to?) How does Isaiah's poetry here make his message more poignant?

What do you learn about God from this brief snippet of poetry?

7. What's the single rule for understanding proverbs? What danger will you run into if you fail to heed this rule?

How would this rule impact your understanding of Proverbs 16:3's application to your life?

8. Why is it important to know Bible *history* when interpreting prophecies about *future* events?

9. (👥👥👥) What are the two different ways to read all the prophetic passages about the future restoration of the nation of Israel?

10. Find out the occasions (purposes) that prompted Paul to write the following epistles. You will need a study Bible to locate this information

    Romans

    1 Corinthians

    Galatians

    Philippians

    1 Thessalonians

    Philemon

11. How might you retain the rules you learned in this chapter for future use as you read the Bible?

{ 3 }
The Theological Setting

YEARS AGO, SUE AND I were visiting my parents in the town where I grew up. I'd heard about a new church in town, so on Sunday I suggested to Sue that we check it out. It was only about a mile from my parents' home and a balmy summer day, so we decided to walk. When we got there we discovered that the church was meeting in a converted warehouse—which we thought was pretty cool!

There were only thirty to forty people in attendance, mostly young like us, and everybody seemed to know each other. The worship band was decent, kicking off the first part of the service.

And then the pastor got up to preach. His text was from Exodus 28. Before I ask *you* to read it, let me give you some background to the passage. God has just instructed His people, as they're traveling from Egypt to the Promised Land, on how to build a large tentlike tabernacle for the purpose of worship. Now God turns to the subject of designing priestly garments for Aaron. Aaron was Moses' brother and the guy who was going to officiate at the tabernacle.

Here's the text:

Make the robe of the ephod entirely of blue cloth, with an opening for the head in its center. There shall be a woven edge like a collar around this opening, so that it will not tear. Make pomegranates of blue, purple and scarlet yarn around the hem of the robe, with gold bells between them. The gold bells and the pomegranates are to alternate around the hem of the robe. Aaron must wear it when he ministers. The sound of the bells will be heard when he enters the Holy Place before the Lord and when he comes out, so that he will not die. (Exodus 28:31–35)

When the pastor finished reading this text, I wondered: *Where's he going to go with this? And how could he possibly draw any meaning from this passage for our lives?* I didn't have to wonder for long. The pastor immediately zeroed in on the gold bells and the pomegranates that adorned the hem of Aaron's robe. (Buckle up. You're about to go for a ride.) Beginning with the pomegranates, he made the observation that these are a type of fruit. (Uh-huh.) And elsewhere in the Bible, he pointed out, the apostle Paul talks about godly character as the *fruit* of God's Spirit, which consists of "love, joy, peace, patience, kindness, goodness, faithfulness, gentleness and self-control" (Galatians 5:22–23).

The pastor said that our lives should be marked by this sort of fruit. I thought to myself: *I understand what Galatians 5:22–23 says about the fruit of the Spirit—but I'm still not sure what that has to do with the pomegranates on Aaron's robe in Exodus 28.* But the pastor wasn't finished. He turned from the pomegranates to the golden bells. He said that the golden bells represented the *gifts* of the Spirit "because bells are something that we give each other as gifts." This was news to me. I'd never given anybody a bell as a gift in my entire life.

By now the pastor had picked up a head of steam, and he was really getting into his sermon. He said that of all the gifts or special abilities that God's Spirit gives us, the most important one is tongues—that supernatural enablement to speak in an unknown language. The pastor spent the better part of the next hour (yes, *hour*) telling us why this gift was a *must* for every Christ follower. And then he closed by asking us to bow our heads in prayer. While our heads were bowed, he invited us to lift a hand in the air if we wanted to signal a desire for the gift of tongues.

He repeated the invitation again and again . . . and again. The band began to play softly. I was quietly hoping that some poor soul would lift his hand, so the pastor would wrap things up. And that's when it dawned on me: *We're the only outsiders in this group. He's waiting for Sue and me to lift our hands.* I suddenly felt like there was a huge bull's-eye painted on my chest. At that point, I leaned over to Sue and whispered: "We're outta here!" And with that, we slinked out of our seats, burst out the back door of the place, and didn't stop running for about three blocks—because we were sure they were gonna come after us!

Question: What's to keep people from reading whatever they want into the Bible? What's to keep them from making the Bible say whatever they want it to say (even about pomegranates and bells)? There must be some rules to follow in order to interpret the Bible correctly. There are! These rules are called hermeneutics, and they're founded on the major premise: *You must understand the context.*

> WHAT'S to keep people from reading whatever they want into the Bible?

There are four kinds of context to consider when reading a passage from the Bible. So far, we have considered two of those contexts—the Bible's *historical* and *literary* settings. We are now ready to take a look, thirdly, at the Bible's *theological* setting. Now, don't let the word *theological* scare you off. Theology has to do with the study of various themes that we find in Scripture. I will cover three aspects of what it means to consider the Bible's theological context in the following pages.

The Principle (and Its Application)

There's a very important principle to consider when looking at a Bible passage from a theological perspective. Here it is: *The Bible must always agree with itself because it all comes from the same Mind.* Whose mind is that? *God's* mind! Take a look at a couple of key Scripture verses that back up this truth (they are well worth memorizing):

All Scripture is God-breathed and is useful for teaching, rebuking, correcting and training in righteousness. (2 Timothy 3:16)

For prophecy never had its origin in the will of man, but men spoke from God as they were carried along by the Holy Spirit. (2 Peter 1:21)

These two verses focus on the fact that *God* is the ultimate author of the Bible. There may have been many human authors responsible for the writing itself—but they were writing down exactly what *God* wanted to say.

Now, this is an important point to make, because in the last two chapters we've focused on the *human* authors of Scripture, not the *divine* author. And that focus has tended to highlight the Bible's diversity. That diversity is seen, first of all, in the unique historical setting (recall chapter 1) of each human author. As I point out in *Foundation* (the second book in the Bible Savvy series), forty different human authors contributed to the Bible, writing at different times over a 1,500-year period, on three different continents, in three different languages. That's diversity! And when these human authors put pen to parchment, they expressed themselves through diverse literary settings (chapter 2), including laws, narratives, poetry, and prophecy.

But now as we come to the Bible's theological setting, we move from an emphasis on *diversity* to an emphasis on *unity*—because we move from a focus on the Bible's *many* human authors to a focus on the Bible's *one*, ultimate Author: God. This is the basis of the principle for interpreting the Bible with theological accuracy: *The Bible must agree with itself because it all comes from the same Mind.*

Maybe an analogy would be instructive here. I love to read mysteries. And my favorite kind of mystery writer is one who lays out several threads of storyline before beginning to weave them together. So, in the first chapter of the book, we're introduced to a few characters and the circumstances of their lives. But as we begin to read chapter two, there may be no mention of these original characters. Instead, we may be introduced to some entirely new people and some entirely new circumstances. It's almost as if we're beginning to read an entirely new book.

However, we're certain that as we continue to read, all

these different characters and their different circumstances are going to fit together, right? How can we be so sure of that? Because we know that the same author is behind the entire story. So, if we read something in one part of the book that seems to conflict with something in another part of the book, we can rest assured that it will all jibe . . . eventually. The apparent conflict will disappear.

What does this have to do with interpreting the Bible? Recall the main principle behind our consideration of the Bible's theological setting: *The Bible must always agree with itself because it all comes from the same Mind*. God is not going to disagree with Himself! What He says in one portion of His Word will not be out of sync with what He says in other portions.

That's why the best way to check if your interpretation of a Bible passage is correct is to compare that interpretation with what the rest of the Bible teaches on the same subject. Are there supporting passages that back up what you think you're seeing in a particular text?

This leads to the critical application of the theological principle that I've been driving home: *The best tool for interpreting the Bible is the Bible.* If the Bible must always agree with itself (the principle), then we should constantly be comparing our understanding of specific texts with what the Bible teaches elsewhere (the application).

This, by the way, is why the leaders of the church's

Reformation in the sixteenth century put such an emphasis on getting people into the Bible. At the time, the popular notion was that only those in the church's hierarchy (priests and theologians) could accurately interpret God's Word. So people were discouraged from trying to read the Bible on their own. If they did, it was argued, they were bound to misunderstand it. "Baloney!" objected the Reformers. (Only they said "Baloney!" in Latin). Their objection was captured in a rallying cry: "*Sola Scriptura!*" ("The Bible alone!"), which is just another way of saying: The Bible itself can keep readers from misinterpreting the Bible.

THE BIBLE itself can keep readers from misinterpreting the Bible.

It's the best tool we have for understanding God's Word.

Now, before I move on to some examples of how to use the Bible to interpret the Bible, let me add a note of clarification to the basic principle that *the Bible must always agree with itself because it all comes from the same Mind.* Sometimes that agreement is not apparent. And that's frequently due to what theologians refer to as *progressive revelation.*

What do Bible scholars mean by *progressive revelation?* Well, there are many things that God reveals to us in Scripture *over time.* In other words, the earlier writings in the Bible may introduce a concept to us that isn't further developed until later writings. So, if we compare this concept in the Bible's earlier writings with the same concept in the later writings, it may seem as if the Bible *disagrees* with itself. But it's not disagreement—it's development. It's *progressive revelation*.

Let me give you a couple of quick illustrations of *progressive revelation*. The first illustration has to do with the Bible's major storyline. If you read *Epic*, you hopefully can recall the single word that sums up that storyline: *redemption*. From the beginning of time, people have gotten themselves into trouble with a Holy God because of their sin. Fortunately, God has a plan for redeeming us from the penalty and the power of our sin. And that plan revolves around a Savior.

Now, when that Savior is first introduced to us in the third chapter of the Bible, the introduction is very cryptic. All that we're told is that one day a descendant of Adam and Eve (i.e., a human being) will crush Satan—but in the process of doing so, he will be severely wounded (Genesis 3:15). That's a foreshadowing of Jesus Christ and His death upon the cross, but we don't get all that information in Genesis.

However, if we keep reading the Bible, we learn some additional things about the coming Savior. We learn that He's going to come from the line of Abraham, the people of Israel, and yet He will be a blessing to the entire world (Genesis 12). Later we learn that He will eventually be a great king like David, whose reign will last forever and ever (2 Samuel 7). Still later we learn this Savior will die a violent death—but in doing so, He will pay the penalty for people's sins (Isaiah 53).

And then we come to the New Testament. The opening four books—the Gospels—describe the actual arrival of this Savior. His name is Jesus Christ. He does miracles. He dies on a cross. He rises from the dead. Amazing events—but their full significance is not explained in the Gospels. It's not until we get to the New Testament epistles that Paul and a few other apostles tease out what was accomplished by the life, death, and resurrection of Jesus—and how it applies to our lives. And it's not until the very last book of the New Testament, Revelation, that we get a riveting picture of Christ's future reign over an eternal kingdom.

What's the point of my brief Bible survey here? To demonstrate that God sometimes reveals things to us in His Word a little bit at a time. This is *progressive revelation.* So, when you're using the Bible to interpret the Bible—keep that in mind. Don't assume that one part of the Bible is at odds with another part of the Bible, when it may just be a case of God gradually unfolding some truth to us.

> **GOD SOMETIMES reveals things to us in His Word a little bit at a time.**

Let me give you another, far less grand illustration of *progressive revelation.* It has to do with monogamy: one man married to one woman. This is God's design for every marriage, right? Well, Kody Brown doesn't think so. Kody has his own TV reality show called *Sister Wives*. He's a fundamentalist Mormon who is married to four women.[1] But when I say *fundamentalist Mormon*, don't think of a guy in bib overalls, living in a cabin in northern Utah. Kody is a forty-one-year-old ad salesman, sporting feathered hair and a goatee, who drives a Lexus two-seater sports car.[2] And his latest wife is fairly good looking. (Not that I noticed.)

Where does Kody get the bizarre notion that it's OK with God to be married to four women at one time? He probably thinks he gets it from the Bible. So let me quickly review what the Bible has to say about monogamy. For starters, it seems this is God's original plan for marriage, since Genesis 2:24 says that "a man will leave his father and mother and be united to his wife, and they will become one flesh." That's *one* man and *one* woman becoming *one* flesh—a not-too-subtle endorsement of monogamy.

However, it wasn't long after Adam and Eve fell from grace that men started taking multiple wives. And some of these polygamous husbands were heroes of the faith: Abraham; Jacob; David; Solomon. Surprisingly, nowhere does Scripture condemn their behavior! I'm sure that Kody is taking his cues from guys like these. So, should we let go of our insistence on one-wife-per-husband? NO! Consider God's *progressive revelation* on this score.

To begin with, even though the Bible describes some of the heroes of the faith as taking multiple wives, it also describes this pattern as always leading to trouble. Solomon's many wives even turned his heart against God! (See 1 Kings 11:3–4.) Next, when Jesus arrives on the scene, He reiterates what Genesis 2:24 says about a husband and wife becoming *one* flesh. And then He adds this line (Matthew 19:6): "So they are no longer two, but one." Did you catch that? Jesus did *not* say, "So they are no longer three, but one" (or "five, but one," as in the case of Kody Brown).

And the Bible has still more to say about monogamy. By the time we get to the epistles of the apostle Paul, we read that monogamy is a mark of spiritual maturity (1 Timothy 3:2). Please keep in mind that Paul wrote that to people who were living in a polygamous culture. So the biblical standard for marriage is one man joined inseparably to one woman.

The complete picture of God's plan comes into total focus through progressive revelation. While we use the Bible to interpret the Bible, we must always make sure that we've read God's *latest* word on any subject.

The Examples

OK, let's take a look at three examples of how we can use the Bible to interpret the Bible, as we consider the topics of prayer, hell, and baptism.

Prayer. Our first test case has to do with prayer. In Luke 11, Jesus' disciples observe Him praying one day. They're so impressed by what they see that they ask Jesus to teach *them* how to pray.[3] In the middle of Jesus' ensuing tutorial on prayer, He says, "Ask and it will be given to you; seek and you will find; knock and the door will be opened to you. For everyone who asks receives; he who seeks finds; and to him who knocks, the door will be opened" (Luke 11:9–10).

Now, what if this were the only passage in the Bible that we had on prayer? Jesus promises, "Ask and it will be given to you." And He repeats His promise in the next verse, "Everyone who asks receives." So I fold my hands, close my eyes, lift my voice to God, and pray, "Lord, please give me a million dollars!" Does that work? It hasn't worked for me.

You may object, "Well, you can't ask God for something like a million dollars. It has to be something legit." But where does Luke 11 say *that*?

Luke 11 *doesn't* say that. However, there is more than one passage in the Bible on prayer, and 1 John 5:14–15 *does* say that! First John 5:14–15 reads: "If we ask anything according to [God's] will, he hears us. And if we know that he hears us—whatever we ask—we know that we have what we asked of him." So, it's not simply a case of "ask and it will be given to you"—like we read in Luke 11. No, what we ask God for has to be *in accord with His will*, as we learn in First John 5.

You see what I just did? I used the Bible to interpret the Bible. But we're not yet finished with this topic of prayer. Let's say that I pray and ask God for something that's *in accord with His will*. Let's say, for example, that I'm out of work and pray for a job. I think it's reasonable to assume that God would want me to be employed. So, based on Luke 11, combined with 1 John 5, I pray for a job, and next week I'm hired, right?

Not so fast! Let me tell you a few more things that the Bible says about getting answers to prayer. Luke 18:1 says that sometimes I've got to keep on praying and not give up. Evidently, the answers aren't always right around the corner. So God may want me to pray for a month for that job . . . or a year. Mark 11:24 says that I've got to pray with faith. I've got to believe that I've already received from God what I've prayed for. What else does the Bible teach about getting answers to prayer?

James 4:1–3 says that I must be free of selfish motivations when I pray. If I want that job strictly so that I have money to spend on me and my family—and if I don't have a track record of giving a portion of my income to the Lord's work—my prayer may fall on deaf ears. And, finally, John 15:7 says that my prayers are most effective when I am personally maintaining a close relationship with Christ. "If you remain in me," says Jesus, "and my words remain in you, ask whatever you wish, and it will be given you." Do I desire to spend time in God's Word (i.e., allowing Jesus' words to remain in me) as much as I desire the new job I'm praying for?

We've just constructed a *theology* of prayer. Instead of misinterpreting what one verse in Luke 11 teaches about prayer ("ask and it will be given to you"), we've surveyed other passages in the Bible on the topic as well. Now, we've got the full scoop. We've used the Bible to help us interpret the Bible.

INSTEAD OF misinterpreting what one verse teaches about prayer, survey other passages in the Bible to get the full scoop.

Hell. Here's another example of how this works. The topic is hell. It's a topic that occasionally makes it into the secular news. Not too long ago a very popular megachurch pastor wrote a book on the subject that became headline material. I watched him launch this book on the Internet, as he was interviewed by the religion editor of *Newsweek* magazine in New York City. It was said that more viewers were watching this interview than any previous Internet event of a similar kind.

According to the book's author, God *loves* people so much that He's going to see to it that nobody winds up in hell—unless they really, really want to go there. Love will carry the day. God's love will triumph over human resistance.

(The book's title, *Love Wins*, underscores this notion.) The author told his interviewer that he was not just making this stuff up. This is what the *Bible* teaches. I'm sure he had in mind verses like John 3:16: "God so loved the world that he gave his one and only Son." God *loves* the world. And John 3:16 concludes by saying that the aim of God's love is to see to it that people "shall not perish but have eternal life." So, it is obvious that God wants people to have eternal life and not spend eternity in hell.

However, is that *all* the Bible teaches on the topic of hell? *God loves people*—is that it? Interestingly, if we drop down just two verses below John 3:16, this is what John 3:18 says: "Whoever believes in him [Jesus Christ] is not condemned, but whoever does not believe stands condemned already because he has not believed in the name of God's one and only Son." Those who don't believe in God's Son—Jesus—stand condemned. What happened to God's *love*?

We need to keep in mind that love is not God's only attribute. God is also holy, righteous, and just—which means that He must punish wrongdoing; He must punish sin. The only way to avoid that punishment is to

LOVE IS NOT God's only attribute. God is also holy, righteous, and just—which means that He must punish wrongdoing.

put our faith in the Savior that God has provided. Jesus is that Savior, because Jesus took the punishment we deserve when He died on the cross. That's why those who reject Jesus stand condemned before God. They're hell-bound.

And speaking of Jesus—nobody in the Bible talked more about hell than Jesus. Jesus frequently warned His listeners not to end up there. He told them to fear the one who has the power to "destroy both soul and body in hell" (Matthew 10:28). That's a strange teaching if this contemporary author's dismissive view of hell is true.

We can't pull out isolated Bible verses on a topic. We've got to consider what the *whole* Bible says about the matter. That's the *theological* context.

Baptism. One final example of how this works. Let's look at a Scripture passage about baptism. In Acts 2, the apostle Peter preaches the first Christian sermon on record. This is just a month and a half after Jesus' resurrection from the dead and His return to heaven. Peter is on the streets of Jerusalem, a huge crowd is in town for a religious holiday, and Peter is preaching like there's no tomorrow. Look at these closing words of Peter's sermon.

"Therefore let all Israel be assured of this: God has made this Jesus, whom you crucified, both Lord and Christ." When the people heard this, they were cut to the heart and said to Peter and the other apostles, "Brothers, what shall we do?" Peter replied, "Repent and be baptized, every one of you, in the name of Jesus Christ for the forgiveness of your sins. And you will receive the gift of the Holy Spirit." (Acts 2:36–38)

Aren't you a little surprised by what Peter tells the crowd to do in order to be forgiven by God, "Repent and be baptized"? The *repent* part makes sense to us—that just means to turn away from our sins and turn toward Christ. That's a faith decision. And the Bible tells us that we're saved by faith. But what about the *be baptized* part of Peter's response? Is Peter adding some sort of religious ritual, some sort of good deed to the salvation equation? Must people be baptized in order to have their sins forgiven? (Some Protestant denominations teach this, based upon verses like Acts 2:38.)

Let me review what other Bibles verses teach on how we are saved:

For it is by grace you have been saved, through faith—and this not from yourselves, it is the gift of God—not by works, so that no one can boast. (Ephesians 2:8–9)

He saved us, not because of righteous things we had done, but because of his mercy. (Titus 3:5)

However, to the man who does not work but trusts God who justifies the wicked, his faith is credited as righteousness. (Romans 4:5)

Verses like these make it clear that God saves us on the basis of our faith in Christ—not because we've been baptized (or on the basis of any other good work). Then how are we to understand Peter's emphasis on baptism in Acts 2:38? We must conclude that Peter is *not* saying that baptism is a requirement for forgiveness. That would be out of sync with what the rest of the Bible teaches. On the other hand, Peter *is* saying that people who genuinely put their faith in Christ for forgiveness will be eager to publicly affirm that decision by getting baptized. Baptism ought to be a slam dunk (sorry) for *true* Christ followers.

The Tools

As you were tracking with my three examples (*prayer, hell, baptism*) of how to use the Bible to interpret the Bible, perhaps you were thinking to yourself: *This is easy for Jim to do with his theological training. But I could never do this.* Oh, yes you could! It just takes the right tools.

It's amazing how much easier a job becomes when we have the right tool for it. Years ago, I decided to save some money by changing the oil in my car by myself. I'm not very mechanically inclined, but fortunately there's not a whole lot to this process. It's just a case of draining out the old oil, replacing the filter, and putting in a few quarts of fresh oil. Simple! Except for the fact that my filter was screwed on very tightly and wouldn't budge. Besides that, it was in an awkward place to reach and extremely difficult to get a grip on with my oily hands. I must have tried for an hour to get that sucker off before giving up and going to the auto supply store for some advice. Their advice was to buy one of their oil filter wrenches. Which I did, and took it home. I had my filter off in twenty seconds!

When it comes to correctly interpreting the Bible *theologically*, it helps to have the right tools for the job. The apostle Paul told his friend Timothy that he should approach the Bible like a skilled workman "who correctly handles the word of truth" (2 Timothy 2:15). In the same way that a carpenter knows how to use his miter box and a surgeon knows how to wield her scalpel and a baseball player knows how to swing his bat, Christ followers should know how to use the tools that make them expert Bible handlers.

Here are four tools that will help you understand the Bible's *theological setting* of any significant topic that you come across in your reading.

Cross-references. Your Bible probably has a column that runs down the middle (or perhaps the margin) of every page.

That's the list of cross-references. When you're reading a verse that raises an interpretive question in your mind, look to see if there is a tiny letter of the alphabet above any of the words or phrases in that verse. That letter corresponds to one or more cross-references listed in the middle column (or margin).

FOUR TOOLS will help us understand the Bible's theological setting on any significant topic: cross-references, a concordance, a study Bible, and a systematic theology.

For example, we looked at Luke 11:9 while discussing prayer. The second phrase of that verse says, "Ask and it will be given to you." Now, in my Bible, there's a tiny *j* above that phrase. So, I go to the middle column of the page. I look for verse 9 of chapter 11. I find the tiny *j*. And it gives me one cross-reference. A cross-reference is a verse in another part of the Bible that says something about the same topic.

Great! Next to the tiny *j* it says: Matthew 7:7. So I look up Matthew 7:7. Now, unfortunately, this is not initially very helpful, because Matthew 7:7 says the exact same thing, with the very same words, as Luke 11:9. So this was a waste of my time, right? Nope. Hang in there with me. There's a tiny *q* in the middle of Matthew 7:7. So I go to the tiny *q* in the middle column of cross-references, and you know what I find? No less than 11 other Bible passages that deal with the topic of how to ask God for stuff in prayer. By looking up these other verses and noting what they teach about prayer, I am kept from misinterpreting Luke 11:9's promise: "Ask and it will be given to you."

A concordance. Most Bibles have a concordance at the back. (They're located just before the maps that most of us never look at.) A concordance is an A–Z list of the most common words that appear in the Bible. After each word, you'll find a bunch of Bible verses that use that word. So if you want to know what else the Bible has to say about prayer, after reading Luke 11:9 you can turn to the *p*'s in the concordance and look up *prayer, pray, praying.* There are a lot of verses on that topic.

Or, if you want more information on *hell,* you can look up *hell* under the *h*'s in your concordance. However, let me mention an interesting side note with regard to this particular topic. When I looked up *hell* in my Bible's concordance, I discovered that all the references are in the New Testament. Should that bother me? Is the contemporary author, whom I referred to earlier, correct when he says that we make too big a deal out of hell (i.e., since it isn't even mentioned in the Old Testament)? No. Instead, this is another instance of *progressive revelation.* The fact is the Old Testament has little to say about the afterlife—hell or heaven. That's a matter that God reveals in greater detail in later books of the Bible.

A study Bible. This is a wonderful tool for interpreting God's Word. The footnotes and book introductions in a study Bible typically include theological insights. For example, if you'll go to the passage in Acts 2 where Peter tells his audience that they need to *repent and be baptized* in order to be forgiven, you'll find a footnote (in the *NIV Study Bible*) that offers the very explanation that I gave you a moment ago for how baptism fits with a salvation that is received by faith alone.

I've found the *NIV Study Bible* to be so helpful that I purchased a second copy of it for my iPhone. It was worth the $25 to have this electronic tool at my fingertips whenever I want it.

A systematic theology. This is a textbook that covers almost any Bible topic you could think of. You just look up the topic in the index at the back of the book and it will direct you to the pages where the author discusses that topic. There are many systematic theology textbooks from which to choose. My favorite is written by Wayne Grudem and entitled, appropriately, *Systematic Theology* (Zondervan), and I recommend it frequently to others (all of our church's staff members and elders have a copy) for several reasons.

First, Dr. Grudem is a highly respected theologian and Bible scholar. Second, he is fair and gracious when presenting differing positions on controversial issues. Third, he knows how to put the cookies on the bottom shelf for the average reader. His book is very understandable—even enjoyable and devotional.

Keep in mind, too, that this is not a volume you must sit down and read cover to cover; it is over 1,200 pages. It's more like a reference tool that you'll keep on your bookshelf and turn to when you have a theological question about something you've read in Scripture. In fact, I encourage the leaders of our 300-plus small groups to keep a copy of Grudem's *Systematic Theology* on their shelf, so that they can find answers to the tough questions that pop up in any good Bible study.

Don't Know Much About Theology?

An old love song occasionally resurfaces in a retro version, called "Don't Know Much about History." The singer confesses that while he doesn't know much about history, biology, geography, or other school subjects, he *does* know that he loves his girl. Cute. Most of us smile when we hear those lyrics, because we identify with a guy who feels limited in his knowledge of academic subjects. Such ignorance is usually not a big deal (unless you're a doctor who's singing "don't know much about biology"). It's much more important to be in love.

Unfortunately, many Christ followers have a similar attitude toward theology. They view it as an academic subject that they don't know much about—but, hey, they love God. And that's all that matters, right? Not quite. The problem with such a cavalier dismissal of theology is that it fails to recognize the fact that we theologize every time we pick up a Bible and read it. We come to conclusions about what each passage says about God, or about various other topics. Those conclusions may be accurate or they may be seriously flawed. In other words, we may have good theology or bad theology—but we all come away from the Bible with a theological perspective on what we've read. Theology is unavoidable. So it's imperative that our theology be accurate.

Hopefully, this chapter has challenged and equipped you to become a skilled workman (or workwoman), who "correctly handles the word of truth."

Study Guide
The Theological Setting

Icebreaker

Does the word *theology* have a positive or negative ring in your ears? Explain.

1. Why must the Bible, given its wide diversity of human authors, always agree with itself? What is the practical application of this principle? Explain why this is so.

2. How does progressive revelation account for the fact that sometimes the Bible seems to disagree with itself?

3. Write out a theology of prayer based upon the Scriptures and insights covered in this chapter.

4. Using the concordance in your Bible, summarize what Jesus teaches about hell.

5. (icon) Read John 3:1–21. Choose three words that you find interesting and that are cross-referenced in your Bible. Write down what you learn about each of these three words from looking up the cross-references.

First word:

Second word:

Third word:

6. (icon) Read Colossians 2. Now, read it a second time, along with all the corresponding footnotes in a study Bible of your choice. Record the top three insights that you gleaned from these footnotes. (Remember that you can purchase an *NIV Study Bible* app for your iPhone and begin using it in the next five minutes!)

7. (icon) Jesus says in Mark 10:11 that "anyone who divorces his wife and marries another woman commits adultery." Period! If this were the only biblical text on divorce, you would have to conclude that divorce is always prohibited—no exceptions. But using your Bible's concordance, cross-references,

and footnotes, construct a fuller theology of divorce (i.e., especially noting if there are any circumstances in which God
permits it).

8. In what sense is every Bible reader a theologian?
Why should this motivate you to pay attention to theology as
you're reading the Bible?

{ 4 }
The Immediate Setting

A FRIEND RECENTLY SENT me a humorous article he'd found on the Internet entitled: "Reasons Why the English Language Is Hard to Learn."[1] Here are some of the compiler's observations about the strange way in which we use words:

There is no egg in eggplant nor ham in hamburger.

Why is it that writers write but fingers don't fing, grocers don't groce, and hammers don't ham?

Doesn't it seem crazy that you can make amends but not one amend?

If a vegetarian eats vegetables, what does a humanitarian eat?

In what language do people recite at a play and play at a recital?

How can a slim chance and a fat chance be the same, while a wise man and a wise guy are opposites?

You have to marvel at the unique lunacy of a language in which your house can burn up as it burns down, in which you fill in a form by filling it out, and in which an alarm goes off by going on.

The writer makes a sharp point: Words, in any language, can be difficult to interpret. And for Bible readers that creates problems, because the Bible is made up of words. In order to avoid misunderstanding what these words are meant to communicate, we must follow some basic ground rules of interpretation: *hermeneutics.*

Do you recall the foundational principle behind hermeneutics? *You must understand the context.* And so far we have considered three important contexts that will help us accurately interpret God's Word. The first of these has to do with the *historical* background of any passage we read. Where did the events take place? What was happening at the time?

The second context worth noting is the *literary* setting of each passage. Is it a narrative, or a poem, or an epistle? There are different rules for interpreting each literary genre.

Third, there are *theological* issues raised in every biblical text. We must be careful not to read too much into what one passage says about a topic without comparing our interpretation with what other Bible passages say about the same topic.

We are now ready to take a look at a fourth, and final, interpretive context. This is the *immediate setting* in which we find the words that we read in Scripture. Words cannot be understood in isolation. Only when they are used in a sentence does their meaning becomes apparent.

Let me illustrate what I'm talking about with the word

spring. (I owe this illustration to Duvall and Hays' excellent book on hermeneutics, *Grasping God's Word*.[2]) This English word may refer to one of four things: a season; a metal coil; an act of jumping; or a source of water. It's impossible to answer the question, "What does *spring* mean?" with any precision until it is used in a sentence.

If I say, "I hope we don't run into a dry *spring* ahead," two of the four possible definitions are eliminated right away. It's obvious that I'm not talking about a metal coil or an act of jumping. However, there are still two definitions remaining. I could be referring to the approach of a season that's lacking in rainfall, or I could be leading a caravan through the desert to a worthless watering hole. Which dry *spring* is it? Let me add one additional sentence to the immediate context of my original statement: "I hope we don't run into a dry *spring* ahead. The grass and flowers need lots of rain before the heat of summer. " Aha! Now you know that the *spring* I have in mind is a season of the year.

What determined the meaning of this word? Its *immediate setting*—the way it was used in a sentence, followed by the way that sentence was used in conjunction with a second sentence. In this chapter we will explore how a word's setting in a particular Bible passage helps us interpret that word accurately.

Many Bible words—some very important ones—can be

just as difficult to pin down as the English word *spring*. Take, for example, the Greek word *sarx*. A very succinct and literal translation of this word is *flesh*. What does *sarx/flesh* mean? The New Testament uses this word in a variety of ways.

In Romans 3:20, the apostle Paul writes that "no one [*sarx*] will be declared righteous in his [God's] sight by observing the law." Paul is obviously referring to humanity in general by his use of *sarx* in this verse. But that's clearly *not* what he means by *sarx* when he tells the Corinthians that "there was given me a thorn in my flesh" (*sarx*, 2 Corinthians 12:7). This is a reference, no doubt, to Paul's body. Jesus also used *sarx* to refer to His body—but not to His body as a whole. He spoke specifically of the non-skeletal parts of it: "a ghost does not have flesh [sarx] and bones, as you see I have" (Luke 24:39). And then there is the spiritual use of *sarx* that Paul regularly employs to speak of our sinful nature: "Those controlled by the sinful nature [sarx] cannot please God" (Romans 8:8).

One word, multiple meanings. Now you can understand why it is important to determine which particular meaning of a word is being used in a given passage. How can we figure that out? Here are some practical steps to consider when interpreting words.

Choose a Balanced Bible Translation

There are three basic philosophies of Bible translation and I will illustrate each with a popular contemporary version of Scripture. At one end of the spectrum are the renditions that pride themselves on being *word-for-word* translations of the original languages. This very literal approach is best represented today by the English Standard Version (ESV). The publisher of this translation is an acquaintance of mine and an extremely generous man. He recently gave me a calfskin-covered copy of the *ESV Study Bible* that's worth hundreds of dollars. So, I would be ungrateful not to speak highly of the ESV. I mean, what's not to like about it?! Seriously, gift or not, the English Standard Version is an example of an effective word-for-word translation.

A word-for-word translation (the *King James Version* and *New American Standard Bible* are also representatives of this approach) is extremely helpful when doing in-depth Bible study that focuses on tracing certain words throughout Scripture. However, a word-for-word approach occasionally sacrifices something by way of readability. At times the text can be a bit stilted or wooden because of the effort to match every Hebrew and Greek word with a corresponding English word.

Perhaps an illustration totally unrelated to Bible translation would help here. Several years ago, Sue and I were eating out at a Mexican restaurant. This was a very authentic place, and we overheard a lot of Spanish being spoken around us. After our meal was served, a guy in a sombrero stopped by our table to serenade us with his guitar. The first verse of his song was sung in Spanish. Then he stumbled through a second verse in somewhat broken English. No doubt the translation was his own, as he warbled that his love was coming from "the bottom of my gut." *Gut* was probably a literal and accurate rendering of the Spanish at that point. But it didn't quite convey the same sentiment in English.

Word-for-word Bible translations, similarly, can sometimes leave us with an English version that is less than a smooth read. But perhaps this is just a matter of taste. Go ahead and take a look at the ESV for yourself. You may love it.

At the opposite end of the continuum from literal translations are the paraphrases. Instead of attempting a word-for-word correspondence between the biblical languages and English, paraphrases (sometimes called *free* translations) endeavor to make a *thought-for-thought* transference from the original language. The most popular representative of this approach today is probably Eugene Peterson's *The Message*. (Many Bible scholars would say that the *New Living Translation* is also a paraphrase. But its publisher rejects such a categorization, declaring it to be a *translation* by its very title.)

While paraphrases provide us with an easier-to-read text and minimize the cultural differences between the Bible's world and ours, they tend to sacrifice something by way of accuracy. And they don't make for good study Bibles, because they're not as concerned with translating *words* with consistency as they are with translating *ideas*.

The New International Version (NIV) represents a translation philosophy that stands midway between the literal (word-for-word) and the paraphrase (thought-for-thought) approaches. Bible scholars refer to it as a *dynamic equivalent* rendition. That is, it attempts to "translate words, idioms and grammatical constructions of the original language into precise equivalents in the receptor [i.e., English] language"—so says New Testament scholar Gordon Fee.[3] Dr. Fee declares this to be the best translational theory. And I tend to agree with him. The NIV combines a literal translation's emphasis on accuracy with a paraphrase's strength of readability.

Whatever Bible translation you choose to use (and I'm not shy about recommending the NIV, with my second favorite being the ESV), let me encourage you to stick with it for the long haul. Feel free to consult other versions when studying a passage. But choosing to "own" one as your primary version will result in a greater familiarity with the text over time. It will also encourage your memorization of Scripture.

Note: The publisher of the NIV recently updated its translation (2011). I must tell you, however, that I'm a fan of the older edition (1984) and don't care for many of the changes made to "improve" it.[4] Hasn't the NIV publisher heard of the debacle created by Coke some years ago when they tried to make us swallow a new recipe for our favorite cola? We rebelled and the soda maker gave us back our original drink as Coke Classic. How 'bout we all demand an NIV Classic? Just a thought, but we'll probably have to bite the bullet and make a transition to the new NIV.

Focus on Interpreting the Most Significant Words

Because the Bible declares itself to be inspired ("God-breathed"; 2 Timothy 3:16), it follows that all its words are inspired. So a word study of a key phrase is often helpful. You don't need to ruminate, however, on every use of "the" or "tree" or "go" in the text. Just look for the key nouns, verbs, and adjectives that seem to be crucial to the passage. Look for important words. Note, too, repeating words. If the same word is used several times within a few verses, it may indicate a theme that God wants to draw your attention to. You may also want to focus on words that are unclear or puzzling to you.

Let's say that you're reading in the second chapter of John's first epistle, and you come to verse 15: "Do not love the world or anything in the world. If anyone loves the world, the love of the Father is not in him." One of the significant words in this verse is certainly *world*—first, because it's repeated three times, and second, because it's a bit puzzling. Why puzzling? Well, doesn't this verse seem to be at odds with the most familiar verse in the Bible, also written by the apostle John? John 3:16 tells us: "God so loved the world that he gave his one and only Son." Yet 1 John 2:15 commands us: "Do not love the world." So, *God* loves the world but *we* shouldn't? Don't you find that puzzling?

IF WE PAY some attention to the word *world* we can deduce that John is using it in two different ways.

The apparent conflict between these two verses is easily resolved once we pay some attention to the word *world* and deduce that John is using it in two different ways. What does *world* mean in each of these two immediate settings?

World in John 3:16 is a reference to people in general. God loved humanity so much that He gave us His Son. But *world* in 1 John 2:15 is a reference to anti-God behaviors and attitudes held by the surrounding culture. How do we know that? Keep reading. The very next verse says: "For everything in the world—the cravings of sinful man, the lust of his eyes and the boasting of what he has and does—comes not from the Father but from the world" (1 John 2:16). So loving the *world* of people is a good thing, while loving the *world* of sin is not. Do you see the benefit of considering a word's immediate setting?

Avoid Faulty Interpretive Approaches

Some preachers (including me, on occasion) love to expound on particular words in the text that they've chosen for their sermon. The minute they say, "The Hebrew (or Greek) for this word is actually . . ." their listeners are wowed. It's assumed that what is said next will be deep and scholarly. But not every approach to interpreting words is helpful. In fact, some of the common approaches can be downright misleading. Watch out for four approaches.

First, putting too much emphasis on individual words. I know, here I've been promoting the study of words while reading the Bible, and now I'm going to tell you not to overdo that sort of thing! Let me explain by citing a passage that far too many preachers have misinterpreted because of their overemphasis on a distinction between two words.

In John 21:15–17, Jesus is having a postresurrection conversation with Peter. Three times Jesus asks Peter, "Do you love me?" The first couple of times Jesus asks the question, the Greek word He uses for love is *agapao*. But Peter uses a different Greek word for love, *phileo*, when he responds, "Lord, you know that I love you." So, the third time Jesus asks the question, he switches to Peter's word: "Do you love [*phileo*, not *agapao*] me?"

Some preachers (and Christian authors) have made a big deal of a supposed distinction between these two words, suggesting that the former (*agapao*) is a reference to divine love, while the latter (*phileo*) connotes human love or friendship. From this distinction they then sermonize that Jesus was hoping for some divinely inspired love (*agapao*) from Peter, but He eventually had to lower the bar and settle for Peter's human affection (*phileo*).

Unfortunately, a more extensive survey of these two Greek words for love indicates that they are not quite so distinct from one another in meaning. In fact, God the Father even uses *phileo* to speak of His love for His Son (John 5:20)! Of course, you're probably wondering how you could be expected to catch stuff like that. Do you have to know the biblical languages or conduct exhaustive searches of every significant word to make sure that preachers and authors aren't exaggerating their meaning?

No. Just be a bit suspicious when too much emphasis is placed on particular words. In the case of *agapao* versus *phileo* in John 21, it's simply not reasonable to conclude that the proper understanding of this passage should come down to our ability to distinguish between two Greek verbs that are both translated into English as *love*. Surely a correct interpretation will not depend on catching something so subtle.

Second, *relying on the etymology of words. Etymology* is just a fancy way of referring to a word's history. It sounds scholarly to hear someone describe what a Bible word originally meant, but that sort of an allusion can be terribly misleading. That's *not* how we discover what a word means in its immediate setting.

Let me illustrate why the etymology approach is faulty. Suppose you and I are sitting on a bench at the mall and you say, "Look at that cute girl." I pull out my iPad, do a quick Google search of the word *cute*, and learn that in Elizabethan England it meant *bowlegged*. (I'm not making this up.) Should I be scanning the crowd for a girl who looks like she just got off a horse? Of course not! The etymology of *cute* does not help me understand what you meant by it.

Dr. Grant Osborne, who's written a comprehensive book on hermeneutics, says: "Words are not used according to their historical value." It's unrealistic, he adds, to suppose that Bible authors would have in mind the semantic evolutions through which words have passed when selecting such words for their writings. "Words always have a current value," Osborne concludes, "limited to the moment when they're employed."[5] How words have been used in the past may give us some clues to their meaning, but how they are being used in the passage where we find them is what's most important.

Third, *taking apart compound words.* Once again, this is a favorite device of some preachers. They announce that a certain word in the text is a *compound word*, and then they proceed to break it down into its parts and define each part. Try doing that with an English compound word and see where it gets you. What about *butterfly*? Well, *butter* is the product of churned milk, and *fly* is the activity of sailing through the air. So, a *butterfly* must be a soaring lump of lard, right? The same sorts of misinterpretations will ensue if we break down the compound words *broadcast* or *hamburger* or *fellowship*.

However, lest we throw the baby out with the bathwater, it must be admitted that on occasion we may be able to learn something about the meaning of a compound word by dissecting it. A *houseboat*, for example, is a residence that floats on water. Similarly, the Greek New Testament word for church—*ekklesia*—aptly describes a group of people who have been called (*klesia*) out of (*ek*) the world to follow Christ.

So it's occasionally insightful to discover what each of the component parts of a compound word in the Bible means. But it would be dangerous to apply this method uncritically, especially if the rendered meaning is not supported by the immediate setting.

Fourth, *using multiple meanings for words*. Now that you know that many Bible words have multiple meanings, it may be tempting to ascribe significance to every definition of whatever word you choose to focus on in a passage. But you don't need to pay attention to multiple definitions of a word that you are studying. Simply select the single definition that fits its setting best. (In other words, *more* is not *better.*)

Moises Silva illustrates this point in his book on hermeneutics by asking us to imagine a foreign visitor who has just heard his American friend complain of an acute pain in her knee. The overseas guest wants to know what is meant by *acute.* Would the following response be helpful?

> In geometry, the word is used of angles less than 90 degrees, while in music it many indicate a high-pitched sound. It also is used to describe an accent mark in some languages and scripts. In objects it indicates a sharp point. The word can be used as a synonym for "keen, discerning, shrewd." Things of great importance can be said to be acute. In medicine, it may describe a disease that is approaching a crisis. Finally, the word can mean "severe."[6]

You may be wondering why I even bother to make this point. It's obviously absurd to latch onto every possible meaning of a word that you are studying in a passage. Of course you would select the single definition that best fits the context. Who couldn't figure this one out? Well, evidently the folks behind *The Amplified Bible* haven't figured it out. Here's how John 3:16 reads in the Amplified version: "For God so greatly loved and dearly prized the world that He [even] gave up His only begotten [unique] Son, so that whoever believes in (trusts in, clings to, relies on) Him shall not perish (come to destruction, be lost) but have eternal (everlasting) life."

This approach to Bible translation is almost humorous. Let me say (tell, declare, affirm) that this is no way (manner, form, custom) to communicate (correspond, talk, signal, disseminate information). Not only does such complexity make the text difficult to read, it also subtly suggests that when we come across a significant word in our Bible reading, we are free to choose whatever definition we like the most from a handful of possibilities. No! We must look for the single definition that is best suited to the context.

Enough about faulty approaches to be avoided. Here's a fifth *positive* rule for interpreting words accurately:

Interpret Words in Light of How They Are Used in Sentences, Paragraphs, Books, and the Bible as a Whole

This is the word's most *immediate setting* and often provides the best help you'll need for determining the meaning of that word. Moving out from the bull's-eye, the next ring represents the paragraph (or cluster of paragraphs) in which the sentence appears that contains your word. What is the gist of that paragraph and how does your word fit into it?

Once you understand how a word functions within its immediate paragraph, you can broaden your investigation of its meaning by examining how it's used elsewhere in the same Bible book. After that, the next step is to study its import in other books by the same author. Keep in mind that Moses wrote five books, Solomon three, Luke two, Paul thirteen, John five, and Peter two (plus an assist on the gospel of Mark). The assumption is that an author will use a word consistently within his own writings—but in a way that may differ from how others use that word.

The final setting in which to consider a word is the Bible as a whole. The fact that there is one divine Author behind the entire Book suggests that there will be some degree of consistency in what words mean throughout Scripture, even though each human author will have his own distinct vocabulary. The tool that will be most helpful in carrying out your contextual study of a word is the concordance at the back of your Bible. As I explained in the last chapter, a concordance lists alphabetically the most common words in the Bible with their Scriptures.

A Study of the Word *Yeast*

Are you ready to put into practice what you've just learned? Let's see how it works with a couple of words. We'll start with what appears to be a fairly straightforward word: *yeast*.

What does *yeast* mean? I'm sure that your quick response

is to identify yeast as the ingredient in bread dough that makes it rise. And that's exactly how Moses used the word when giving the Israelites instructions about Passover preparations: "For seven days you are to eat bread made without yeast" (Exodus 12:15).

But does it seem likely that Jesus has the literal meaning of *yeast* in mind when He warns His disciples, "Be on your guard against the yeast of the Pharisees" (Luke 12:1)? Hardly! Jesus was not conducting a cooking class for His followers. So what did He mean by His use of the word *yeast*? Fortunately, Jesus Himself defines the word at the sentence's end: "Be on your guard against the yeast of the Pharisees, which is hypocrisy." Hypocrisy is a two-faced behavior that can permeate a person's character like yeast working its way through a lump of dough.

This negative meaning of yeast, however, could not be what Jesus had in mind on another occasion when He used the word to describe the kingdom of God.

Then Jesus asked, "What is the kingdom of God like? What shall I compare it to? It is like a mustard seed, which a man took and planted in his garden. It grew and became a tree, and the birds of the air perched in its branches."

Again he asked, "What shall I compare the kingdom

of God to? It is like yeast that a woman took and mixed into a large amount of flour until it worked all through the dough." (Luke 13:18–21)

Doesn't it help to look at the entire paragraph here to determine how Jesus is using the word *yeast*? The kingdom of God is spreading, just as yeast spreads through dough. And in case we might miss the analogy, Jesus precedes it with a description of a mustard seed growing into a tree. Same idea, confirming our understanding of *yeast*: God's kingdom is getting bigger and bigger.

But sometimes even the immediate paragraph is no help when interpreting a word. This is the case when Jesus cautions His disciples: "Be on your guard against the yeast of the Pharisees and Sadducees" (Matthew 16:6). At first glance, this seems like a repeat of the Luke 12:1 warning to steer clear of hypocrisy. But *yeast* isn't identified as hypocrisy on this occasion. In fact, *yeast* isn't identified at all, leaving the disciples to speculate about what Jesus means. They initially conclude that He must be using the word literally—Jesus is chiding them for forgetting to bring bread on their outing across the lake (v. 5). They must be at fault for having nothing to eat.

But this is not what Jesus means by *yeast* in this setting. We have to keep on reading if we want to find out what He has in mind. After He reminds His disciples that on two previous occasions He had fed thousands of people with only a few loaves of bread, they realize that *yeast* couldn't possibly be a reference to Jesus' concern that they lacked bread. The lightbulbs begin to go on. Jesus is using the word metaphorically. "Then they understood that he was not telling them to guard against the yeast used in bread, but against the teaching of the Pharisees and Sadducees" (Matthew 16:12). So *yeast* means false teaching in this passage—a definition only arrived at after reading a couple paragraphs of text (vv. 7–12).

Now that we've looked at a few instances where Jesus used the word *yeast*, let's see what Paul does with it. In 1 Corinthians 5:6–7, Paul writes: "Your boasting is not good. Don't you know that a little yeast works through the whole batch of dough? Get rid of the old yeast that you may be a new batch without yeast." What is the *old yeast* that Paul wants the Corinthians to get rid of? We won't find an answer to that question in the sentence that the word appears in. Nor in the surrounding paragraph.

If we want to find out what Paul means by *old yeast* we need to read the entire chapter of 1 Corinthians 5. Here's the skinny: sexual immorality is rampant in Corinth—and not just in the city, but in the local church. The worst case is that of a guy who's sleeping with his stepmom! Paul tells these believers to kick this guy out of their congregation if he's not willing to repent of his sin. Otherwise, his promiscuous behavior will spread to others. Getting rid of the old yeast is finally spelled out near the close of the chapter with these words: "You must not associate with anyone who calls himself a brother but is sexually immoral" (1 Corinthians 5:11). So *yeast* in this case refers to a professing Christ follower who is unrepentantly engaged in flagrant sin.

One final example, also from Paul, of the use of *yeast*:

> You were running a good race. Who cut in on you and kept you from obeying the truth? That kind of persuasion does not come from the one who calls you. "A little yeast works through the whole batch of dough." I am confident in the Lord that you will take no other view. The one who is throwing you into confusion will pay the penalty, whoever he may be. Brothers, if I am still preaching circumcision, why am I still being persecuted? In that case the offense of the cross has been abolished. As for those agitators, I wish they would go the whole way and emasculate themselves! (Galatians 5:7–12)

Paul's concern, expressed in these verses, is that the Christ followers in Galatia are allowing certain false doctrines to lead them away from the truth that he had preached to them. This heresy (and the people who promoted it) is the *yeast* that Paul warns them against. What exactly does this dangerous teaching consist of? You can pick up a hint of it in this paragraph. It's got something to do with an emphasis on the Jewish ritual of circumcision. But if this paragraph were all you had to go on, you would be somewhat in the dark with regard to all Paul means by *yeast* in this setting.

So, what do you do? You sit down and read through the six short chapters of Galatians. Don't forget to start with the one-page introduction to this epistle that you'll find in your study Bible. By the time you're finished with Galatians (thirty minutes, tops), you'll have a thorough understanding of the heresy of the *Judaizers*, who taught that faith in Christ is not enough for salvation. Faith must be accompanied by good works—especially certain Jewish rituals. This is the *yeast* that Paul did not want permeating the church in Galatia.

We're done with our survey of the word *yeast*. It's used in a wide variety of ways in the Bible. You've seen how its meaning sometimes lies on the surface (i.e., the actual ingredient in bread dough, Exodus 12:15). But on other occasions, we couldn't discover the word's meaning until we searched the host sentence (hypocrisy, Luke 12:1); or the surrounding paragraph (the kingdom of God, Luke 13:18–21), or a cluster of several paragraphs (false teaching, Matthew 6:6–12); or an entire chapter (sexual immorality, 1 Corinthians 5); or a complete book of the Bible (the Judaizers' heresy, Galatians).

A Study of the Word *Justify*

Allow me to give you a second example of researching a word's meaning in its immediate sentence, then paragraph(s), then book of the Bible, and then Bible as a whole. We will study a key verb in the Bible: *justify*.

I promise not to take as much time with this word as I did with *yeast*. But it *is* one of the most important words in the Bible! The reason I've chosen this word is because a failure to correctly interpret what it means in its specific context could result in a misunderstanding of how a person is able to experience God's salvation.

Let's jump right into the thick of it. I'm going to pit Paul's use of *justify* against that of James. In Romans 3:28, Paul writes: "For we maintain that a man is justified by faith apart from observing the law." Contrast that with James 2:24: "You see that a person is justified by what he does and not by faith alone." Could any two statements be more at odds with each other than these?

One conclusion we might be tempted to draw from this comparison is that the Bible contradicts itself. Paul, the author of thirteen Bible epistles, says that justification is the result of faith *plus nothing*. James, also the author of a Bible epistle, says that it is the result of faith *plus works*. So it seems that the Bible occasionally disagrees with the Bible. However, we've previously concluded that this can never be the case, since the Bible is ultimately the product of the same Divine Mind: God's! God is not going to disagree with Himself.

The only other conclusion we can draw from this seemingly major rift between Paul and James is that they're talking about two different matters. Proving this conclusion looks, initially, like an uphill battle, not only because both writers use the same key word (*justify*), but also because they use the same Bible character (Abraham) to illustrate what they mean by the word. It doesn't look like they're talking about two different matters. It looks like they're talking about the same thing and spouting contradictory viewpoints!

But when we take a closer look at the paragraphs around Romans 3:28 and James 2:24, we see signs that Paul and James are addressing two different issues. Even in their citing of Abraham as a role model they draw from two separate incidents in this great patriarch's life. (See Romans 4:9–25 and James 2:20–23.) Paul recalls how Abraham, though he was advanced in years, believed in God's promise of a son. It was on the basis of this faith that God justified him. James, on the other hand, references Abraham's willingness to offer up that son, Isaac, years later on an altar. It was by this action, James says, that Abraham was justified.

These two events in Abraham's life tip us off that Paul and James are making completely different points. Paul is concerned with how we begin a relationship with God. There's nothing we can do to earn this status. We must put our faith in God's promised Son—not Isaac, but Jesus. When we do that, God *declares* us to be righteous in His sight based upon the forgiveness which Christ purchased for us on the cross.

In contrast, James is concerned with what we do *after* we decide to put our trust in Christ. How can we be sure that our faith is the real deal? Abraham demonstrated the genuineness of his faith in God by a willingness to sacrifice his son, Isaac, as God had commanded. Are our lives producing a similar obedience that confirms an authentic faith in Christ?

So when Paul speaks of what it means to be justified, he has in mind *God's declaration* of our righteousness, which is based solely on our faith in Jesus Christ. But when James speaks of what it means to be justified, he has in mind *our demonstration* of righteousness, which will result from a true faith in Jesus Christ. So Romans 3:28 and James 2:24 are not contradictory, they're complementary. And the only way to figure that out is by studying *justify* in the immediate contexts of Paul's and James's epistles.

Our surveys of the Bible's use of *yeast* and *justify* have underscored how important it is to interpret the meaning of individual words with respect to their immediate setting. How do they fit into their sentence, paragraph (and surrounding paragraphs), book, and the Bible as a whole? This question should also be asked when we are seeking to interpret concepts that are expressed by groups of words. In order to ascertain whether we correctly understand these concepts, we must take a closer look at the immediate settings in which they appear. Let's do that with a couple of examples.

A Closer Look at Two Phrases

Jesus taught His disciples, "For where two or three come together in my name, there am I with them" (Matthew 18:20). Some have interpreted this statement to be the simplest definition of a church. What constitutes a church? All it takes, they say, is for two or three believers to be in the same place at the same time.

One popular Christian pollster even cites this passage to suggest that we need a revolution in how we do church today. It's time, he says, for us to give up our outdated notion of the local church, with its worship services, Bible studies, and ministries. Local churches are now passé. As we head into the future, the church will exist wherever two or three Christ followers are hanging out together. According to this pollster's definition, even a couple of buddies playing golf on a Sunday morning would qualify as a church.[7]

139

But before you abandon your local church for eighteen holes with a friend next weekend, let me push back on this interpretation of Matthew 18:20. If your Bible is handy, open it and turn to the verse. It serves as a wrap-up to a lesson that began in verse 15. What's the topic of the lesson? The paragraph heading in my Bible reads: "A Brother Who Sins Against You." Jesus is teaching about how to resolve a conflict with someone who wrongs you. The first thing you do is go to him privately and discuss the problem. If that doesn't work, you return with a friend to back you up. And if the offender still stubbornly resists your attempt to reconcile with him, get the *church* (presumably a few leaders) involved.

This is the point at which Jesus makes the statement about two or three gathering in His name. He's not explaining to us what constitutes a church. He's not talking about getting together for worship services—or golf. He's laying out a strategy for resolving conflict. Do you see how important it is to check out the *immediate context* of a concept that you encounter in Scripture?

Here's a second phrase: "One will be taken and the other left." This phrase appears twice in a lesson that Jesus taught about His future return. Jesus describes a coming day when two men will be working in a field and one will be taken and the other left. The same thing will happen to two women who are grinding away with a hand mill (Matthew 24:40–

41). What event does Jesus have in mind here? Some say that this is a vivid description of the rapture—that secret coming of Christ, when He whisks believers off the planet before the Great Tribulation strikes. Jesus' full return to earth, they say, will occur visibly and gloriously seven years later. So, those *taken* in the Matthew account are raptured Christ followers.

This interpretation became so popular in the early 1970s that pioneer Christian rocker Larry Norman wrote a song based on it, "I Wish We'd All Been Ready." (DC Talk later did a retro version of the tune.) The lyrics warn us about the following scenario:

"Two men walking up a hill,
one disappears and one's left standing still,
I wish we'd all been ready.
There's no time to change your mind,
the Son has come and you've been left behind."[8]

This song is near and dear to my heart, because I was a high school student when it hit the charts. So, I chose to sing it as a duet with a friend of mine at our public high school's annual talent show. This led to my being "discovered" by the choir director, followed by a couple years of fame (OK, I'm slightly exaggerating) in various school musical performances. But on a more serious note (awful pun), this song reflects what I would argue is a misinterpretation of Matthew 24.

Take a look at the immediate context of the line: "one will be taken and the other left." Just before Jesus describes one of two men being taken from a field and one of two women being taken from the mill, he references the story of Noah: "For in the days before the flood, people were eating and drinking, marrying and giving in marriage, up to the day Noah entered the ark; and they knew nothing about what would happen until the flood came and took them all away" (Matthew 24:38–39).

What people are described by the phrase *took them all away* in this account? Noah and his family—who were carried to safety by the ark? No, this is a reference to the wicked people who were *taken away* in judgment by the flood.

So, when Jesus speaks, in the very next verses, about a man who is *taken* from a field and a woman who is *taken* from her mill, He is not alluding to believers who will be raptured [taken away] from the earth to safety before the Great Tribulation begins. Jesus is talking about those who will be *taken* in judgment from the earth when He returns to set up His kingdom. The fact that Jesus goes on to warn His listeners about this judgment in the rest of Matthew 24 seems to confirm this interpretation. "One will be taken and the other left" does not support the notion of a rapture. Those who adopt the concept of a return of Christ to rapture believers into heaven seem to be ignoring the immediate setting.

Now would be a good time to summarize what I've been emphasizing in this chapter with a pithy saying that I heard years ago: "A text without a context becomes a proof text for a pretext." Did you follow that? If a word or concept that we read in the Bible (*text*) is interpreted without reference to its host sentence, paragraph(s), book, and Bible (*context*), we may mistakenly think we've found evidence (*proof text*) for our preconceived beliefs (*pretext*).

You must understand the context! When interpreting the Bible, this means that it is critical to consider the historical, literary, theological, and immediate settings of every passage we read. And now that you've grasped the importance of *context*, you're ready to move on to applying the Bible to your daily life. *Walk* (book four in the Bible Savvy series) will equip you to do this.

Study Guide
The Immediate Context

Icebreaker

How many different meanings for the word "run" can you come up with?

1. Explain the three translation philosophies behind the various Bible versions.

What is the Bible translation that you most often use? Why? Which category of translation philosophy does it fall into? What are the strengths and weaknesses of such a translation?

2.   😊😊😊 If you want to interpret the Bible correctly, you must learn to recognize key words as you read. Take a look at the following passages and note the most significant word(s) or phrase(s) in each:

      Genesis 45:3–9 (this one is so obvious you might miss it, but you can check your answer by comparing it to what you find in Genesis 50:20)

      Deuteronomy 28:1–14

      Ezekiel 33:1–9

      John 15:1–8

      1 Corinthians 9:19–23

      Hebrews 9:11–14

3. *The Amplified Bible* is constructed on what premise? What is the weakness of such a premise?

145

4. Read Joshua 1. What command does God repeatedly give Joshua? From the context of this chapter, how does a person come by these two characteristics?

5. The opening declaration of Jesus' ministry, recorded in Mark 1:15, is: "The time has come. The kingdom of God is near. Repent and believe the good news!" If the kingdom of God was the first thing out of Jesus' mouth, this must be a very important biblical topic. Using your concordance, briefly summarize what the gospel of Mark teaches about this subject.

Based upon what you have learned about the kingdom of God in Mark, is this a present or a future reality? Explain. (The *NIV Study Bible* has an extremely helpful footnote along these lines for Luke 4:43.) What bearing does this have on your life today?

6. In Matthew 5:14, Jesus announces to His followers, "You are the light of the world." But this verse doesn't say what is meant by that metaphor. You'll need to look at a wider context to discover what it means to be *light*. How would you define being *the light of the world* according to the context of:

   a. the Matthew 5:14–16 paragraph?

   b. Jesus' Sermon on the Mount in Matthew 5–7 (cite broad categories)?

   c. other New Testament writers in 2 Corinthians 4:5–7; Ephesians 5:8–13; 1 Peter 2:9; 1 John 1:5–9; 2:9–10?

7. The apostle Paul seems to express a negative viewpoint toward God's law in Romans 7, noting that Christ followers have both "died to the law" (7:4) and been "released from the law" (7:6). This has led some believers to conclude that God's law has no relevance for their lives today. But read Romans 7 in its entirety and sum up this chapter's *balanced* perspective on God's law.

This same balanced perspective can be seen in the broader context of the epistle of Romans. Note what Paul says, positively and negatively, about the law in Romans 3:20, 31.

Evidently, there is a very specific sense in which Christ followers are to see themselves as released from the law. In what sense is it no longer applicable to you? In what sense does the law still have a role to play in your life?

What additional positive remarks do other Bible writers make about God's law—most notably, the psalmist (Psalm 119:1, 18, 44–45, 52, 62, 72, 92, 97–98, 136, 156, 165) and two of the major prophets (Jeremiah 31:33; Ezekiel 36:26–27)?

8. *Cessationists* believe that the biblical gift of tongues is no longer given to believers by the Holy Spirit today. A key text that is used to support this position is 1 Corinthians 13:8: "Where there are tongues, they will be stilled." Cessationists say that the apostle Paul is looking to his near future when the New Testament canon would be completed and there would no longer be a need for revelation from God through tongues.

Read 1 Corinthians 13:8–12. What time frame does this context suggest for when tongues would be stilled? Explain.

Now read the context of the following chapter, 1 Corinthians 14. Is there any mention of the cessation of tongues in this passage? What *does* Paul say about tongues by way of guidelines for using this gift?

Notes

About the Bible Savvy Series

1. Thom S. Rainer, *The Unchurched Next Door* (Grand Rapids: Zondervan, 2003), 200.

Chapter 1: The Historical Setting

1. R. C. Sproul, *Knowing Scripture* (Downers Grove, Ill.: InterVarsity, 1977), 64.

Chapter 3: The Theological Setting

1. Legally, Kody Brown has a civil marriage with one of the four women; he calls the other three "sister wives." When Utah law enforcement officials began investigating whether Brown had violated state law banning polygamy, the Browns threated a lawsuit to challenge the polygamy law. Charges were later dropped. See John Schwartz, "Polygamist, Under Scrutiny in Utah, Plans Suit to Challenge Law," *New York Times*, July 11, 2011; "Polygamy Charges Against Sister Wives' Kody Brown Dropped," *US Weekly*, June 1, 2012.

2. See http://hollywoodlife.com/celeb/kody-brown.

3. If you too aspire to be a better pray-er, I recommend James L. Nicodem, *Prayer Coach* (Wheaton: Crossway, 2008).

Chapter 4: The Immediate Setting

1. From Kip Wheeler, "Reasons Why the English Language Is Hard to Learn," http://web.cn.edu/kwheeler/English_hard_2learn.html. Dr. Wheeler, an associate professor of English at Carson-Newman University in Jefferson City, Tennessee, compiled his listing from various articles by Richard Lederer and the anonymous poem "The English Lesson."

2. J. Scott Duvall and J. Daniel Hays, *Grasping God's Word* (Grand Rapids: Zondervan, 2001).

3. Gordon D. Fee and Douglas Stuart, *How to Read the Bible for All Its Worth* (Grand Rapids: Zondervan, 2003), 35.

4. For example, I read the famous Shepherd Psalm in the new translation and saw that they had changed "the valley of the shadow of death" to "the darkest valley" (Psalm 23:4). *Are you kidding me? Nixing "the valley of the shadow of death"? There are some things you just don't mess with!* And the use of "they" and "them" plural pronouns linked to singular verbs when referring to either sex at times sounds strange to me.

5. Grant Osborne, *The Hermeneutical Spiral*, rev. ed. (Downers Grove, Ill.: InterVarsity, 2006), 70.

6. Moises Silva, *An Introduction to Biblical Hermeneutics* (Grand Rapids: Zondervan, 2007), 58.

7. George Barna, *Revolution* (Carol Stream, Ill.: Tyndale, 2006), 1–2, chapter 7. For a critique of the book, see Kevin Miller, "No Church? No Problem," http://www.christianity today.com/ct/2006/january/13.69.html.

8. Larry Norman, "I Wish We'd All Been Ready," copyright 1969 by Larry Norman. Used by permission of the Larry Norman Trust. All rights reserved.

Bibliography

Driscoll, Mark and Gerry Breshears. *Doctrine: What Christians Should Believe.* Wheaton: Crossway, 2010.

Duvall, J. Scott and J. Daniel Hays. *Grasping God's Word: A Hands-On Approach to Reading, Interpreting, and Applying the Bible.* Grand Rapids: Zondervan, 2005.

ESV Study Bible. Wheaton: Crossway, 2008. Print.

Fee, Gordon D. and Douglas Stuart. *How to Read the Bible for All Its Worth.* Grand Rapids: Zondervan, 2003.

Grudem, Wayne. *Systematic Theology.* Grand Rapids: Zondervan, 1994.

NIV Study Bible. Grand Rapids: Zondervan, 2008. Print.

Osborne, Grant. *The Hermeneutical Spiral: A Comprehensive Introduction to Biblical Interpretation,* rev. ed. Downers Grove, Ill.: InterVarsity, 2006.

JAMES L. NICODEM

Bible Savvy

Epic: The Storyline of the Bible unveils
the single theme that ties all of scripture
together: redemption.

Foundation: The Trustworthiness of the Bible
explains where our current bible came from
and why it can be wholly trusted.

Context: How to Understand the Bible shows
readers how to read the different parts of the
Bible as they were meant to be read and how
they fit together.

Walk: How to Apply the Bible puts the readers
increased understanding of the Bible into real
life terms and contexts.

Too many of us, regardless of our familiarity with the stories of the Bible, are blind to the story of the Bible. We miss the forest for the trees. We fail to recognize how the Bible's many individual stories fit together to tell one mega-story. The macro-story. The story of God and us.

> Phil Vischer
> Creator of Veggie Tales and What's in the Bible? video series

Jim Nicodem's purpose is to lay out, in straightforward, nontechnical language, many of the most important principles of interpretation. He does this so each person may know the foundational principles of biblical interpretation, and so understand many texts. In other words, Jim wants the church he serves, and many other churches, to be filled with men and women who will become better Bible readers.

> D. A. Carson, PhD
> Research Professor of New Testament at Trinity Evangelical Divinity School, Author of New Testament Commentary Survey

As a university professor on a Christian college campus, I can tell you that biblical illiteracy is on the rise. That's why the Bible Savvy series should be a prerequisite reading for everyone. Jim Nicodem puts the cookies on the bottom shelf by making the epic story of the biblical narrative understandable and accessible. The Bible Savvy series lays out the foundation and context for God's Word and then shows us in plain language how to apply the Bible's teachings to our lives step-by-step. It's phenomenal.

> Les Parrott, PhD
> Seattle Pacific University
> Author of You're Stronger Than You Think

The Bible is one of the most precious possessions to a believer living in a restricted nation. I am constantly amazed by the hunger for biblical teaching expressed by those who face persecution daily. Their sacrificial passion should inspire us to rekindle our quest for biblical understanding. Jim Nicodem's Bible Savvy series is the kind of resource needed to reengage our hearts and minds with God's Word, and renew a hunger for God's truth on par with our persecuted brother and sisters.

> James E. Dau
> President, The Voice of the Martyrs

Jim has done a masterful job in the Bible Savvy series! In these four concise books, Jim marches with clarity and skill into topics that would be difficult to tackle in a seminary classroom, much less in an American living room. And rather than a monologue, these books create a dialog among the author, the reader, their small group, and the living Word of God. These practical, approachable resources provide foundational training that is greatly needed by nearly every small group and leader I encounter.

> Greg Bowman
> Coauthor of *Coaching Life-Changing Small Group Leaders*
> Past executive director of the Willow Creek Association

Reading the four books in the Bible Savvy series is like getting a Bible college education in a box! The Lord is calling our nation to a Bible reading revolution, and these books are an invitation to be part of it.

> Hal Seed
> Author of *The Bible Questions* and *The God Questions*
> Lead Pastor, New Song Community Church, Oceanside, California

Living in the land of the Bible is considered a privilege by many, but the real privilege is to let the Bible become alive through us, in whatever land we may live. In the Bible Savvy series, Jim Nicodem not only helps us to understand God's plan to save us, but also His desire to change and shape us through His Word and Spirit in order to be a light in this dark world.

> Rev. Azar Ajaj
> Vice President and lecturer, Nazareth Evangelical Theological Seminary

To ignite a love for the God's Word in others is the goal of any spiritual leader. Communicating God's Word is the most important of all. Pastor Jim's Bible Savvy series is the tool, the guide, and the process for worship leaders to go into deep spiritual places. His biblical scholarship, communicated with such creativity, is exactly what is needed in worship ministry today.

> Stan Endicott
> Slingshot group coach/mentor
> Worship Leader, Mariners Church, Irvine, California

Jim Nicodem leads one of America's finest churches. Jim knows how to communicate the truth of the Bible that brings historical knowledge with incredible practical application. The Bible Savvy series is the best I have ever seen. Your life and faith will be enhanced as you use and apply this material to your life.

> Jim Burns, PhD
> President, HomeWord
> Author of *Creating an Intimate Marriage* and *Confident Parenting*

Pastor Nicodem is like a championship caliber coach: he loves to teach, and he stresses that success comes from mastering the basics. The Bible Savvy series will help you correctly interpret the best Playbook ever written: the Bible. Understanding and applying its fundamentals (with the help of the Bible Savvy series) will lead one to the Ultimate Victory . . . eternity with Jesus.

> James Brown
> Host of *The NFL Today* on the CBS television network

JAMES L. NICODEM

Bible Savvy

Hear from the author by
checking out the videos
on the Bible Savvy Series
with James Nicodem.

biblesavvy.com

Walk

How to Apply the Bible

James L. Nicodem

MOODY PUBLISHERS

CHICAGO

© 2013 by
JAMES L. NICODEM

Published in association with the literary agency of Wolgemuth & Associates,
Inc.

Edited by Jim Vincent
Interior design: Ragont Design
Cover design: Smartt Guys design
Cover image: iStockphoto

Library of Congress Cataloging-in-Publication Data

Nicodem, James L., 1956-
    Walk : how to apply the Bible / James L. Nicodem.
        pages cm. — (The Bible savvy series)
    Includes bibliographical references.
    ISBN 978-0-8024-0636-1
    1. Bible—Hermeneutics. 2. Bible—Criticism, interpretation, etc.
    I. Title.
    BS476.N53 2013
    220.6—dc23

                                                        2012047219

We hope you enjoy this book from Moody Publishers. Our goal is to
provide high-quality, thought-provoking books and products that connect
truth to your real needs and challenges. For more information on other books
and products written and produced from a biblical perspective, go to www.
moodypublishers.com or write to:

Moody Publishers
820 N. LaSalle Boulevard
Chicago, IL 60610

1 3 5 7 9 10 8 6 4 2

Printed in the United States of America

About the
Bible Savvy Series

I MET THE REAL ESTATE AGENT at my front
door and invited him in. My wife and I were about to put
our home on the market and I had called Jeff as a potential
representative. As he sat down at our dining room table and
opened his briefcase, I noticed a Bible perched on top of other
papers. I asked Jeff if he was a Bible reader and he replied that
he was just getting started. What had prompted his interest?
He'd recently come across a list in *Success, Inc.* magazine of
the most influential books recommended by business leaders.
The Bible had been the most frequently mentioned book on
the list. So, Jeff was going to give it a try.

My real estate agent isn't alone in his new interest in the
Bible. According to a recent survey, 91 percent of those who
have lately begun attending church were motivated to do so
by a desire to understand what the Bible has to say to their
lives.[1] That means nine of every ten visitors to church are intrigued by the Bible! But while they are curious about God's
Word, they're also a bit intimidated by it. The Bible is such
a daunting book, written in ancient times and addressed to

vastly different cultures. Is it really possible to draw relevant insights from it for our lives today? People are returning to church to find out.

Ironically, while an interest in Bible knowledge can be detected among those who are new to church, it seems to be on the wane among many veteran churchgoers. When my oldest daughter enrolled at a Christian college, the president of the school addressed parents on opening day. He told us that the Bible comprehension exams of each incoming class of freshmen show less and less knowledge of God's Word. And then he added: "These kids are growing up in *your* churches." Evidently, many churches are not doing a good job of teaching committed believers how to read, interpret, and apply the Bible.

The Bible Savvy series has been written to help a wide spectrum of Bible readers—from newbies to seasoned Bible study leaders—get their arms around God's Word. This multi-book series covers four essential Bible-related topics that Moody Publishers has made available in one set as a comprehensive manual for understanding God's Word and putting it into practice. *Walk* is the final book of the four-book series.

An added bonus to the Bible Savvy series is the Study Guide that follows every chapter of each book. These questions for personal reflection and group discussion have been crafted by a team of small-groups experts. The Study Guide is also available online at biblesavvy.com and may be downloaded and used for personal study or reproduced for members of a small group.

Four Things You Must Know to
Get the Most out of God's Word

The four books of the Bible Savvy series will give you a grasp of the following topics, allowing God's Word to become a rich resource in your life:

1. *The storyline of the Bible.* The Bible is actually a compilation of sixty-six books that were written over a 1,500-year period. But amazingly there is one central storyline that holds everything together. You'll trace this storyline in *Epic* from Genesis to Revelation, learning how each of the sixty-six books contributes to the overall plot.

2. *The reliability of the Bible.* How did God communicate what He wanted to say through human authors? What are the evidences that the Bible is a supernatural book? How do we know that the *right* books made it into the Bible and that the *wrong* books were kept out of it? Isn't a text that was hand-copied for hundreds of years bound to be filled with errors? *Foundation* will give you answers to questions like

these—because you won't get much out of the Bible until you're certain that you can trust it.

3. *How to understand the Bible*. People read all sorts of crazy things into the Bible, and have used it to support a wide variety of strange (and sometimes reprehensible) positions and activities. In *Context* you will learn the basic ground rules for accurately interpreting Scripture. (Yes, there are rules.)

4. *How to apply the Bible*. It's one thing to read the Bible, and it's another thing entirely to walk away from your reading with an application for your life. Even members of Bible study groups occasionally do a poor job of this. Participants leave these gatherings without a clear sense of how they're going to put God's Word into practice. *Walk* will equip you to become a Bible doer.

Do You Have Savvy?

The dictionary defines *savvy* as *practical know-how*. It is my hope and prayer that the Bible Savvy series will lead you into an experiential knowledge of God's Word that will transform your life.

Many people have contributed to my own love and understanding of the Bible over the years—as well as to the writing of this book. I owe a huge debt of gratitude to them.

Mom and Dad made God's Word central to our family life, encouraging my siblings and me to memorize big chunks of it.

When I got to high school, I was a bit turned off to church, but I started attending a youth ministry in a neighboring suburb that was led by Bill Hybels. (These were pre–Willow Creek Community Church days, when dinosaurs roamed the earth.) Bill had (and still has) an incredible ability to open the Bible, read a passage out loud, and then drive home its application to the lives of his listeners. After a year of hearing him teach God's Word in such a life-impacting way, I went away to college and decided to major in biblical studies.

Two professors (among many) fanned the flame of my love for the Bible during my college and seminary years. Dr. Gerry Hawthorne taught me Greek New Testament at Wheaton College, and there are thousands of men and women in ministry around the world today who still remember his simple-but-powerful class devotions. He'd put one verse on the chalkboard (remember chalk?) and then tease out its significance for our lives—often with tears in his eyes. Dr. D. A. Carson taught me the Bible at Trinity Evangelical Divinity School. His books (and occasional phone and email exchanges) continue to shape me today. I aspire to have even a quarter of his passion for God's Word!

After school, as I started out in youth ministry, I began listening to cassette tapes (same era as chalk) by Dr. John

MacArthur. John is internationally famous for his verse-by-verse teaching of Scripture. Although he is occasionally more adamant about certain doctrines than I am (we agree on the essentials), his love for the Bible is infectious. John has set the bar high for all pastors who want to faithfully teach their churches God's Word. As my ministry has continued, I have found other communicators who whet my appetite for Scripture—many of them through their books, some of them currently through their podcasts. Thank you Lee Strobel, Joe Stowell, John Ortberg, Mark Driscoll, Francis Chan, Tim Keller, and many others.

Today, my desire to get people into the Bible is fueled by the five thousand-plus eager learners whom I have the privilege of pastoring at Christ Community Church of St. Charles, Illinois, and its regional campuses. I am especially grateful for both the staff and volunteer leaders who oversee almost four hundred Community Groups that are studying God's Word. And one of those leaders, who writes incredible Bible curricula and teaches scores of Bible-hungry women, is my wife, Sue. Her devotion to Scripture is a constant inspiration to me.

Lastly, a special thanks to my faithful assistant, Angee Jenkins, who helped to edit my manuscript, track down footnotes, and protect my writing time; and to my agent, Andrew Wolgemuth, who found a great publisher in Moody to make the Bible Savvy series available to you.

To watch Jim's personal introduction to Walk,
scan the QR code below with your smartphone or go to
www.biblesavvy.com/video/#walk1.

Contents

Foreword

JIM NICODEM HAS done a great job in the Bible Savvy series of demonstrating that the Bible is a special book whose storyline is compelling, whose content is reliably authoritative, and whose history and theology is understandable. But as good as the first three books have been, it would be of no avail if Jim hadn't made it all the way to this closing volume in the series. Digesting the earlier books equips us to move confidently into Scripture to harvest fascinating truths about God and ourselves. But if all we have at the end is a bucket load of knowledge, we have missed the point!

God never intended that the Bible would simply make us smart—although that is a part of the process. If all we have is knowledge of what is true and right from God's point of view, then we are in a dangerous place. Knowledge left to itself will make us proud of what we know and judgmental toward those who are biblically ignorant. Instead, God gave us the His Word to transform our lives—to move us from assimilation to application so that in the end we can reflect His glory by becoming conformed to the image of Jesus Christ.

But applying the transforming truth of Scripture is a challenge. A challenge because the process begins with the convicting power of God's Word which, like a mirror, shows us what we really are like and what needs to be changed. When you got up this morning and looked in the mirror you immediately knew that you needed to do something about it . . . and everyone around you was glad that you did.

Do your world and the testimony of Christ through you a favor and surrender to the life changing influence of the Bible. In our fallen state we are not prone to forgiveness, grace, mercy, patience, generosity, unconditional love and a host of other virtues that make your life a blessing to others and a credit to God. Applying divine truth to our anything-but-divine lives will in the end make us humble about ourselves and compassionate toward others.

With the assistance of the indwelling Spirit, an open Bible on your lap and Pastor Nicodem's handy volume nearby, open your heart and let the transforming work of God's Word do its work!

JOSEPH STOWELL
President, Cornerstone University

Introduction:
"So What?"

I WENT STRAIGHT FROM being a biblical studies major in college (where I wrestled with Scripture in the original Hebrew and Greek) to being a youth pastor in a church (where I taught the Bible to middle school and high school students). What an abrupt transition!

Those kids weren't particularly interested in how the tense of a Greek verb impacted something Paul wrote in one of his epistles. They were preoccupied with gaining popularity at school, making it onto the basketball team, following their favorite band, and finishing their homework before the weekend was over. How could I teach them God's Word in a way that would be relevant to their everyday lives?

Being newly married at the time, I took advantage of my wife's wise input as I prepared my weekly talks for these students. I remember sitting Sue down on the threadbare sofa in our sparsely furnished apartment and making her listen to parts of each message before I went public with them. Then I would ask her for feedback.

Almost always, the first thing out of her mouth was a two-word question: "So what?"

"What do you mean, 'so what'?" I would shoot back, feeling defensive.

She would then patiently explain that my talk hadn't clearly called for an application. What was my text from the Bible challenging these students to do? What was the *so what* of my presentation?

While I was frequently annoyed with Sue for pointing out this recurring deficiency in the rough drafts of my talks, I knew she was putting her finger on something very important. James warns us in his New Testament epistle, "Do not merely listen to the word, and so deceive yourselves. Do what it says" (James 1:22). The end result of exposure to the Bible—whether by listening, reading, or studying—should be the application of what it teaches. What will we put into practice? How will we *walk* the Word?

Walk is the final book in the Bible Savvy series. It is the culmination of everything that has been taught in the first three books about grasping the Bible's storyline (*Epic*), trusting the reliability of the Bible's text (*Foundation*), and interpreting each Bible passage according to sound hermeneutics (*Context*). Yet none of this has lasting impact on our lives if we don't walk away from each encounter with God's Word prepared to do something in response to it. Unfortunately, what the text is asking you to do will not always be readily apparent. Coming up with applications that fit your life's circumstances is a learned skill. *Walk* will give you the steps for acquiring that skill.

{ 1 }

Light for the Path

IF YOU EVER GET THE opportunity to visit Israel, make sure you visit Hezekiah's Tunnel—but bring a flashlight with you! Otherwise you will walk in complete darkness during your tunnel tour. The tunnel, located on the south side of the old city of Jerusalem, was constructed back in 700 BC by Israel's King Hezekiah as he was getting ready for an Assyrian invasion.

Jerusalem's major water supply at the time was the Gihon Spring, which, unfortunately, was located *outside* the city walls. That's not a good spot for your major water supply if your city is about to come under siege!

So King Hezekiah covered over the Gihon Spring and began building an underground aqueduct to divert the water to a pool (the Pool of Siloam) *inside* the city walls. One team of underground diggers started at the spring, while the other team started at the pool—and they somehow managed to meet in the middle! The finished aqueduct, five hundred yards long, was an engineering marvel in 700 BC.

Besides bringing a flashlight for your tunnel tour, be ready to walk through knee-deep, icy cold water for forty-five minutes. I emphasize that flashlight because I remember Sue and I didn't have one when we made our trek through the tunnel a couple of summers ago. We were enrolled in a course at Jerusalem University College with forty other students, so we were counting on others in the class to come prepared. Only a few of them were. (Where are the Boy Scouts when you need them?)

It was a really, really dark and claustrophobic walk for most of the way. Our only consolation was knowing that if we kept moving forward—and the walls were so narrow and the ceiling was so low at times that forward was the only direction we *could* move—we would eventually end up at our destination. Yup, next time we'll bring a flashlight!

Turn On the Light!

Hezekiah's Tunnel is a metaphorical picture of our lives. On any given day, we can feel like we're in desperate need of light. There's a big decision looming in front of us, or we're in the middle of a crisis, or we're struggling in our parenting, or we're trying to figure out a career path, or there's conflict and confusion in some important relationship. And we're just not sure what to do next. We're *in the dark*, as the saying goes. We wish somebody would shine a little light on our path.

Well, that's exactly what God offers to do. The light that He shines is the light of His Word. In Psalm 119:105, the psalmist says to God: "Your word is a lamp to my feet and a light for my path." God has given us His Word to *illuminate* our lives. In this chapter we are going to take a look at three important aspects of that illumination.

Illumination's Source

A few years ago, the elders of our church were wrestling with a difficult situation. One of them mentioned a passage in the gospel of Matthew that he thought might be relevant to our discussion. We all turned to that text to take a closer look at it. But after we read the verses together, we weren't quite sure how to interpret them correctly. No problem. I just pulled a commentary on Matthew's Gospel off my shelf (a book of several hundred pages, written by a Bible scholar) and read aloud what it had to say about our passage. Unfortunately, we didn't understand what the *commentary* had to say about the passage in Matthew that we didn't understand. (Understand?)

Now what? Fortunately, the New Testament expert who had written that Matthew commentary is a friend of mine. He was one of my professors in graduate school. So I called him up. And I asked him for an explanation of his commentary's explanation of our passage. We had a very enlightening conversation, after which I was able to guide our elders in applying an important principle from Matthew to our difficult situation.

Now, wouldn't *you* love to have the phone number of your very own Bible scholar/friend on speed dial? When you're reading the Bible this week and come across something you don't understand, you could just punch that number and Bob-the-Bible-Brain would pick up. Then you could ask him: "What's the deal with all those funky dietary laws that Moses recorded in Leviticus?" Or, "What does Paul mean by 'justification' in Romans 3?" Imagine having your very own Bible scholar/friend—just a phone call away.

Hey, I've got an even crazier idea! Instead of calling some modern-day Bible scholar, what if you could text your question to the *original* author of any portion of Scripture? What if you could contact Moses *directly* about those funky dietary laws in Leviticus, or ask the apostle Paul *himself* to explain justification in Romans 3 to you?

OK. I'll go one better than that—better than a modern-day Bible scholar at your service, better than a direct connection with one of the Bible's original authors. What if God Himself—who inspired those original human authors to write what they wrote—were available to explain Bible passages to you? Cool!

Well, I'm not making up this last option. Look at what the apostle Paul wrote to the Corinthians about God's assistance in illuminating our understanding of what He's communicated to us:

For who among men knows the thoughts of a man except the man's spirit within him? In the same way no one knows the thoughts of God except the Spirit of God. We have not received the spirit of the world but the Spirit who is from God, that we may understand what God has freely given us. This is what we speak, not in words taught us by human wisdom but in words taught by the Spirit, expressing spiritual truths in spiritual words. The man without the Spirit does not accept the things that come from the Spirit of God, for they are foolishness to him, and he cannot understand them, because they are spiritually discerned. (1 Corinthians 2:11–14)

Now, there's a ton of stuff in these verses that I would love to unpack—but I'm only going to take the time to explain the basic flow of what the apostle Paul is teaching here. First, Paul points out that nobody knows or understands God quite like God's own Spirit (verse 11: "No one knows the thoughts of God except the Spirit of God").

Second, Paul reminds his readers that, if they're now Christ followers, they have God's Spirit living on the inside. This is one of the benefits that Jesus promises those who surrender their lives to Him. When you ask Jesus to forgive your sins and rule your life, He gives you the Holy Spirit as a signing bonus (verse 12: "We have not received the spirit of the world but the Spirit who is from God").

Third, Paul explains that this is the reason that some people understand the things that come from God (e.g., the Bible) and other people don't. If you've begun to follow Jesus and have God's Spirit on the inside, God's Spirit helps you understand God's Word. On the other hand, if you're not yet a Christ follower, then the Holy Spirit doesn't indwell you and it's not surprising that you find the Bible to be confusing, boring, unrelated to your life, or just plain not worth reading.

This means that if you want God's Word to shine light on your path, you first need the Holy Spirit to shine light on God's Word. (That last sentence is so important that I'm going to ask you to go back and read it a second time. Thanks.) Theologians have a name for the truth that I'm describing here. They call it the *doctrine of illumination*. God wants to speak to you. He speaks through His Word, the Bible. But you won't be able to make sense of what God's saying until you surrender your life to Christ and the Holy Spirit comes to live in you.

YOU CANNOT make sense of what God's saying until you surrender your life to Christ and the Holy Spirit comes to live in you.

Have you done that yet?

Now, please don't misunderstand me here. You don't need the Holy Spirit in order to make sense of the Bible from an *external* standpoint. Anybody can read a Bible and understand it externally. Anybody can follow the meaning of its words, or the structure of its sentences, or the logic of its passages. However, as Martin Luther, the great reformer and theologian of the sixteenth century, put it: there's a big difference between the *external* clarity of the Bible, which anybody can grasp, and the *internal* clarity of the Bible—what it means for our lives personally—which only those with God's Spirit on the inside can grasp. (I haven't been able to track down where Luther said this. But trust me—I'm sure he said it.)

And only when you are able to grasp God's Word does it begin to grasp you. Are you experiencing this? When you read the Bible, do things jump off the page at you? Do you get excited as you come across truths that have direct bearing on your life? That's God's Spirit *illuminating* the text for you.

In fact, every time you pick up your Bible to read it, or study it in a small group, or listen to it in a sermon, it's a good idea to offer a quick prayer: *God, may Your Spirit help me understand and apply to my life what I'm about to encounter in Your Word.* I can't emphasize strongly enough how important it is to approach God's Word by prayerfully inviting the Spirit to speak to you. If you're a Christ follower, the Holy Spirit is now your internal tutor.

Of course, this doesn't mean that everything you come across in the Bible is going to be easy to understand. Yes, the

Holy Spirit is going to help you. But like any good teacher who uses an assortment of pedagogical tools to get the job done (e.g., visual aids, textbooks, lab experiments), the Spirit uses a variety of means to help you understand and apply the Bible to your life: a study Bible, a good small group curriculum, the teaching pastors of your church, and so on. But you will still be amazed—once you have the Holy Spirit on the inside—at how much of the Bible comes alive to you with no outside help.

THE UNDERLYING source of all biblical understanding is the Holy Spirit. He is what you need most.

You may have been raised in a church tradition where you were taught *not* to study the Bible on your own. Without the assistance of a priest, or a minister, or a rabbi—you were warned—you would not be able to make sense of the Bible. While I would certainly agree that gifted teachers are a tremendous asset when it comes to gaining insight from God's Word, let me repeat my point that the underlying source of all biblical understanding is the Holy Spirit. He is what you need most. And if you have Him, a good portion of the Bible is going to be clear to you without any additional input.

Theologians call this the *doctrine of perspicuity.* (It's closely related to the *doctrine of illumination,* which I mentioned earlier.) I'll bet you don't know what *perspicuity* means. Give up? It means *clarity*. You gotta love theologians—they choose an obscure word like *perspicuity* to talk about clarity.

The *doctrine of perspicuity* expresses a great truth. Here it is (in my own words): God's Word will be clear, for the most part, to those who have put their trust in Jesus Christ. Why? Because the Spirit, as your resident tutor, will illuminate the Bible (see John 14:26; 16:13–15). And once the Spirit begins to illuminate the Bible for you, the Bible will be able to illuminate your life. You will discover, as the psalmist did, that God's Word is "a lamp to [your] feet and a light for [your] path" (Psalm 119:105).

Illumination's Condition

Let me tell you an Old Testament story about a guy named Naaman. (You can find it in 2 Kings 5 if you want to read it for yourself.) Naaman was the commander of the king's army in Aram, one of Israel's adversaries. The Bible describes him as "a great man in the sight of his master and . . . a valiant soldier" (v. 1). But in spite of all that Naaman had going for him, he had one horrific problem: *leprosy*. Leprosy was an incurable disease that could take his life.

As God would have it, in Naaman's household there was a Jewish servant girl who was familiar with the miracle-working ministry of an Israeli prophet named Elisha. When

29

the servant girl told her master about this potential source of healing, Naaman pulled together some money, got a letter of recommendation from his king, and made a beeline for Israel.

Arriving at Elisha's home and expecting to be personally welcomed by the prophet, Naaman was a tad insulted when a servant was sent to the door to greet him. And what was worse—the servant delivered these bizarre instructions to Naaman: "Go, wash yourself seven times in the Jordan, and your flesh will be restored" (v. 10). Well, Naaman was a proud man and the Jordan River was a dirty and unimpressive stream, so he rejected Elisha's secondhand counsel. There was no way that he was going to obey this humiliating directive. Naaman revved up his chariot and prepared to return home to Aram.

But Naaman's servants wouldn't let their boss throw in the towel. They said (my paraphrase of verse 13): "Yeah, it looks like a stupid command—dunk in the Jordan River seven times. But what harm would it do to give it a try?" So Naaman gave it a try. And he came out of the water completely cleansed of his leprosy.

Here's the point that I want to draw out of this story. As long as Naaman refused to heed Elisha's instructions, those instructions had zero impact on his life. In fact, those instructions seemed ridiculous (unreasonable, absurd, preposterous) to him. But once Naaman made up his mind to *obey* the words of

God's prophet, those instructions changed his life. It will work the same way in your life. Only when you come to the Bible with a submissive attitude will the Bible truly impact you.

If you approach the Bible with an unsubmissive attitude, not only will you gain nothing from it, you may even conclude that some of its instructions are just plain stupid. So illumination's condition is a submissive attitude. God's Word is not going to make sense to you until you approach it with a willingness to do what it says. The Holy Spirit is eager to illuminate the Bible for those who are eager to obey it. Note the close connection between illumination and obedience in the following passage:

> Jesus replied, "If anyone loves me, he will obey my teaching. My Father will love him, and we will come to him and make our home with him. He who does not love me will not obey my teaching. These words you hear are not my own; they belong to the Father who sent me.
>
> "All this I have spoken while still with you. But the Counselor, the Holy Spirit, whom the Father will send in my name, will teach you all things and will remind you of everything I have said to you." (John 14:23–26)

ONLY WHEN you come to the Bible with a submissive attitude will the Bible truly impact you.

One of the Bible interpretation rules presented in *Context* is to look for repeating words or ideas. Three very significant words pop up several times in this little clump of verses you just read. Can you pick them out? One of them is "teaching" (or "teach"). Jesus is pointing out something that we already noted in 1 Corinthians 2: the Holy Spirit has been given to Christ followers as an internal *Teacher.* He is *illumination's source.* One of His jobs is to help us understand God's Word.

What are the other two repeating words in this passage? *Love* and *obey.* If we expect the Holy Spirit's teaching to make sense to us and impact our lives, then we need to approach God's Word in an attitude of loving obedience. That's the condition for receiving illumination.

Let me illustrate the importance of meeting this condition with something Jesus said to a group of His detractors who failed in this regard: "You diligently study the Scriptures because you think that by them you possess eternal life. These are the Scriptures that testify about me, yet you refuse to come to me to have life" (John 5:39–40).

Do you follow Jesus' accusation here? He's telling a bunch of religious leaders that they don't "get" God's Word. Specifically, they don't grasp what the Bible has to say about eternal life. Why not? Well, it wasn't because they hadn't studied the Bible. They were Bible experts! No, the problem was that they didn't meet the *condition* for Bible illumination. What's the condition? You've got to approach the Bible with a submissive attitude—with a willingness to obey whatever it says. The religious leaders didn't meet that condition, as demonstrated by the fact that they refused to come to Jesus for eternal life even though that's exactly what the Bible instructed them to do!

What about *you*? What disposition do you bring to the Bible? Do you approach the Bible like it's an all-you-can-eat buffet, where you are free to take what you want and leave the rest? Don't expect the Holy Spirit to illuminate God's Word and God's Word to light your path if *that's* your attitude. In fact, I'd encourage you to confess any such attitude to God as sin. Tell God you're sorry for the arrogance of picking and choosing which parts of the Bible you're going to obey. Ask Him to forgive you, and to give you a submissive, eager-to-obey-everything-He-says spirit.

A number of years ago, I attended a pastors' conference at a well-known megachurch in California. In fact, the church had recently been in the news. A large group of pro-choice protestors had picketed one Sunday morning because the church had a reputation for teaching a pro-life position.

News reporters and camera crews from nearby Los Angeles TV stations were recording the action. The senior pastor told us of one reporter's comment and subsequent conversation. The TV reporter had stuck a microphone in the pastor's face and said,

"I must admit that I've been a little surprised by your church. I wasn't familiar with it before today, so when I heard that you were being picketed by a pro-choice group, I just imagined a different sort of church than the one I've found."

The pastor politely asked, "What sort of church did you imagine?"

"Well, I'll tell you what I *didn't* imagine," the reporter replied. "I *didn't* imagine a church that would have so many attenders. Why, even the local mayor goes here . . . and lots of young, well-educated women! How did you manage to get so many people to buy into a pro-life position?" (There's no such thing as media bias, right?)

Here was the pastor's explanation. He said (my paraphrase): "The issue is not getting people to buy into a pro-life position. The issue is getting people to submit to the authority of God's Word. Because once they are willing to do whatever God says, then all we have to do is teach them what God says and they're eager to obey it. So, if the Bible says that God knits a baby together in its mother's womb before the child is ever born [Psalm 139], then our church's members are going to protect that unborn baby!"

Did you follow that? You must choose between two approaches to the Bible. Either God's Word is going to stand in authority over you (i.e., you're willing to obey whatever it says), or you are going to stand in authority over God's Word (i.e., you'll pick and choose what you want to obey).

EITHER GOD'S Word is going to stand in authority over you, or you are going to stand in authority over God's Word.

Let me encourage you to go with the first of those two positions. Determine that you will submit to the authority of God's Word. Only then will God's Spirit illuminate the Bible for you. And only then will the Bible illuminate your life.

Beware of any traces of an unsubmissive attitude—any tendencies to dismiss the Bible's directives as outdated, or ridiculous, or not worthy of serious consideration. Watch for rebellious thoughts. The Bible on sexual purity? *Nobody follows those standards anymore!* The Bible on tithing? *Who'd be crazy enough to give 10 percent of their paycheck to the church?* The Bible on forgiving those who abuse you? *You don't know my boss!* The Bible on training your children in Scripture? *When is there time to do that between sports and music lessons and family getaways?*

Keep in mind that *illumination's condition* is a submissive attitude.

Illumination's Aim

We're about to take a look at one of the word pictures the Bible uses to describe itself. But before we look at this word picture in the epistle of James, let me mention several other Bible metaphors that appear throughout Scripture. Significantly, they all describe the Bible as something that's very active, very dynamic. The Bible is not just a book that's intended to sit on a shelf or coffee table or kitchen counter gathering dust. It's God's means of accomplishing His purposes in our lives.

Psalm 119:105 describes God's Word as a lamp that lights our path. Jeremiah 23:29 depicts it as both a fire that purifies and a hammer that breaks up the hardness of our heart. Ephesians 6:17 calls it a sword that we're to use when fighting our spiritual enemies. First Peter 2:2 portrays it as milk that nourishes us. And James 1:21 paints it as a seed that sprouts to eternal life in us.

You get the idea. God intends the Bible to work us over. God's Word is meant to do something *to* us, or *in* us, or *for* us.

> **GOD'S WORD is meant to do something *to* us, or *in* us, or *for* us.**

Now let's look at the word picture in James:

Do not merely listen to the word, and so deceive yourselves. Do what it says. Anyone who listens to the word but does not do what it says is like a man who looks at his face in a mirror and, after looking at himself, goes away and immediately forgets what he looks like. But the man who looks intently into the perfect law that gives freedom, and continues to do this, not forgetting what he has heard, but doing it—he will be blessed in what he does. (James 1:22–25)

What metaphor is used to describe the Bible in these verses? *A mirror.* How can we use the Bible like a mirror in our lives? Well, there are a couple of ways to look into a mirror. The first is to cast a quick glance into it as you're walking by. You might wink at yourself, or smile . . . but that's about it. The other way is to gaze intently into the mirror in order to make some adjustment to yourself. You comb your hair, or shave your face, or pick the spinach leaf from between your teeth, or practice the hand gestures for your presentation at school or work, or evaluate how many pounds you have to lose, or try on a new outfit. Whatever. You look into the mirror with the *aim* of improving yourself.

In a similar fashion, there are two ways of looking into God's Word. The first is to look into it and do *nothing.* The other way is to look into it and do *something.* James says that we should always look into the Bible with the aim of doing *something*—making some God-pleasing improvement to our lives. The final goal of reading or studying or listening to a sermon from the Bible is not *knowledge.* It's *life-change.* Gaining

Bible knowledge is important, but only as a means to an end. The end is to do something with what we've just learned.

I am constantly promoting Community Groups (small group Bible studies) at our church. I love to see men, women, and students commit to a weekly venue where they'll dig into God's Word with friends. But surprisingly, I also do a fair amount of talking people *out* of Community Groups. Why would I talk somebody out of Bible study? Because I frequently run into people who are in multiple groups. Now, I suppose that on rare occasions it's beneficial to be in *two* groups at once (especially if you're married, and one of the groups is a couples group). But I get concerned when people confuse Bible *knowledge* (learning lots of "deep" Bible factoids in multiple groups) with Bible *life transformation* (putting what's been learned into practice).

One of my constant mantras is: *It's not how much of the Bible you get through that matters, but how much of the Bible gets through you!* If you're taking in more Scripture than you can put into practice, it would be better to scale back to one small group meeting and to focus on *walking* the Word. The same goes for the amount of Bible you import through Christian radio and the sermon podcasts of your favorite communicator. The aim of being illuminated by God's Word is to *apply what you've learned* to your life.

My best buddy in college was the wide receiver on the

football team. One day I was talking to him about the upcoming NFL playoffs—what teams I thought would win, who my favorite players were . . . that kind of stuff. Suddenly it dawned on me that this guy wasn't participating in the conversation. In fact,

DON'T SETTLE for merely reading the Bible or studying it or listening to it preached. Put the Bible into play in your life.

he didn't seem to know very much about the National Football League. So I gave him a hard time. "You're a football player and yet you hardly know anything about professional football!" He quickly retorted: "I'd rather *play* football than *watch* it!"

He's right. Participating beats observing. Don't settle for "watching" the Bible—merely reading it, or studying it, or listening to it preached. Put the Bible into play in your life. Let it always be your *aim* to come away from God's Word with an application for your life. You could even do that right now with something you learned in this chapter about *Illumination's Source* (the Holy Spirit), *Illumination's Condition* (a submissive, eager-to-obey attitude), and *Illumination's Aim* (to put something into practice). What's your application?

Perhaps you're thinking: *I'm not sure how to craft good applications from what I learn in the Bible. How do I go from text to life?* Good question. That's what we're going to cover in the next chapter.

Study Guide

The *Study Guide* questions at the end of each chapter have been designed for your personal benefit. *All* questions can be used for personal study and, if you're part of a discussion group, for preparation for your group meeting. If you are part of a small group, you will find that the questions preceded by the group icon (👥) are especially useful for discussion. Your group leader can choose from among those questions when the group meets.

Icebreakers

- Describe a time in your life when you were caught in the dark—without a light.
- When you read the Bible on your own, how often do you come away from it with a specific application for your life? (Explain your answer.)

    Always

    Frequently

    Sometimes

    Seldom

1. If a person regularly finds the Bible to be confusing, boring, or difficult to apply to their life, what might that indicate? Why?

2. Read Ephesians 1:13–14. How does a person get the Holy Spirit? What picture does Paul paint in these verses about the Holy Spirit's role in the lives of believers? Why should this be encouraging to a Christ follower?

3. Read 1 Corinthians 2:11–14 and Romans 8:5–17. Make a list of ways in which the Holy Spirit demonstrates His presence in a person's life. Circle the evidences on the list that you see in your own life.

4. What do you learn in John 14:15–17, 26 and John 16:7–15 about the Holy Spirit's role as your personal Bible teacher?

If the Holy Spirit has been given to you as a resident tutor, how might that impact the way in which you approach reading, studying, and applying the Bible?

5. What is the *condition* you must meet in order for the Holy Spirit to illuminate God's Word for you? What might be some indications of such an attitude on your part?

6. What has been one or two of the hardest lessons for you to learn from God's Word? Why were they so difficult to apply?

7. What does Paul warn us *not* to do to the Holy Spirit in Ephesians 4:30? Read the surrounding context to this verse (vv. 25–32) and note the sorts of behaviors that would do this to God's Spirit.

How might grieving the Holy Spirit affect His role as your teacher and illuminator of God's Word?

8. (image) Explain how the Bible serves as a mirror in the life of a Christ follower.

What are some tips for using the Bible as a mirror that you pick up in James 1:22–25?

In the very next verses (James 1:26–27), what are some of the changes that James says should be made in our lives after looking into the mirror of God's Word?

9. (image) What is something you will *start* doing or *stop* doing as an application of this chapter?

{ 2 }

From Text to Life

MY TWENTY-FIVE-YEAR-OLD son, Andrew, is a Pied Piper when it comes to younger kids. Children love to hang out with him. He's a good time. So it didn't surprise me when Andrew, after graduating from college, landed a job as a sixth-grade teacher. Nor was I surprised when he turned out to be one of the most popular teachers in the school. Not many teachers would take on thirty kids in a game of playground dodge ball! But this became a favorite pastime of Andrew, along with engaging students in personal conversations and making English literature cool.

As Andrew began his first summer break as a teacher, he decided to make some extra income by offering to tutor students. A few of his own kids were immediately interested. So were a couple of their friends from other schools. But Andrew quickly noticed a big difference between his own kids and their outside friends. His own kids were used to his interactive teaching style. He'd trained them to contribute to lively discussions.

This wasn't the case with their outside friends. Andrew was incredulous when he asked one young girl some questions about her reading assignment and her eyes glazed over. She didn't have an answer. This was new territory for him.

As he was telling me this story, he said, "She just looked at me, Dad. She just looked at me! I could tell she hadn't read her assignment very thoroughly—because she had nothing to say."

Maybe you feel like that little girl when you read the Bible. Maybe you have a hard time paying attention. Maybe you don't get anything out of it. Maybe your eyes glaze over. Maybe you're not reading the Bible with any regularity . . . because you're just not drawn to it. In the last chapter I cautioned that if this is true of you, it could be an indication that you don't yet have a personal relationship with Jesus Christ. Because once you begin a relationship with Jesus, the first thing He does is give you the Holy Spirit. God's Spirit comes to live inside of you. And one of the Spirit's jobs is to make God's Word come alive to you. He gives you a love for the Bible and helps you understand it and apply it to your life.

So if you are not experiencing this yourself, it *could* be that the Holy Spirit isn't presently living on the inside. You need to surrender your life to Christ. That's *one* possibility. Another possibility is that the Holy Spirit *does* live in you, but you've just never been taught how to put the Bible into practice. You'd really like to be able to do this, but it seems like a daunting task. The reason your eyes glaze over is *not* because you're disinterested in the Bible; they glaze over because you don't know how to *walk* the Word. You don't know how to move *from text to life*.

This chapter will offer you a step-by-step process for doing that—four steps in all. And you're not going to forget these four points, because I'm going to give them to you in the form of an acronym. Taken together, the first letter of each step spells a word: *COMA*. Follow these instructions and you'll break out of a spiritual *coma* as you read the Bible. Instead of your eyes glazing over, you'll sense God prompting and empowering you to *do* something. (Just for the record, the COMA acronym is not original with me. I don't know who first came up with it, but it's been used by Christ followers for years as a reminder of how the Bible application process works. I just like COMA because it's memorable.)

C: Context

When you're reading a passage from the Bible, before you can apply that passage to your *own* life, you need to understand what it meant to its original audience. What was their *context*?

Let me illustrate why context is so important. Stephen Covey, author of the bestselling book *The 7 Habits of Highly Effective People*, tells the story about a time he was riding a train in the city. There was a father on the train with three young kids—and those kids were really acting up. They were running up and down the aisle, banging into people. And the dad just sat there, oblivious to the havoc his children were causing.

Finally, Covey couldn't take it any longer. He tapped the dad on the shoulder and said, "Sir, your children are really disturbing a lot of people. I wonder if you couldn't control them a little more?" The dad looked up and replied, "Oh, you're right. I guess I should do something about it. We just came from the hospital where their mother died about an hour ago. I don't know what to think, and I guess they don't know how to handle it either." Covey immediately felt like a total jerk. He had jumped to the wrong conclusion because he hadn't taken the time to understand this dad's context. And so Covey warns us, in his book, not to make the same mistake. Don't read your autobiography into other people's lives.[1]

That's good advice to follow when you're reading the Bible. Don't try to figure out what God is saying to *you* until you've figured out what God was saying to the original audience. What was the context of that audience? We covered this topic in detail in book three of the Bible Savvy series (*Context*), which dealt with the rules of Bible interpretation. The basic premise behind these rules is: *You must understand the context.*

And there are four contexts that you need to consider for

every Bible passage. The first is the passage's *historical setting*. Who wrote the book of the Bible that you're reading? Who were they writing to? When did the action in this book take place? (1400 BC? AD 60?) What was going on in the world at the time? What problem was the author addressing in the lives of his readers? You can easily acquire this information by reading the brief introduction to any Bible book in your study Bible.

Second, you need to consider your passage's *literary setting*. There are at least six different kinds of literature in the Bible, and different rules for interpreting each one. You don't interpret, for example, an Old Testament law in the same way that you interpret one of David's psalms—or a prophecy in Isaiah, or a parable in Matthew's Gospel, or a directive in one of Paul's epistles. Let me remind you of why the rules of interpreting these various genres are so important by relating an amusing anecdote.

Several years ago, a guy wrote a bestseller called *The Year of Living Biblically*. The author decided that he would try to obey all the Old Testament laws for an entire year. Now, if you read *Context*, you may recall that one of the rules for interpreting Old Testament laws is to differentiate between laws that were only meant for ancient Israel and laws that are still in force today. Well, this guy obviously didn't know about that rule. He tried to obey *all* the laws—from not cursing others to not shaving his beard. (The not-shaving-the-beard law turned out to be a real bummer, because his beard itched like crazy and it kept getting him stopped at airport security checkpoints.)

But the funniest story this guy told was about the time he met a man in the park, who asked him why he was dressed so strange. He told the man that he was trying to obey all the Old Testament laws—from dressing a certain way, to stoning adulterers. The man became indignant. He admitted, "I cheated on my wife years ago. So are you going to stone me?" Well, the author of the book was prepared for a scenario like this. He reached into his pocket and took out a handful of pebbles and began to toss them at the adulterer. The adulterer was not amused. He grabbed the pebbles from the author's hand and began throwing them back.[2]

A passage's *literary setting* is important. It helps if you know the rules for interpreting laws or prophecies or narratives or proverbs or whatever. (For a detailed discussion of the literary setting, see chapter 2 of *Context*.)

"ASK AND IT will be given to you" doesn't mean that you can pray to win the lottery and God will grant your request.

Third, you must consider your passage's *theological setting*. Consider what the *whole* Bible teaches about whatever topic you come across in the passage that you happen to be reading. In *Context*, we explored the topic of prayer along these lines. Just because you read in Matthew 7:7, "Ask and it will be given to you," doesn't mean that you can pray to win the lottery and God will grant your request. No, the Bible has more to say about prayer than what you find in Matthew 7:7. Whatever topic you come across in a Bible passage—don't jump to any conclusions about that topic until you've considered what the rest of the Bible has to say about it.

Fourth, look at a passage's *immediate setting.* Don't view a Bible word in isolation. How does that word fit into the sentence you found it in? How does that sentence fit into its host paragraph? How does that paragraph fit into the surrounding chapter, and that chapter into the book of the Bible that you're reading?

Before you can apply a Bible passage to your own life, you must understand what it meant to its original audience. What are the *historical, literary, theological,* and *immediate settings* of your passage? Don't be overwhelmed by this assignment. Much of the information you're looking for, as I've repeatedly said, can be culled from the book introductions and the page footnotes of a good study Bible.

O: Observations

Once you've scoped out the *context* of the Bible passage that you're about to dive into, your next step is to read the passage and make as many *observations* about it as you possibly can.

A couple of months ago, I was working out at the health club and I began talking about books with one of the guys I had met there. Gary, a corporate attorney, loves to read mystery novels. Recently, he'd been reading Erle Stanley Gardner mysteries—the author who wrote the stories that the old *Perry Mason* TV series was based on. When he finished the books, he went to the library and checked out the black-and-white DVDs of that series.

Soon Gary had me hooked on *Perry Mason*. It took a little bit of work to get into a dated courtroom drama, but it eventually grabbed me. Maybe it was the '58 Ford T-Bird that Perry drove around in. Whatever, this crime-solving lawyer taught me how to look for clues in a murder mystery. As I watched each episode, trying to beat Perry to the punch, I got better and better at making astute observations.

That's what you want to do when you read a passage in the Bible. You want to make insightful *observations*. What should you be looking for? Let me suggest four things to keep your eyes open for: *the theme, repeating words or ideas, something striking,* and *truths about God*.

Theme. If you had to summarize the passage you just read in a word or phrase, what would it be? Is this passage about: *Jesus' power to do miracles? How to resolve conflicts? The sins of Moab and Edom? God's help in trouble?* What's the theme of the passage? If you've got a study Bible, you might want to note what it calls the passage you've just read. Your Bible gives every section a title.

Just a word of clarification here: If you sit down and read an entire chapter from the Bible, that chapter may contain multiple themes. For example, if you're reading one of the New Testament Gospels, one chapter may recount three different episodes from a day in the life of Jesus (each with its own theme), or four different parables that Jesus tells. If you're reading a chapter from the book of Proverbs, there may be a dozen or more different themes in that single chapter.

AN ENTIRE chapter from the Bible may contain multiple themes.

What should you do when your passage contains multiple themes? Well, if your end goal is to make an application from that text to your personal life, just choose *one* of the themes to work with. Which theme are you drawn to? Each theme will have its own application. You need to focus on one of them.

Repeating Words or Ideas. If God repeats the same word or idea in a chapter, you can count on the fact that He wants you to pay attention to it. This past week, as I was following my daily Bible reading schedule, I found myself in First

Timothy. In chapter 2 of that epistle, Paul talks about the importance of *prayer* several times. *Aha!* I thought: *God's got something to say to me about prayer.* That's how it's done. Keep your eyes open for repeating words or ideas. Circle them in your Bible. Draw a line between them, connecting them.

Something Striking. I'm not always sure why certain things jump out at me when I'm reading the Bible—but they do. That'll happen to you, too. Something may strike you because it's unexpected. Or maybe it's something you never knew before. Perhaps it catches your attention because it's strange (like, *Why did the prophet Elisha make that axhead float?*). Sometimes it addresses a problem you're currently facing or puts a finger on a sin you've recently been guilty of.

If a line or a verse in a chapter strikes you—for whatever reason—underline it, or put an exclamation point in the margin next to it. A couple of weeks ago, my Bible reading schedule took me to the book of Second Samuel. I read an entire chapter that listed the names of King David's key fighting men. My first reaction was: *Not a lot in this chapter to apply to my life today.* But then something struck me. The chapter noted that among the hundreds of warriors that followed David, there was a special group referred to as The Thirty. Not only that, there was a select group within The Thirty who were called The Three.

Here's the observation that popped into my head: *David*

focused his attention on a handful of guys that he gave extra time and attention to. And then I recalled that Jesus did the same thing, right? The Gospels tell us that Jesus had seventy committed followers, and twelve disciples within that group of seventy. Finally, within those twelve were three guys (Peter, James, and John) with whom He was especially close.

Wow! It was really helpful to make that observation in Second Samuel. I'm glad I noted something that struck me. (I'll come back to this in a moment.)

Truths about God. This is always a good observation to make. Whatever passage you read in the Bible—what does it tell you about God? If the Bible is revelation from God about God and His plans, then many Bible passages will be telling you and me truths about God. Mark them down in your Bible's margins (or personal notebook or journal) when you see them. Note any attributes that describe what God is like, or any actions that recount what God has done.

So when it comes to observations, look for themes, repeating words or ideas, something striking, and truths about God. Now let's go back to COMA: C stands for *Context*. O stands for *Observations*. *M* stands for . . .

M: Message

What is the basic *message* that God wants to communicate to you through the passage you're reading? Before you can answer this question, you *must* complete the first two steps of COMA. You must consider the passage's context and make as many observations about the passage as possible. The *context* and the *observations* steps will help you understand what the passage meant to its original audience. What was God saying to *them*? Until you know the answer to that question, you're not ready to determine what God is saying to *you*. You're liable to read into the text something that isn't there. You'll read your autobiography into it.

So the C and the O steps of COMA focus on the original audience. But the *M* and the *A* steps shift the focus to you. *M* stands for *message*. What is the basic message that God seems to be communicating through this passage? This message will come out of one of your observations.

What happens if you make multiple observations? Suppose you read a chapter in the book of Acts and note three different themes, four repeating words, two things that really strike you, and one big truth about God. Just choose *one* of these observations to work with—whichever one you feel most drawn to. (Hopefully, the Holy Spirit will be influencing this decision, because He knows exactly what you need to get out of the Bible on any given day.) This observation will lead to the specific message that you are about to take away from the text.

Let me say it again: The message you draw from your daily

dose of the Bible will be based on *one* of the observations you make while reading your passage. Let me show you how this works. Earlier, under "Observations," I mentioned that while reading a chapter in Second Samuel I was struck by the fact that David had a special group of followers called The Thirty, and a subset within that group called The Three. That was my observation. What message might I draw from such an observation? Here's the one that occurred to me: "No leader can mentor everybody. So good leaders pour time and attention into a handful of followers."

Do you see how I did that? When you're drawing a message out of one of your observations, try to construct that message in the form of a timeless principle. What I mean by a timeless principle is a lesson that can be applied to everyone who ever reads that text. It's the sort of thing that could be stated on a wall plaque. "Good leaders pour time and attention into a handful of followers." Wouldn't that make a catchy saying for a wall plaque or a great caption for a leadership poster?

If you have a hard time *seeing* a timeless principle behind one of your observations, it may help to put on your SPECS. SPECS is another acronym (as well as a nickname for spectacles or glasses). Now, I don't want to confuse you by piling up acronyms in this chapter, but I think you'll find SPECS to be very useful. (Like COMA, I have no idea who to credit for coming up with it. It's been around for some time.)

You put on your SPECS by asking yourself five questions. In the Bible passage do you see a:

> **S**in to confess?
> **P**romise to claim?
> **E**xample to follow?
> **C**ommand to obey?
> **S**tatement about God (i.e., some truth about who He is or what He's done)?

Those are your SPECS!

Let's go back to my observation in Second Samuel about David and his groups of The Thirty and The Three. Which letter of SPECS did I use to get a message out of that observation? *E*: an *example* to follow. David modeled a wonderful leadership strategy that I should adopt: "Good leaders pour time and attention into a handful of followers."

One final thought about getting a message out of the text. This is something creative for you to consider doing (and it's strictly extra credit for overachievers). See if you can capture your message (timeless principle) in the form of a pithy title. If you were going to write a book or preach a sermon on your message, what would you call it? Here's what I titled the message on leadership that I drew out of Second Samuel: *My Guys*. A bit trite? Perhaps, but *My Guys* captured the essence of the message that God's Word spoke to me. That title stuck in my mind as a reminder to identify a few men in whose lives I might make a significant investment.

I do this, by the way, every time I read the Bible. I give a title to the message that I've drawn out of an observation from the passage. I taught my kids how to do that during family devotions as they were growing up. I also taught the guys in my Community Group how to do it. And now I've taught *you* how to do it. You'll find it to be a creative and memorable way to sum up the message you take away from a passage.

A: Application

The application is where the rubber meets the road. This is where you come away with something to put into practice. This is where you actually begin to *walk* the Word. Let me give you three couplets that can help to make this happen. They all start with the letter *P* so they'll be easier to remember (and because the preacher in me can't resist the urge to alliterate on occasion).

Personal and Specific. It's time to take that message (timeless principle) you came up with—the one that applies to everybody—and bring it home to your own life. Let's say, for example, that you've just read a Bible passage that emphasizes the importance of prayer. The message you drew out of the text was: *Prayer is important.* Great! What are you going to do about it? You reply: "I need to pray more." Wonderful! That's *personal*. But it's not *specific*. And applications that lack specificity are seldom put into practice. When are you going to pray more? You decide: "I'm going to get up ten minutes earlier each day and spend that extra time before work in prayer." Much better! That's both *personal and specific*.

Let me give you something harder to apply to your life. Let's say that you've just read a Bible passage and one of the observations that you made was: *God is merciful.* (This is one of those *truths about God* that you're keeping an eye out for.) A terrific observation! But observation is only the second step in the COMA process. What's the third step—the *M*? Is there a message (timeless principle) to be drawn from the observation that *God is merciful?*

You could probably come up with several messages. *Because God is merciful, He forgives sins. Because God is merciful to us, He expects us to be merciful to others. Because God is merciful, He is worthy of our praise.* Those are all messages that could be drawn from the observation that *God is merciful.* But they're not yet applications—because they're not yet *personal and specific.*

Take the first message: *Because God is merciful, He forgives sins.* How could you make that personal and specific? You could say: "I'm going to take time to confess my sins right now and ask God to forgive me." And then you do it. Or, take the second message: *Because God is merciful to us, He expects us to be merciful to others.* A great message—put it on a wall plaque—but it's not yet an application. Make it personal and specific: "Today, I am going to extend mercy to Jason (or Tammy or Adam or some other person who's offended me), because God has extended mercy to me."

What if you had come up with the third message? *Because God is merciful, He is worthy of our praise.* That's so

> **A MESSAGE becomes an application when you make it personal and specific.**

true! But it's not *personal and specific.* How could you praise God for His mercy in a way that's personal and specific? You could sing along with a worship CD on your way to work. You could tell three people about how God has been merciful to you. You could make a list of all the ways that God has shown you mercy. Those are true applications.

Paper and Pen. Write out your application. You won't come up with a definitive application unless you write something down. Really, you won't! At best, you'll come away from your Bible reading with an ambiguous insight. But you won't actually put something into practice, because you haven't explicitly stated what that something would be.

Write out your application. Go to Walgreens or CVS. Buy a cheapo, spiral-bound notebook or a fancy journal. And write out each application that you get from the Bible. As a matter of fact, there are several things you'll want to write out. (This is all really simple and basic.) Begin with the day's date and the text that you're reading from the Bible (e.g., "Wednesday, 8/24: Hebrews 1"). Then just summarize the O, M, and A steps of COMA for your passage (i.e., the specific *observation* that led to the timeless *message* that led to your personal *application*). This may sound like a lot of writing, but it actually adds up to about a paragraph's worth of print.

Let me illustrate how this works with the passage that I keep referring to in Second Samuel. I read that passage on June 11. So I wrote in my journal, "Saturday 6/11: II Samuel 23."

Then I spelled out my *observation* (O): "Although David had many followers, he had a special group called 'The Thirty' and a group within that group called 'The Three.'"

Next I wrote down the *message* (M) that came out of the observation: *Good leaders pour time and attention into a handful of followers.*

Finally, I wrapped up my entry with an *application* (A): "I'm going to personally mentor three guys this next year by meeting with them once a week over coffee." (I even listed the names of the three guys.)

Less than a paragraph of writing. (Oh, I almost forgot. I also put the title I'd created, "My Guys," next to "II Samuel 23" at the start of my entry. But that's it.) When you take the time to do this, it crystallizes your takeaway from God's Word. Another benefit of writing something down is that it helps you remember it. I'll bet that if you read the Bible first thing in the

WHEN YOU take the time to write it down, it crystallizes your takeaway from God's Word.

morning—before you go to school or work—and you *don't* write something down, you forget what God's Word said to you by lunchtime. Right? So grab a *paper and pen* and write out your application.

Pray and Pray. I know that this sounds obvious—but it's the part of application that I most often forget to do (which is why I'm stating it twice in this couplet). I frequently write out my observation, message, and application, but then forget to ask God to help me put it into practice. And when I forget to *pray*, what I've written down ends up being just words on a page. It never gets translated into real-life action. I don't *walk* the Word.

Well … you've covered a lot of ground in this chapter. Now it's time to put COMA to work. In the next chapter, you'll take a look at several Bible passages and *walk* them through the steps of *context, observations, message,* and *application.*

To watch Jim's midpoint comments about Walk, scan this QR code with your smartphone or go to www.biblesavvy.com/video/#walk2.

Study Guide

Icebreakers

- Describe the most and the least relevant courses you took in school. What made them so?
- What have been your biggest challenges in getting practical applications from the Bible for your life?

1. What does COMA stand for? Describe what is meant by each letter of this acronym.

2. What are the four kinds of *contexts* to consider when reading a Bible passage? Explain why each of these is important to consider when interpreting Scripture.

3. With the help of the introductions provided for each Bible book by your personal study Bible (or a similar tool), briefly sketch out the historical contexts for the following books:

   Deuteronomy

   Nehemiah

   Hosea

   Philemon

   James

4. Read Deuteronomy 8. Make some observations about this chapter in each of the four observation categories *(theme, repeating words or ideas, something striking, and truths about God)*.

5. 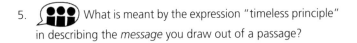 What is meant by the expression "timeless principle" in describing the *message* you draw out of a passage?

What is the danger in skipping the *C* and *O* steps of COMA—and moving right to the *M*?

6. 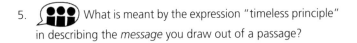 What five things will SPECS help you see when crafting a *message* from a Bible passage?

Why is it beneficial to put your *message* in the form of a pithy title?

7. (icon) Choose one of your *observations* from Deuteronomy 8 (see above) and draw a *message* (timeless principle) from it. Next, put that *message* in the form of a title.

8. Write out the four couplet-tips for making *applications* and explain why each one is important.

9. (icon) Craft a personal *application* based upon the *message* that you drew out of Deuteronomy 8.

10. (icon) What was the most difficult step in COMA to get the hang of as you applied it to Deuteronomy 8? Why?

{ **3** }
Coming Out of a COMA

MY SON HAS RECENTLY BECOME a photo-journalist for a missions organization. (I don't know what he'll say when he discovers that I've used him as the opening illustration for two consecutive chapters in this book. But there's an old saying about it being easier to get forgiveness than permission. So sorry, Andrew.) His ministry moves him from one foreign country to another. This past week he Skyped me from Romania.

I almost didn't connect with him because I can never remember how to use Skype when it's finally time to put it to work. Yes, it's partly because I'm technologically challenged. But in my defense let me point out that there are a lot of things I forget how to do if I don't do them with some amount of frequency.

In the last chapter, I taught you the COMA steps that will enable you to start with a Bible passage and end up with a practical application of that text to your life. What are the chances that you'll remember and use these steps? Like communicating by Skype, the chances of remembering are slim to none if you don't review and practice them. That's exactly what you're about to do in this chapter. I will walk you through COMA for a couple of passages, using different genres of biblical literature as examples. If you would like to maximize your learning from this exercise, feel free to push the pause button *before* reading my insights for each text and do your own COMA study of it. Then you can compare what you've discovered for yourself with what I've come up with.

A Quick Review of the COMA Steps

COMA is a lot easier than it looks. Honest! I've read a number of books that teach Bible study methods and I've never put them to good use because of their complexity. They're too busy. But COMA is different—at least, once you get the hang of it. Let me walk you through the steps again, explaining why each is really quite simple.

Context only has to be determined when you're beginning a new book of the Bible. Let's say, for example, that you're starting to read through the epistle of First Corinthians. I recommend (and explain why in the next chapter) that you don't cover more than one chapter per day. Since there are sixteen chapters in this New Testament letter, you will be working your way through it for the next two to three weeks. But you only have to figure out the context once. And, as I've constantly reiterated, it's already spelled out for you in the brief introduction to the book that you'll find in an

NIV Study Bible. Read about the author, the recipients, the historical setting, and the purpose of First Corinthians before you delve into chapter 1—and you won't have to do so again for another few weeks. (Unless, of course, you need to refresh your memory about these details.)

The *observations* step probably seems a bit more intimidating because I've given you four things to look out for: *theme, repeating words or ideas, something striking,* and *truths about God.* But let me say a few words about this step that will make it more manageable. It is not necessary for you to squeeze every possible observation out of each chapter you read. Just note three or four that are obvious to you—even if there are several observations in each of the four categories that could be detected if you looked long and hard enough. This is not a test for which you will be graded (in case you're worried about your GPA).

When I walk you through a couple of Bible chapters in a moment, I will go overboard in making observations—but that is only to stimulate your thinking. When I'm reading a chapter for my own benefit, I typically come away with only a handful of observations. In fact, often I won't make a single observation in one or two of the four observation categories (e.g., I may not detect a repeating word or spot some great truth about God in the text). And on occasion, I am hard-pressed to find even one observation of any kind in the entire chapter (although I usually stick with it until I do). So don't go OCD trying to get all four observations in every passage you read.

The *message* step is then built on *one* of your observations. Just *one*! Which one? That's for you to decide. I try to maintain an attitude of prayer when I'm reading God's Word, so it's not unusual for me to say out loud: "Lord, there are several things in this text that have caught my attention and which I could apply to my life. Please help me choose the one that You know I need most." And then I select the observation that seems to be pregnant with significance for me personally and I craft a message from it. I jot that message down in my journal in the form of a timeless principle—most often in one sentence. A single sentence! (Although, if you're an incurable overachiever you might recall the extra credit points you can rack up by restating your message as if it were the title of a book you're writing on the subject. That title will help the message stick in your mind throughout the course of the day.)

Finally, the *application* step requires that you get specific about how to put the message of the text into practice in your life. But once again, though there may be many ways in which you might flesh things out, you only have to articulate *one*. What could be more simple? An occasional *context*, a few *observations*, a one-sentence *message*, and a single *application*. About a paragraph of writing in your journal.

Of course, if you want something that is more complex, there are plenty of Bible study methods and tools out there to choose from. Once I heard a presentation by a Bible software company. When the rep finished explaining all that his top-of-the-line product could do, I was in awe. This resource would enable its users (for a sum of money slightly less than the purchase price of a foreign car) to trace every occurrence of a word's Hebrew root throughout the Old Testament, study dozens of commentaries on any passage in Scripture, read full-page articles on Bible-related topics, yada, yada, yada.

You can go the Bible software route if you want to. But my guess is that you'll rarely use it. And you'll feel like David in King Saul's armor when you do. David couldn't wait to shed that cumbersome suit, exchanging it for five smooth stones and a simple slingshot.

Here's why I wouldn't recommend the Bible software approach to you. First, it will deluge you with information—a bazillion times more information than you could possibly digest. And besides that, your goal should not be Bible *knowledge*, right? It's the *application* of Scripture that you're shooting for. Second, if you're like most people, you have twenty to thirty minutes a day to spend in God's Word. If half that time is taken up reading an article about the bronze basin in the temple (interesting, but probably not life changing), you will walk away from your study without a sense of having connected with God. Third, Bible software is not helpful on a desert island. OK, that's a strange way to put it, but I call it my *Desert Island Principle.* I want to equip you to draw nourishment from God's Word with nothing but a Bible (admittedly, an *NIV Study Bible*), a notebook, and a pen. If you're ever abandoned on a desert island, with no Wi-Fi available, you'll still be able to glean rich insights from Scripture (which you might want to share with Tom Hanks, if you run into him and his volleyball). And speaking of a Bible, notebook, and pen—why don't you get those out, turn to 1 Kings 16, and take fifteen or twenty minutes to complete a COMA study of this chapter. I'll wait . . .

Now, be honest . . . Did you complete your COMA? I'm aware that when most of us begin reading a chapter in a book, our goal is to complete that chapter without interruption. But allow me to point out that there is no value in finishing this present chapter unless you have gotten a handle on COMA along the way. Why did you pick up *Walk* in the first place? Wasn't it because you desire to get more out of God's Word for your daily life? I promise you that this exercise will help you accomplish your goal. So if you haven't done so, please run 1 Kings 16 through COMA on your own before reading the following.

A COMA for 1 Kings 16

Hope you enjoyed doing your own COMA. Here's mine. (Of course mine is not better than yours. It's just different. The important thing is that we both found messages and applications that impact our lives and honor our God.)

Context. The book of First Kings was originally part of a single volume that included Second Kings and First and Second Samuel. Scholars are not sure who wrote this collection, although Jewish tradition credited Jeremiah (mistakenly) as the author. These books tell the tragic story of Israel's monarchy—which, ironically, began on a high note, with the reigns of Saul, David, and Solomon. But Solomon's son split the united kingdom in two, north and south, due to his foolish leadership.

The northern country, consisting of nine and one-half tribes, continued to be called Israel. It had one wicked king after another, until God allowed Assyria to destroy Israel in 722 BC and carry many of its people into captivity. The southern country, consisting of the remaining two and one-half tribes, was called Judah. Occasionally, its succession of wicked kings would be interrupted by a godly leader who would return Judah to the Lord. But these revivals didn't last for long, so in 586 BC God allowed Babylon to demolish Judah and exile many of its citizens.

The purpose of First Kings is not to give its readers a detailed historical account of Israel's monarchy. In fact, some of the kings who reigned the longest (e.g., Omri) are barely mentioned. First Kings is focused, instead, on pointing out the close connection between Israel's welfare and the people's obedience to God. Obedience brings blessing. Disobedience brings trouble. This correlation is illustrated, especially, by the lives of Israel's kings. And it's heralded, in First Kings, by two prominent prophets—Elijah and Elisha.

You didn't need me to tell you any of the above—not if you have an *NIV Study Bible.* I just summed up a few highlights from the four-page introduction to First Kings (which, by the way, is a much longer introduction than for other Old Testament books). Now, if you have a different study Bible, that's OK. If you looked at the opening page for First Kings in your study Bible, it's likely some of this background info popped up to offer valuable context.

Observations. The *theme* of this chapter is the summary of the reigns of five wicked kings from northern Israel. I learned that from the five section headings in the chapter in my *NIV Study Bible,* which list the kings by name. (The first section heading is actually found above 1 Kings 15:33: *Baasha King of Israel.* But Baasha's story is continued in the opening verses of 1 Kings 16.) This theme is not particularly scintillating, but at least it prepares me for what I'm going to find in the chapter.

There are a number of *repeating words or ideas* in 1 Kings

16. Did you notice them as you were reading the text? They occur in several clumps. But it's worth taking the clumps apart and paying attention to a few repeating ideas in each. One of these ideas is expressed by the line: "he did evil in the eyes of the Lord" (15:34; 16:7, 19, 25, 30). Another idea that pops up in the same clumps is that Israel's wicked kings were *walking in the ways of Jeroboam*. Did you see that? And what about the recurring statement that these leaders *caused Israel to commit* similar sins by their bad example? Each of these three repeating ideas is an observation from which a message could be drawn—which I'll get to in a moment. But first, a few more observations.

Did you come across *something striking* as you read 1 Kings 16? A couple of things jumped off the page at me; they really fall into the *repeated ideas* category, since both of them occur more than once in the chapter. But I'm identifying them as *something striking* because . . . well . . . they struck me. The first is that the particular sin for which these wicked kings were notorious was *idolatry* (see vv. 13, 26, 31). Evidently, not all sins are equal. Some are especially offensive to God. Which leads me to my other striking discovery: each succeeding wicked king was worse than the previous one.

EACH OF these three repeating ideas is an observation from which a message could be drawn.

This is indicated by the word *more* in describing the latest king's level of sinning (see vv. 25, 30, 33).

Any *truths about God* in this chapter? You probably picked up some that I missed. But I'll tell you the one that really caught my attention—probably because it's also a *repeating idea* in 1 Kings 16. God gets angry. Majorly angry! Especially at idolatry (see vv. 2, 7, 13, 26, 33).

Just a quick tally of my observations: one *theme*; three *repeating words or ideas*; two *something striking*(s); and one *truth about God*—for a grand total of seven observations. There are probably numerous additional observations that

ANY TRUTHS about God? . . . God gets angry. Majorly angry! Especially at idolatry.

could be made about chapter 16. But remember—my goal is *not* to squeeze every possible observation out of the text. I'm not after quantity. Besides, seven observations are more than I typically will come up with. I outdid myself so as to stimulate your ability to spot these things.

Message. I am now ready, according to the COMA approach, to select one of my seven observations and draw a message out of it. But in order to give you a better idea of how this transition from observation to message goes, I will spell out a message for every one of my observations (with the exception of the *theme* observation).

Please note that you may have made a similar observation to one of mine. This does not guarantee, however, that we both drew the same message from that observation. Often observations lend themselves to a variety of life lessons. So, if we came up with different messages for the same observation, don't assume that you've done something wrong (or, that I have). Here are the messages (timeless principles) that I derived from my observations:

Observation: The wicked kings *did evil in the eyes of the Lord.*

Message: Our sins are never done in secret but are committed in full view of God.

Observation: The wicked kings were guilty of *walking in the ways of Jeroboam.*

Message: Bad leaders leave an indelibly bad legacy.

Observation: The wicked kings *caused Israel to commit sins* similar to their own.

Message: Sins are never strictly personal—they set a bad example for others to follow.

Observation: Idolatry is a horrible sin.

Message: Rivals to God are not to be taken lightly.

Observation: Each succeeding wicked king sinned *more* than the previous one.
Message: Unchecked sin just keeps on getting worse.

Observation: God is angered by idolatry.
Message: Recognize and remove idols or face God's discipline.

Application. As with the message, it is only necessary at this point to come up with *one* application from 1 Kings 16. This application should be built on the message (drawn from one of your observations) to which God's Spirit seems to be directing your attention. Did any of your observation-message insights elicit such a response from you? Did any of them seem especially relevant to something that's currently going on in your life? Did it possibly even get an *Ouch!* out of you? Bring that message home by determining to *do* something about it—something personal and specific.

Crafting applications from messages is more art than science, which means it's easier to describe the product than explain the process. So, allow me to describe some of the possible applications that came to my mind from the messages I drew out of 1 Kings 16 (even if I can't fully explain how I came up with them).

When I meditated on the message that *our sins are never*

done in secret but are committed in full view of God, I began to wonder if there are sins in my own life that I've been treating as if they are hidden from God. My application would be to sit quietly before the Lord for a minute or two, inviting Him to identify any unconfessed and unrenounced transgressions. Then I would pray through 1 John 1:9. (I'll let you look that one up for yourself.)

A couple of the messages that I drew out of First Kings 16 have to do with the tendency of a leader's sins to be picked up by their followers. As a dad, I can certainly vouch for this unfortunate propensity in my family. While I constantly hope that my kids follow in the steps of my good qualities, I occasionally observe that they have become imitators of my negative traits. An application along these lines would be to identify and pray about any bad-dad fruits I see growing in my children's lives. God's

SOME IDOLS are lurking in my life. What are they? How can I dethrone them? My application should answer these questions.

Spirit might even prompt me to own up to one of my contagious faults in conversation with my kids.

Here's one final stab at an application from First Kings 16. Two of my messages touch on the danger of idolatry. If I define an idol as anything that gets an excessive amount of my time, energy, and affection, I am sure that there are some idols (or potential idols) lurking in my life. What are they? How can I dethrone them? My application should answer these questions—*specifically*. I might also determine to do something that would exalt God to His proper place of prominence in my heart, such as singing a worship song or lifting up a prayer of thanksgiving.

How did you do with 1 Kings 16? Are you ready to try COMA with a new text? I know, I know, you're never going to finish *Walk* at this rate. But tell yourself that it's not important to read the remaining pages of this chapter before the sun goes down. Instead, make up your mind that the rest of your reading time today will be devoted to working through another passage with the help of COMA. Grab your Bible and turn to John 5.

I will take a much more abbreviated approach in presenting my COMA musings for this new text (i.e., no more rambling commentary as with 1 Kings 16). But I hope that you will be able to follow my train of thought as I move from *context* to *observations* to *message* to *applications*. Please keep in mind, once again, that I will be noting more observations than I typically come up with (like an overzealous bird-watcher who keeps handing you his binoculars so you won't miss a single species). And I'll be drawing a message out of every observation—even though COMA requires that I choose just one observation to convert into a poignant message.

A Different Genre of COMA

A final word about the passage I've selected. I'm moving from an Old Testament narrative (1 Kings 16) to a New Testament Gospel (John 5). As I've taught people how to study the Bible *a la* COMA over the years, I've noticed that many of them do better with some kinds of literature than with others. For example, they may love Old Testament stories and find it easy to spot life lessons in such—but have a hard time getting into the densely worded theological arguments of Paul's epistles. Others, however, can't get enough of Romans or Colossians—but they really struggle to squeeze something for their lives out of the prophets Amos or Obadiah. (OK, who *doesn't* struggle to squeeze something out of Amos or Obadiah?)

So I am giving you a taste of two different biblical genres in this chapter. You may gravitate more to one than the other, but I hope you'll get a feel for how COMA works with both. In fact, in the appendix you will find the results of a COMA study of three additional kinds of biblical literature: Old Testament poetry (Ecclesiastes 2), Old Testament prophecy (Isaiah 14), and New Testament epistle (Hebrews 2). The Study Guide at the end of this chapter will ask you to do your own COMA studies of these passages. After you've completed your work, you can compare it with what I've provided in the appendix.

As you're working on the Study Guide passages, you may want to pull out (or purchase) your copy of *Context* and turn to the chapter on *literary settings.* Each kind of biblical literature comes with its own rules of interpretation. These rules are covered quite simply in *Context* and may shed some light on the passages you'll be studying. Are you ready to COMA John 5?

A COMA for John 5

Context. The author of this Gospel is John, who repeatedly identifies himself as "the disciple whom Jesus loved" (13:23; 19:26; 20:2; 21:7, 20, 24). Don't think of this as one-upmanship on John's part (like the child who boasts, "Mom loves me best"). He's not comparing himself with the other disciples; he's just noting the closeness of his own relationship with Jesus. That makes this Gospel a very intimate, firsthand account. It is written by someone who saw what Jesus did and heard what Jesus taught. John wrote down these eyewitness observations some time before the end of the first century. His Gospel has a different feel than the Gospels of Matthew, Mark, and Luke and includes things that the others leave out.

John tells us the purpose for his book in 20:30–31: "Jesus did many other miraculous signs in the presence of his disciples, which are not recorded in this book. But these are written that you may believe that Jesus is the Christ, the Son of God, and that by believing you may have life in his name." John wants to lead people to faith in Christ. To that end, he describes some of Jesus' miracles, which point to His true identity and saving power.

John calls these miracles "signs." There are seven of them described in this Gospel. And the healing of the lame man, at the beginning of chapter 5, is one of them. This event took place during "a feast of the Jews" (v. 1), which probably refers to one of three annual celebrations that brought thousands of religious pilgrims to Jerusalem. The location of the healing was a pool called Bethesda that had a reputation for curative powers.

Observations-Meanings-Applications. This is a long chapter (forty-seven verses) and it contains many, many details that might be cited as observations. A person could spend an entire week in John 5. But if you're following the four-year Bible reading schedule (available at *biblesavvy.com*), you must cover it in a single day. Is this too fast a pace?

Well, first let me point out that this is why I don't care for the read-through-the-Bible-in-a-year schedule. If you were on that plan, you'd not only be reading John 5 in a day but would also be reading a couple of Old Testament chapters and a psalm or two on the same day! At the other extreme, if you insist on taking several days to read and study, say, John 5 because of its rich content, it will be years before you make it through the entire Bible. So one chapter of reading per day is about the right pace (i.e., the four-year Bible reading schedule)—even though passages like John 5 will be a challenge to cover in the time allotted.

Remember that your goal is not to observe every possible detail of the text. Make a handful of observations and choose one of them to develop into a message and application. Here is a sampling of what I saw in John 5.

> *Observation:* Jesus repeatedly referred to Himself as one who had been *sent* by the Father (vv. 23–24, 30, 36–38). This verb reminds us that He came to earth for a special purpose. Jesus was on a mission from God.
>
> *Message:* Jesus lived with a keen consciousness that He had been *sent* to save the world.
>
> *Application:* Elsewhere Jesus says that He sends His followers into the world in the same way that the Father had sent Him. Am I keeping my *sent*-ness in the forefront of my thinking? My life purpose must be to bring the good news of salvation to others. Pray for opportunities to talk about Christ today.

Observation: Jesus was very careful to do only what the Father wanted Him to do (a *repeated idea* in vv. 19, 30, 36). He had a very focused agenda.

Message: The temptation to do too much, to pack a schedule too full, will wear a person out! Let God set the agenda.

Application: Look over the day's "To Do" list. Is there anything on it that is a *good* idea but not a *God* idea? Only engage in tasks to which God is calling me. Don't add another activity to my schedule without asking: *Lord, is this something You want me to do?*

Observation: The following all bore testimony to Jesus (circle the numerous occurrences of *testify/testimony*): John the Baptist (v. 33); Jesus' works (v. 36); God the Father (v. 37); Scriptures (v. 39); and Moses (v. 46). There is plenty of evidence to substantiate that Jesus is who He claims to be.

Message: Be confident and bold in asserting Jesus' claims for Himself!

Application: This observation brings to my mind the books of apologist Lee Strobel. I will pick up an extra copy of *The Case for Christ* or *The Case for Faith* and pass it on to an unbelieving friend.

Observation: My curiosity is piqued (*something striking*) by the question Jesus asks the lame man: "Do you want to get well?" (v. 6). Isn't the answer to this inquiry a no-brainer? Of course; why would a lame man *not* want to get well? My footnote suggests a couple of reasons why Jesus asked the question. First, the man might have found begging to be a profitable profession. And second, he might have given up on ever being healed.

Message: Sometimes we don't really want or expect God to intervene in our lives.

Application: Is there something I'm not praying about (or have stopped praying about) because I've concluded that God is just not going to do anything about it? Where have I accepted the status quo—instead of challenging it in prayer?

Observation: Something else grabs my attention: after Jesus healed this guy He told him to stop sinning or something worse would happen (v. 14)! I know that sickness is not necessarily the result of sin in a person's life (see John 9:1–3). But evidently, on occasion, it *is.*

Message: God sometimes uses illness or hardship to get our attention about sin in our lives.

Application: Ask God if there is something behind my health problems. Any sin to be acknowledged and uprooted?

Observation: The religious rulers were such weenies! (Sorry, it was the first derogatory name that came to mind.) In verses 9–10 they accost the healed man for carrying his mat on the Sabbath—something which they claim is against Moses' law. It really isn't a transgression of the law. It just violates their interpretation of how the Sabbath law should be lived out.

Message: Beware of man-made rules—and don't let them become a yardstick by which others are measured.

Application: I must be especially careful that spiritual disciplines (e.g., Bible reading, tithing, serving the poor) don't become legalistic rules by which I attempt to earn God's favor.

I've just listed six observations from John 5 that led to messages and applications for my life. And yet I haven't scratched the surface of this chapter of John's Gospel. Without taking the time to develop the following thoughts, let me point out several other observations I made while reading the passage. In the category of *something striking*, I was struck by how much the religious leaders were diligent Bible students—yet blind to what the Bible taught about Christ (vv. 39, 40). I was also unsettled by Jesus' accusation that His antagonists preferred the praise of one another to the praise that comes from God (v. 44; ouch! that hits close to home).

And here are a few *truths about God the Son* (i.e., Jesus) I noted: He sovereignly chose to heal the lame man, in spite of there being no mention of faith on the guy's part (vv. 8–9); He called God by the intimate name of *Father*—something that Jews avoided doing, and which was interpreted as a claim to being equal with God (vv. 17–18); He referred to Himself as the source of life (vv. 21, 26); and He warned that mankind would face Him as judge (vv. 22, 27).

Wow! Any one of these observations is worth running with. Significant messages could be drawn from them and life-transforming applications made of those messages. What did you come up with?

Now it's time to try your hand at using COMA with a few more passages of different genres. Turn to the Study Guide and go for it. And when you're finished, don't forget to compare your results with the COMA insights from these Bible chapters that are provided in the appendix.

Study Guide

Icebreaker

What kinds of things are you most observant about (i.e., you notice details)? In what areas of life do you wish you were more observant?

1. Do a COMA study of Ecclesiastes 2. (Compare your results with the appendix.)

   Context:

   Observations (theme; repeating words or ideas; something striking; truths about God):

   Message (from one of your observations):

   Application:

2. (●●●) Do a COMA study of Isaiah 14. (Compare your re-
    sults with the appendix.)

    Context:

    Observations (theme; repeating words or ideas; some-
    thing striking; truths about God):

    Message (from one of your observations):

    Application:

3. (●●●) Do a COMA study of Hebrews 2. (Compare your
    results with the appendix.)

    Context:

    Observations (theme; repeating words or ideas; some-
    thing striking; truths about God):

Message (from one of your observations):

Application:

4. 🗣 Do a COMA study of Leviticus 4, or Psalm 139, or 1 John 4. (Your pick. How big a challenge do you want? You won't find any help in the appendix. It's just you . . . and the Holy Spirit.)

Context:

Observations (theme; repeating words or ideas; something striking; truths about God):

Message (from one of your observations):

Application:

A Daily Discipline

I WAS FLIPPING THROUGH the TV channels after watching the news one night, and I came across a lady preacher. Her name was Pastor Bambi. No offense to any reader of this book named Bambi, but if I were a lady preacher with that name, who was trying to draw a television audience, I think I would change my name to something that has more gravitas. Maybe something with a biblical ring to it—like Pastor Esther or Pastor Rachel.

There was something else about her program that caught my attention. Pastor Bambi was offering her viewers miracles. Splashed across my TV screen in big bold letters were the words: *Miracle Healings!!* Well, I believe that God sometimes miraculously heals people today. So I had no problem with that. But the next set of big bold letters read: *Miracle Debt Cancellations!!* Really? Miracle debt cancellations? No doubt a lot of people who flip through TV channels late at night are struggling with debt. That's a big problem in our country today. But how should we be addressing the problem?

Should you and I be hoping for "miracle debt cancellations"? Should we watch Pastor Bambi's TV program, pray with her at the end of the show for our debt to be removed, and then expect to hear the next day from Visa Card, or our home mortgage company, or the government's student loan department: "Good news! You don't owe us anything! Somebody paid your bill!"?

Well, I'll tell you how we fix people's debt problems at our church. We encourage men and women to sign up for a nine-week Financial Peace University small group. FPU is a very practical study that's been put together by financial expert Dave Ramsey.[1] It trains people—in a small-group setting with other eager participants—how to make money, save money, budget money, and give money. This requires a lot of hard work and discipline! But we've seen scores of people climb out of debt and begin to enjoy life. These people weren't waiting around for some miracle debt cancellation.

Don't get me wrong. We believe in miracles at our church. And God does do *financial* miracles in our lives from time to time. But God also seems to expect from us a certain amount of hard work and discipline—in whatever area of our lives we hope to grow in. This is even true of our spiritual development. Look at what the Bible says about this: "Train yourself to be godly. For physical training is of some value, but godliness has value for all things" (1 Timothy 4:7b–8a).

The first sentence is straightforward: "Train yourself to be godly." The word *train* in these verses is the Greek verb *gymnazo.* Now, you don't have to be a Bible scholar to deduce that *gymnazo* is the word from which we get *gymnasium*—the place where we go to exercise and work out. That's what's required for godliness, Paul says. That's what's necessary for spiritual growth: exercising and working out.

The apostle Paul even likens *godliness* training to *physical* training in these verses. The same sort of discipline is required for both endeavors. In other words, spiritual growth isn't something that just happens to us. It's something we've got to work at. This is especially true when it comes to the practice of applying the Bible to our lives. Bible application takes work. It takes *daily discipline.* In this chapter you'll discover four factors that will help you develop that discipline.

The Role of the Holy Spirit

My brother-in-law recently told me a story about his five-year-old grandson. Little Cole is a preschooler. And he's a bit on the hyperactive side, which means he's always getting in trouble at the Christian school he attends. When Cole's mommy arrives to pick him up each day, he's frequently seated in the principal's office.

That's where she found him a couple of weeks ago. His mom looked at him sternly and asked, "What's the problem, Cole?" Now, Cole has a hard time saying his *v*'s—they come out as *b*'s. So, he looked forlornly at his mommy and replied,

"I can't get da debil out of my heart."

Cole isn't the only one who's got a problem with the debil in his heart. We all do! And no amount of effort on our part is going to remove the debil from our hearts. This is something that only God can do. Only God can liberate us from Satan's death-grip and make us spiritually alive.

In John 3, we read the story of a religious leader by the name of Nicodemus (I like that name), who visited Jesus one night. Nicodemus approached Jesus under the cloak of darkness because he didn't want anyone to see him soliciting spiritual input. After all, Nicodemus was supposed to be a guy with spiritual *answers*, not spiritual *questions*.

Jesus cut right to the chase with Nicodemus. He told Nick that if he wanted spiritual life, he'd have to be born again. And then Jesus explained that being born again isn't something you can do to yourself. It's something that only God's *Spirit* can do to people. But God's Spirit won't do this to you (we learn elsewhere in Scripture) until you surrender your life to Jesus Christ. Only when you sincerely ask Jesus to forgive your sin and lead your life, will the Holy Spirit come to live on the inside and make you spiritually alive.

Just as the Holy Spirit is the force behind your spiritual *birth*, He is also the power behind your spiritual *growth*. Remember those verses we looked at in 1 Timothy 4 a few moments ago? They said that "training to be godly" requires hard work. Spiritual growth won't just *happen* to you—you'll have to go after it. But where do the desire and the discipline to "go after it" come from? From the Holy Spirit.

> YOU'LL HAVE to go after it [spiritual growth]. But the desire and the discipline to "go after it" come from the Holy Spirit.

Let me give you an analogy: growing spiritually is like sailing a boat. Can you picture yourself doing that? Sue and I lived on Cape Cod years ago, and we occasionally went sailing with friends. So, it's not too hard for me to picture the scene I'm about to describe to you. Your sails are hoisted, you've got a sunshiny day, you've got miles of open water in front of you, and you've got the basic skills of sailing under your belt. What's the only thing you lack? A good breeze!! Have you ever been on a sailboat when there was no wind? You didn't go anywhere. Boooooring.

The Holy Spirit is the wind in the sails of your spiritual growth. (Jesus used wind as a word picture to talk about the Holy Spirit with Nicodemus in John 3—maybe because *wind* and *spirit* come from the same Hebrew word, *ruach*.) The daily discipline you need to apply God's Word to your life—to pick up a Bible, read it, and put it into practice—must come from the Holy Spirit. If you try to do this by sheer personal willpower, you'll give it up in no time. It'll be about as enjoyable as sailing on a day with no wind.

Here are a couple of verses from Galatians 3 that back up this point that I'm making: "I would like to learn just one thing from you: Did you receive the Spirit by observing the law, or by believing what you heard? Are you so foolish? After beginning with the Spirit, are you now trying to attain your goal by human effort?" (Galatians 3:2–3).

Do you follow Paul's argument here? He asks the Galatians how the Holy Spirit came into their lives in the first place. Was it the result of observing the law, Paul asks. In other words, was it the result of their personal effort? Was it the result of keeping God's rules? Was it the result of pulling themselves up by their spiritual bootstraps? No! The Galatians initially received the Holy Spirit by simply believing—by simply surrendering their lives to Jesus Christ, as I've already explained. That's how the Holy Spirit comes to live in people.

OK, Paul continues, if that's how you Galatians experienced spiritual *birth*, how do you think you experience spiritual *growth*? Is it now all up to you? Does the discipline that's required for training in godliness come from within you? Are you supposed to just suck it up and get 'er done? Is it a case of "three yards and a grass stain"? No! You need to depend on the Holy Spirit for both the desire and the discipline to grow spiritually.

If the reading, journaling, and applying of the Bible is not yet a part of your daily routine—or if it comes and goes—you need to ask the Holy Spirit to put wind in your sails. You will never consistently walk the Word until the Holy Spirit motivates and empowers you to do so. Make this a matter of prayer. (But keep in mind that you won't even be able to pray earnestly for this discipline unless the Holy Spirit enables you to pray earnestly. Start your asking there.)

The Role of Personal Effort

OK. I may be confusing you. My first point has been that spiritual growth must come from the Holy Spirit, *not* from personal effort. Now, my second point is that spiritual growth comes from personal effort. Huh?

Let me illustrate this second factor with an anecdote, an unusual story that appeared in a news magazine (so it must be true). The owner of a new recreational vehicle had a traffic accident after making a rather poor choice. According to the news report, the guy put his RV on the interstate for the first time, got it up to speed, and then pushed the cruise control button. At this point, with his RV in an automatic mode, and with nothing in front of him but open road, this guy decided to get up from his seat and make a sandwich for himself in the kitchenette.

Too late, he realized that driving his RV required some involvement on his part. Big mistake!

I know some Christ followers who make a similar blunder with regard to their spiritual journey. They assume that since the Holy Spirit now indwells them, they are on some sort of spiritual "autopilot." There is no need for them to do anything. They don't believe that training in godliness should involve rigorous exercise. It's simply a matter of waiting for the Holy Spirit to overwhelm them with the urge and the power to do the right thing.

Years ago, one of the elders in the church that I pastored out East lived by this approach. As a self-employed commercial artist, he could schedule his day any way he pleased. Well, some days, he would get the urge to study his Bible—so he would. All day! But other days he wouldn't feel inclined to pick up God's Word—so he wouldn't. In fact, he would occasionally go a couple of weeks without reading his Bible at all (not good for a church elder).

The guy drove me nuts. But he was convinced that he should never ever do anything of a spiritual nature unless he felt an overwhelming leading of the Holy Spirit to do so. He believed that if something required effort on his part, it must be wrong. Not surprisingly, his spiritual life was a mess! Totally erratic. Huge ups and downs. The apostle Peter has something to say to those who are tempted to take this approach, who assume that spiritual growth should be an effortless endeavor:

For this very reason, *make every effort* to add to your faith goodness; and to goodness, knowledge; and to knowledge, self-control; and to self-control, perseverance; and to perseverance, godliness; and to godliness, brotherly kindness; and to brotherly kindness, love. For if you possess these qualities in increasing measure, they will keep you from being ineffective and unproductive in your knowledge of our Lord Jesus Christ. (2 Peter 1:5–8, emphasis added)

The theme of the above Bible passage is spiritual growth. Peter identifies eight qualities that ought to characterize the life of a Christ follower "in increasing measure." Please note that one of these qualities is *knowledge.* In fact, Peter mentions knowledge twice in this passage, at the beginning and at the end (v. 5 and v. 8). He exhorts us to grow in our knowledge of Jesus Christ. How do we acquire such knowledge? Doesn't this require getting into the Bible? Absolutely.

And what does Peter say about the way in which we should go about a pursuit of Bible knowledge? Look at the second phrase in verse 5: "make every effort." So spiritual growth requires knowledge of Jesus Christ; knowledge of Jesus Christ requires getting into the Bible; and getting into the Bible requires *personal effort.*

Personal effort is not inconsistent with relying on the Holy Spirit to put the wind in your sails. Personal effort and the Holy Spirit go hand in hand. Of course, if you try to grow spiritually on nothing but personal effort, you're going to feel like you're pushing a rock up a hill with your nose. You need the Holy Spirit's empowerment. But on the other hand, if you try to grow spiritually by always waiting for the Holy Spirit to move you to do the right thing, your growth is going to be erratic, inconsistent, whimsical. You need to *make every effort*—as Peter says.

PERSONAL EFFORT and the Holy Spirit go hand in hand.

Let me give you a picture of how the Holy Spirit and personal effort work hand in hand. It's a picture that God paints for us in the Old Testament. After God delivered His people from slavery in Egypt, He led them to the very edge of Canaan. And then God made them a promise. God promised them victory. God promised to drive out their enemies. God promised to give them the land (which is why it was known as the Promised Land). But right alongside these sorts of promises, God repeatedly challenged His people to be courageous and fight hard!

So, which was it? Was God going to drive out their enemies and give them the land, or were they supposed to fight for it? The correct answer is: YES! Acquiring the Promised Land was a both/and kind of thing. And that's the same way we're to pursue spiritual growth today—by *both* relying on

God's Spirit *and* making every personal effort.

I frequently talk with Christ followers who wonder if something is wrong in their pursuit of spiritual growth, because it feels like such an effort at times. Why don't they leap out of bed in the morning and grab their Bible, eager to meet with God? What's wrong with them? Should they just stay in bed until the Holy Spirit gives them the urge to get up and read God's Word?

Let me answer that question with a story from the life of Harry Ironside. Dr. Ironside was a great Bible teacher in the middle of the twentieth century. On one occasion, he was speaking on the campus of a Christian college, and a student asked him a personal question after his lecture: "How do you manage to get up every morning and study the Bible?" Here was Dr. Ironside's response. (You may have to read this next sentence twice, since it's so profound.) He said: "I just get up."

Deep stuff, eh? If you determine to read your Bible every morning (or at some other set time during the day), there will be many days when you don't feel like doing it. But don't wait for the Holy Spirit to move you. Just get up! The same advice applies to your participation in a small group, where you study and apply the Bible with friends. Personal confession: There are many times that I don't feel like going to my early Wednesday morning men's group when my alarm goes off. (OK, I admit it. And I'm a pastor. But let me finish.) However,

I am always glad to be at my men's group once I'm there. And I'm super pumped by the time I'm driving away from it.

The daily discipline of applying God's Word to your life requires the empowerment of the Holy Spirit, the exertion of personal effort, and . . .

The Role of Godly Habits

Have you ever tried to break a bad habit? Have you ever tried to stop smoking, biting your nails, watching too much TV, texting while driving, or leaving the toilet seat up? It's hard to break a bad habit, isn't it? Habits seem to have a power of their own. Which is why it's so helpful to develop *godly habits*. Godly habits have the power to propel you on to spiritual growth. Whether it's the habit of gathering for worship with other believers *every* week, or the habit of giving God the first 10 percent of *every* paycheck, or the habit of reading your Bible *every* day—godly habits will grow you up in Christ.

Unfortunately, far too many Christ followers fail to develop godly habits. Sometimes it's because they're lazy. Sometimes it's because they get bored with routine. Sometimes it's because they object that godly habits (churchgoing, tithing, Bible reading, etc.) are legalistic—nothing but rules, rules, rules.

I get so tired of hearing that last argument. Why don't

we call it *legalistic* when someone runs ten miles every day in preparation for a marathon? Why don't we call it *legalistic* when someone does homework every day in order to graduate? Why don't we call it *legalistic* when someone brushes their teeth every day so as to avoid cavities? Why is it only *legalistic* when someone practices godly habits out of a desire to grow spiritually?

Let me suggest to you that anyone who ever excels at anything—be it piano, golf, sales, parenthood, gardening—gets there by practicing certain habits. They don't just "wing it." Keep that in mind as you read the following verse: "Do your best to present yourself to God as one approved, a workman who does not need to be ashamed and who correctly handles the word of truth" (2 Timothy 2:15).

What does God want you to excel at? Handling His Word! He wants you to be able to handle the Bible like a skilled workman handles his

WHAT DOES God want you to excel at? Handling His Word!

tools. Now, I'm pretty sure that skilled workmen don't become skilled until they've put hours and hours of practice into using those tools. They become skilled out of *habit*.

And so I want to challenge you to become habitual in your handling of God's Word. Let me give you some key ingredients that would contribute to the development of this godly habit—three pairs of ingredients. (By the way, if these look familiar, it's because I touched on the same ingredients in *Foundation*, the second book in the Bible Savvy series. But I'm not averse to repeating myself in order to drive home an important point.)

A time and a place. Many people find early morning to be the best time of day for getting into the Bible. One advantage of this time slot is that there is typically nothing else competing for your attention—except sleep. Those who try to read their Bibles later in the day often find themselves distracted by other concerns. Or something comes up unexpectedly that bumps their Bible reading. So meeting with God first thing in the morning is often the best plan. However, if a long lunch break or a quiet moment after you get the kids to bed works best for you, go for it. Just remember that there's a better chance of the Bible becoming a habit if you read it *at the same time* every day.

Same with the location. Find a place that works for you and stick to it. It may be in your pickup truck as you sit in the parking lot at work. It may be at a local coffee shop, assuming that you can screen out the white noise. It may be at your kitchen table. It may be on the treadmill—as long as you make time for writing something down after you're done walking or running. What time and place would work best for you? Lock them in, right now. Start tomorrow.

A Bible and a reading schedule. You don't want just any kind of Bible, right? You want . . . (If you're not saying the right answer out loud at this point, all my nagging has been ineffective.) You want a *study* Bible. Make it an *NIV Study Bible*—or a similar study Bible—with all the helpful book introductions, explanatory footnotes, cross-references, a concordance, and maps.

Let's say you're Bible-ready. Where are you going to start reading? Let me give you several suggestions, schedule-wise. Pick whichever one suits you best. If you're brand new to the Bible, you might want to start in a Gospel—one of the four biographies of Jesus. I think Mark is the easiest place to begin. It's sixteen chapters long, so if you read one per day, you'll finish the book in two to three weeks. Way to go!

IF YOU'RE brand new to the Bible, you might want to start reading in a Gospel.

For most people, I'd recommend the four-year Bible reading schedule that you can find on the *biblesavvy.com* website. You'll go through the Old Testament once and the New Testament twice during that time period. It's a very do-able pace—one or two chapters a day, five days a week. The brisk pace of a one-year schedule will frequently leave you falling behind and feeling guilty.

Speaking of avoiding guilt, you can also read through

the Bible without using any schedule at all. You'll never feel pushed or prodded. Simply pick a book of the Bible to begin with, read one chapter a day, put your bookmark between the pages, and the next time you read just pick up where you left off. (If you miss a day or two, you miss a day or two. No pressure to catch up with a predetermined schedule.) When you get done with that book of the Bible, go to the table of contents and check it off. Then start with a new book.

Here's one last reading schedule approach. If you're in a small group and you're using a curriculum that's taking you through a book of the Bible, spread your homework out over the course of a week (i.e., that's your reading schedule). Don't do it all the night before your group meets. It's just like eating. Much better to ingest some food every day than to stuff yourself once a week at an all-you-can-eat buffet.

A notebook and COMA. I would encourage you to go back and review chapter 2, "From Text to Life." Have you begun using COMA in your daily Bible reading? The *context-observations-message-application* approach will ensure that you *walk* the Word. Following the four steps of this acronym may feel as awkward as learning to ride a bike at first. But they say (don't ask me who *they* are) that it takes thirty days to develop any good habit. So, try giving COMA a one-month trial, writing something down each day, and see what it does for your spiritual growth.

Role Models

This fourth factor is icing on the cake. Having role models can strengthen your daily discipline of applying God's Word to your life (alongside of *the Holy Spirit, your personal effort,* and *godly habits*). Positive role models have a way of inspiring us to do the right thing. This is probably why the apostle Paul frequently urged the readers of his epistles to imitate him (see his requests in Philippians 3:17; 4:9; 1 Corinthians 4:16; 11:1; 1 Thessalonians 1:6; 2 Thessalonians 3:7, 9; and 2 Timothy 3:10, 14).

These role models don't even have to be well-known Christ followers if they exemplify good habits. I just finished reading a biography about Ron Santo. Ron was the all-star third baseman of the Chicago Cubs who recently joined baseball's Hall of Fame. He was a boyhood hero of mine. All the infielders on my Little League team tried to imitate Ron's hustle—diving for ground balls, even when they were hit right to us. After Ron's playing days concluded, he became a radio announcer for the Cubs. It was a job that he held right up until he passed away.

Ron had severe diabetes. He had to have one leg amputated . . . and then the other. And his diabetes was complicated by heart trouble and cancer. But as I read Ron's biography, I was so impressed by his upbeat, "can do" spirit. Getting around on two prosthetic legs didn't slow him down.

He bounded up and down the stairways to the announcer's booth at Wrigley Field. He even played a lot of golf and could hit a pretty long tee shot. As I was reading this stuff, I felt convicted about all the times that I complain about my aches and pains. All the times that I complain about having to work out to stay in shape. I decided that Ron Santo is a good role model for me when it comes to pushing myself physically.

WHEN IT COMES to pushing yourself _spiritually_, do you have any good role models?

Do you have any good role models, when it comes to pushing yourself _spiritually_? Do you complain—at least to yourself—that reading and applying the Bible is just too much work? Is that why you've neglected to make it a daily discipline? I want you to consider, as a role model, a guy whose story is told in Robert Sumner's book _The Wonder of the Word of God_.[2]

This is a true story, although Sumner doesn't tell us the guy's name. He lived in Kansas City, and was severely injured in an explosion at work. The man's face was badly disfigured. He lost his eyesight, as well as the use of both hands. Having recently become a Christ follower, his greatest disappointment was that he could no longer read his Bible. But then he heard about a lady in England who'd learned to read Braille with her lips. Unfortunately, the nerve endings in his own lips had been destroyed by the explosion. One day, however, he touched some raised Braille letters with his tongue and found that he could distinguish the characters.

At last count, he'd read through the Bible four times—with his tongue! Now, there's an inspirational role model for you. Do you still think that the daily discipline of reading and applying God's Word is beyond you?

I could tell you many more stories that are far less dramatic. I could tell you about my eighty-something-year-old mom and dad who still read and apply the Bible every day of their lives. I could tell you about a guy who attends my church and informed me that he'd grown up with a reading disorder. Books had never been his friends. But he was determined to befriend *God's* Book. So he picked up a Bible and started working through just one paragraph at a time. Today, he's not only a Bible reader—he's discovered that this daily discipline has given him the skill to read other printed materials as well.

I could tell you about the high school girls that I saw in a coffee shop the other day. They were huddled over their Bibles, and I thought I recognized a couple of them from my church. One girl approached me after their gathering broke up, and explained that since our youth ministry's House Groups were taking a break for the summer, she and her friends were getting together on their own to study the Bible.

I could tell you about some of the guys in my Wednesday morning men's group who are brand new to the Bible—but now they're reading it and coming up with great applications for their lives. As a matter of fact, I'm always personally challenged by the applications they come up with. And it bugs me when I hear people who've been Christ followers for years say that they prefer being in a group of "mature" believers with whom they can do "deep" Bible study. What makes a Bible study deep? Learning the Hebrew meaning of some Old Testament word? Tracing the route of Paul's third missionary journey on a first-century world map? Give me a break! I think "deep" Bible study happens when people put God's Word into practice. That's why some of *my* role models in this regard are beginners.

There are role models all around you—people who are digging into God's Word and applying it to their lives as a daily discipline. What about you? Today would be a good day to start.

Study Guide

Icebreaker

In what areas of your life are you disciplined? In what areas of your life do you wish you were more disciplined? Why are you more disciplined in some areas than in others?

1. Read 1 Timothy 4:7b, 8. In what ways might training in godliness be like physical training?

   Why does Paul say that training in godliness trumps physical training? What might be included on the list of "all things" for which godliness has value?

2. What four factors contribute to your spiritual growth? Briefly describe why each one is important.

3. Explain why the Holy Spirit's empowerment and personal effort must be balanced as you pursue spiritual growth (i.e., what happens when either of these is neglected).

What Old Testament picture portrays this balance?

4. What do you think is the difference between godly habits and legalistic practices? How might you keep the former from morphing into the latter in your life?

5. What would be the best time and place for you to daily spend time with God in His Word? Why?

6. Which Bible reading schedule (i.e., of the several recommended in this chapter) would work best for you? Why?

7. Do a COMA study of 2 Corinthians 4.

Context:

Observations (3–4):

Message (and title):

Application:

8. Why do you think Paul urged others to imitate him?

What do you learn about the example Paul set from the following verses: Philippians 3:17; 4:9; 1 Corinthians 4:15–17; 1 Thessalonians 1:4 6; 2 Thessalonians 3:6–10; 2 Timothy 3:10–11?

9. Who models spiritual growth for you? What can you learn from this person's example?

Why are spiritual role models important?

Appendix:
Additional COMA
Passages

IN THE STUDY GUIDE FOR CHAPTER 3
you did your own COMA study of Ecclesiastes 2, Isaiah 14, and Hebrews 2. As a sample of how it may look, here are my own COMA studies of these passages. (If you haven't completed all three passages at the end of chapter 3, no peeking at these; first finish and then come back.)

Ecclesiastes 2

Context. Although the writer of Ecclesiastes is never identified by name, there are many signs in the book that point to Solomon as its author. He is referred to as: a "son of David" (1:1); a "king over Israel" (1:12); a builder of "great projects" (2:4); a guy who "amassed silver and gold" (2:8); a man who found some women to be "a snare" (7:26); and a teacher of many proverbs (12:9). Sure sounds like Solomon to me—or someone who is putting himself in Solomon's sandals as a writing device.

Solomon reigned over Israel during its golden era (around

900 BC, give or take a few decades). But even though he'd had it all and seen it all, Solomon was pretty cynical about what life has to offer. Ecclesiastes is the reflections of an old man who learned the hard way that only God can give a person lasting satisfaction. Because this is a book of poetry, expect Solomon to use picturesque language to get his point across.

Observations-Messages-Applications. Ecclesiastes 2 is a gold mine of *repeating words or ideas.* Often when I am reading through a chapter of the Bible and come across a repeating word, I will circle that word each time it pops up. But if I come across a second repeating word, I will put a box around every occurrence of it—so as to distinguish it from the circled word. If a third repeating word shows up, it gets bracketed. And so it goes. Well, in Ecclesiastes 2, there are so many repeating words or ideas that I ran out of devices by which to identify them.

Here are six observations from Ecclesiastes 2, each with an accompanying message and application:

Observation. Solomon was a huge pursuer of *pleasure* (a word that's found in verses 1, 2, 10; its synonym, *delight,* is also used)—but it never brought him fulfillment.

Message. Pleasure, in and of itself, is empty.

120

Application. I tend to overuse the renting of a good movie as an escape. The pleasure of such is short-lived. The next time I'm inclined to pick up something at Redbox, I will look instead for a way to connect with God.

Observation. Solomon tried to find meaning in his work—to no avail (see *work/toil/labor* in verses 17, 18, 19, 20, 21, 22, 23, 24—more than twenty-five times in Ecclesiastes overall).

Message. Lasting satisfaction can't be found in a job.

Application. I work too many hours—a habit that to some extent is fueled by the accolades I receive from others and the importance of my vocation. But I must start saying "no" to long hours. I must honor my day off.

Observation. Solomon discovered a wide variety of life-pursuits to be "meaningless" (a word that describes a passing breath and which is used eight times in this chapter and thirty-five times in Ecclesiastes as a whole). Solomon also refers to these life-pursuits as a "chasing after the wind" (three times in this chapter and nine times in the book). It must be noted, however, that the reason these activities prove to be empty is because they are most often pursued as an end in themselves and for benefits in *this* world. Solomon unmasks our all-too-often *present*-world perspective with the repeating phrase "under the sun" (six times in this chapter and twenty-nine times in the book).

Message. Nothing in this world can produce a lasting, joyous sense of significance.

Application. Make a list of five things (or activities) from which I try to gain significance or happiness (family members not included). Acknowledge to God the futility of this pursuit.

Observation. I am struck by the fact (aha! *something striking*) that even *wisdom* (which pops up ten times in Ecclesiastes 2) is derided by Solomon as meaningless (v. 15). Wisdom is meaningless? Only in the sense that, apart from God, it doesn't change a person's ultimate fate.

Message. Wisdom and knowledge shouldn't be pursued as an end in themselves.

Application. I am an insatiable learner, always reading. I need to return to my practice of evaluating and summarizing in an electronic file what I've just finished reading—from the standpoint of what that reading contributes to eternal values and objectives.

Observation. Solomon reached the point of actually *hating* his life and the things he'd worked for (2:17, 18). His honest despair and strong language jumped off the page at me.

Message. When life is in the pits, that's often an indication that the wrong sources have been trusted to provide fulfillment.

Application. The next time I'm discouraged (I probably won't have long to wait), I will ask myself the question: *What am I currently depending on to make me happy?*

Observation. Here's an eye-opening *truth about God* from 2:24–26: Only He can enable us to enjoy anything in this life (i.e., in a thorough and lasting way). The footnote in my *NIV Study Bible* says that these verses are *the heart of Ecclesiastes*, introducing a theme that's repeated in: 3:12, 13, 22; 5:18–20; 8:15; 9:7; and 12:13.

Message. The search for significance must begin and end with God.

Application. Don't let my daily "quiet times" (a.k.a. devotions, appointments with God, personal Bible study, etc.) become mechanical. Evaluate whether I'm just going through the motions or genuinely connecting with God. Am I taking time to worship—since worship rekindles my heart's desire for God?

Isaiah 14

Context. Isaiah was written by a prophet whose name literally meant "the Lord saves"—a fitting name, since he had much to say about God's coming salvation. Isaiah saw the northern kingdom of Israel fall to the Assyrians in 722 BC, and he warned the southern kingdom of Judah that a similar fate awaited them if they didn't repent of their sin and turn back to God. Isaiah spent most of his life in Jerusalem, the capital city of Judah. The prophets Amos, Hosea, and Micah were his contemporaries. Tradition says that Isaiah met his death at the hands of wicked king Manasseh—who sawed him in two!

Isaiah 14 begins with a promise of restoration. Isaiah describes a time in the future when God would bring His people back from foreign captivity and resettle them in their own land. Bible scholars assert that there are three possible interpretations of this resettlement. It could be a description of Judah's return from Babylonian exile a couple hundred years in the future. Or, it could be a figurative description of people being gathered into the church through faith in Christ (who is called God's *Servant* in Isaiah) over the last two thousand years. Or, finally, it could describe the millennial kingdom that Christ will inaugurate when He returns to rule over this earth.

Did I learn all this stuff in seminary? Nope, I picked it up from reading the introduction and various footnotes to Isaiah in my *NIV Study Bible*. That's also where I learned that the *theme* of Isaiah 14 is *a prophecy against Babylon*—a diatribe that began back in chapter 13. What's amazing about such a prophecy is that Babylon was not yet a superpower when Isaiah wrote that it would one day conquer and exile Judah. And what's more, Isaiah prophesied that Babylon, after conquering other nations, would itself be conquered.

> *Observations-Messages-Applications.* Here are five observations about Isaiah 14, followed by corresponding messages and applications.

> *Observation.* Isaiah's prophecy against Babylon, the *theme* of chapter 14 (see the heading in chapter 13), begins a ten-chapter section that describes the coming destruction of one wicked nation after another. God's people were probably cheering when they got this news—but their euphoria was cut short when they arrived at Isaiah 22. Because God had plans to punish wicked Jerusalem as well.

Message. God punishes wickedness wherever it is found —even in His own people.

Application. Make a list of three or four sins that especially aggravate me when I see them in others. Now, look for signs of those same sins in my own life and repent of them.

Observation. The first-person pronoun "I" is repeated, again and again, in verses 13–14. These "I" statements are the arrogant boasting of Babylon—putting itself on par with God!

Message. Bragging is audacious. It takes credit for things that God has done.

Application. Be careful of self-promotion in conversation with others. Do I leave people impressed with me or with God?

Observation. I am struck by what will be the ultimate fate of proud Babylon. The description in verse 11 is one that any middle schooler would love: "Maggots are spread out beneath you and worms cover you." Gross!

Message. The horrific demise of Babylon underscores the fact that God hates pride and will not put up with it for long. (As 1 Peter 5:5 says, "God opposes the proud but gives grace to the humble.")

Application. This heightens the sense of my previous application. Bragging is not only foolish and audacious; it is also dangerous—because it puts me in the same camp as God's enemies. (Did you catch the footnote that points out that this passage has been considered to be a description of Satan's fall? Pride is the identifying mark of God's archenemy!) Be on the lookout for evidences of pride in my life and deal with it severely.

Observation. Throughout this chapter God is described as the one who will deliver His people from bondage and destroy their enemies (a wonderful *truth about God*). But I am especially impressed by the ease with which God does this. He is so powerful that when He deposes the mighty Babylonian empire it will be with the casual whisk of a broom: "I will sweep her with the broom of destruction" (v. 23). In other words: God's enemies are no big deal.

Message. While my enemies may seem formidable, God can quickly and easily remove them.

Application. Identify any current enemies in my life—sins that entangle me, people out to harm me, situations that batter me. Turn these enemies over to God in prayer, reminding myself that while they are huge to me they are small potatoes to God.

Observation. Note the various words in verses 24–27 that underscore God's sovereignty: *sworn, planned, purposed*. God is not pictured in Isaiah 14 as playing defense. He is not waiting for bad things to happen in our lives and then coming up with a way to rescue us. No, God is large and in charge from the very outset. Everything that would happen to the nations that are described in this section of Isaiah would take place exactly as God had planned it.

Message. God has a plan. Nothing happens outside of that plan or outside of God's control.

Application. When bad things happen to me today— whether they are minor irritations or major catastrophes—say out loud: *God has a plan*. Thank and praise Him for His sovereignty. Sing a song that reminds me that He is on His throne.

Were any of your observations similar to mine in Isaiah 14? There is much more to be gleaned from this chapter than the few things I touched on. And even if you made some of the same observations that I did, you probably drew a different message from one of them and applied it to your life in a way that wouldn't have occurred to me. This is what makes COMA such a rich (and simple) curriculum for small groups to use. When your group gathers each week, even though the members have all been studying the same passages, there will be a wide variety of insights to be shared with one another.

Hebrews 2

Context. The author of this epistle does not identify himself by name. For centuries the church attributed the book to Paul—but that is not likely since Hebrews is written in a style that is very different from Paul's. Whoever penned this letter was well respected in the early church, really knew his Old Testament, and had an intellectually keen mind.

The epistle was addressed to Christians who were in danger of slipping back into Judaism because of persecution. To prevent this from happening, the author drives home the truth that Christ is superior to angels, Moses, Joshua, high priests, and temple sacrifices. Hebrews was most likely written before AD 70 since it does not mention the temple's destruction—an event that would have been of tremendous concern to the author's Jewish-Christian audience.

Observations-Messages-Applications. Here are four observations about Hebrews 2, coupled with corresponding messages and applications.

Observation. Jesus became one of us so that He could come to our rescue. His incarnation is mentioned several times in this chapter (vv. 11, 14, 17–18).

Message. Jesus is not aloof. He desires intimacy with His followers and has gone to great lengths to make it possible.

Application. Take time to praise Christ for becoming a man.

Observation. Jesus was made "perfect" through His suffering (v. 10). Now that's definitely *something striking* since I thought Jesus was perfect to begin with, didn't you? Here's where a footnote can really help. Jesus was never imperfect in a moral or spiritual sense. Being *made perfect* for Jesus involved the completing of His identification with us by going through suffering. This is why Jesus can now serve as our sympathetic high priest (vv. 17–18). He understands the trials we endure and the temptations we face—He's *been there, done that.*

Message. In the words of the old hymn, "Jesus knows our every weakness. . . . Take it to the Lord in prayer" ("What a Friend We Have in Jesus").

Application. What am I troubled about today? What sin is especially tempting me? I need to stop assuming that

Jesus doesn't want to be bothered by these things or wouldn't understand what I'm facing. I should call to mind Jesus' incarnation—and pray!

Observation. God (here's a *truth about* Him) confirmed the preaching of the gospel in New Testament times with signs, wonders, miracles, and gifts of the Holy Spirit (v. 4). Such attestations are still helpful today.

Message. God backs up His *truth* with *proof.*

Application. Cry out to God for my gospel preaching and personal witnessing to be accompanied by displays of His power—especially answers to prayer for the healing of bodies, the restoration of marriages, the provision of jobs, and the deliverance from addictions.

Observation. Jesus came to destroy Satan and deliver people from death—and the fear of death (vv. 14–15).

Message. Jesus can break the stranglehold that Satan has on a person's life.

Application: Who do I know that is currently facing death apart from Christ? I must pray for that individual and make an appointment to meet with them to talk about the One who delivers from death.

There is certainly a lot more to be found in Hebrews 2. By now I hope you're getting the hang of COMA. Don't let go of it when you're finished with *Walk*. Make it your daily practice to be a *doer* of God's Word.

Notes

About the Bible Savvy series

1. Thom S. Rainer, *The Unchurched Next Door* (Grand Rapids: Zondervan, 2003), 200.

Chapter 2: From Text to Life

1. Stephen Covey, *The 7 Habits of Highly Effective People* (New York: Free Press, 2004), 30.

2. A. J. Jacobs, *The Year of Living Biblically: One Man's Humble Quest to Follow the Bible as Literally as Possible* (New York: Simon & Schuster, 2008).

Chapter 4: A Daily Discipline

1. Based on Dave Ramsey, *Financial Peace University* (New York: Penguin Group, 2003).

2. Robert L. Sumner, *The Wonder of the Word of God* (n.p.: Biblical Evangelism Press, 1969).

Bibliography

Ortberg, John. *The Life You've Always Wanted: Spiritual Discipline for Ordinary People*. Grand Rapids: Zondervan, 2002.

Warren, Rick. *Bible Study Methods: Twelve Ways You Can Unlock God's Word*. Grand Rapids: Zondervan, 2006.

Whitney, Donald S. *Spiritual Disciplines for the Christian Life*. Colorado Springs: NavPress, 1991.

JAMES L. NICODEM

Bible Savvy

Epic: The Storyline of the Bible unveils the single theme that ties all of scripture together: redemption.

Foundation: The Trustworthiness of the Bible explains where our current bible came from and why it can be wholly trusted.

Context: How to Understand the Bible shows readers how to read the different parts of the Bible as they were meant to be read and how they fit together.

Walk: How to Apply the Bible puts the readers increased understanding of the Bible into real life terms and contexts.